FRANZ JALICS

CONTEMPLATIVE RETREAT

An Introduction to the
Contemplative Way to Life
and to the
Jesus Prayer

Contemplative Retreat
by Franz Jalics

Printed in the United States of America

ISBN 1-594671-56-7

Original Title: *Kontemplative Exerzitien,* published in German by Echter Verlag, Würzburg, Germany, 1994.

First English edition, *Called to Share in His Life*, trans. Sr. Lucia Wiedenhöver, OCD, published by St. Paul's Press, Bandra, Mumbai, India, 2000.

Edited for publication in the United States by Ruth A. Fox, Ph.D.

Except for scripture passages paraphrased by the original author, Bible quotations are taken from The New American Bible with Revised Psalms and Revised New Testament, copyright © 1987 by Thomas Nelson, Inc., Nashville.

To order one or more copies of this book, call
1-866-909-BOOK (2665)
or visit
www.Xulon Press.com

In Europe, order direct from either
www.gardners.com or www.bertrams.com
<http://www.bertrams.com>

CONTENTS

CONTEMPLATIVE RETREAT

INTRODUCTION

My encounters with people over more than thirty-five years of pastoral ministry have convinced me that, behind the most diverse lifestyles, a search for God is taking place in the depth of the soul, and that people make room for the search in their lives. Now and then, however, people experience our organized religious structures as too complicated, impractical, and artificial. Frequently those structures obstruct access to the divine. People are really looking for a simple, spontaneous, and immediate contact with God. Wherever I guided toward simplicity, immediacy, and inner spiritual reality, people were relieved and told me that they had been looking in vain for this simple way for years or decades. Others confessed that they had encountered God secretly in this way without having the courage to say so, because of the fear of not being understood by their pastors.

I believe that this simplicity and directness fulfils a basic need for modern men and women to balance against our hectic and complex world. Pastors and counselors themselves, weighed down by activities, long for quiet and simplicity, at least in their relationship with God. This simple way characterized by immediacy in the relationship with God is called *contemplation*.

My experiences led me to teach those who came to me this simple way to God. After many years in retreat practice, I would like to make my retreat experiences available also in book form (see Endnote 1). I want to offer to all Christians—and especially to those who counsel others—a practical workbook which will help them take this contemplative journey to the center, to the risen Christ and the Father, on their own. Perhaps this book will also be helpful to them in promoting the contemplative way.

1. From pre-contemplative to contemplative prayer

The way to God has been described in many different ways in the long tradition of the Church. The threefold division is well known and widespread: *the Way of Purification* (via purgativa), *the Way of Illumination* (via illuminativa), and *the Way of Union* (via unitiva). (This division has its roots in the Bible and is presented by St. Thomas Aquinas in the *Summa Theoligica.)* In the following paragraphs, my exposition of the three phases of the spiritual life follows the classic handbook by Adolphe Tanquery: *The Spiritual Life: A Treatise on Ascetic and Mystical Theology* (Paris, 1931).

At the beginning there is the Way of Purification. Here the main obstacles which keep us at a distance from God are removed through careful effort. Serious sins must be purged. This is done by discursive [or rational] thinking (see Endnote 2) and concentrated effort of the will. The mind works through analysis, consideration, and reflection on the meaning of life and on ways to achieve goals. The mind, through such thinking, then motivates the will to make changes in life. The human being calls to mind what he or she is here in the world for: what do I want to achieve in life and what consequences will my behavior have for my life? These reflections lead the person to a new orientation toward Jesus Christ.

The second part of the way is the Illuminative Way. This word should not be equated with the concept of illumination in Eastern prayer methods. At this stage we work to progress from good to better in a more subtle way. The predominance of reason is supplemented by delicate inner feeling. We learn to handle our character. We begin to look behind the curtain of our behavior—to try to get to the bottom of the unconscious disrupting factors in our psyche and come to terms with our past. We learn the attitudes that belong to love and true humanity. We begin to savor the good and to deal gently with ourselves. We orient ourselves mainly by the example of Jesus Christ and the saints. According to the traditional formulation in the Church, the goal of the Illuminative Way is the acquisition of "virtues." We might say, to use modern idiom, that we try to become more human and also more Christ-like in our feelings and behavior. We strive for Christian perfection.

These two first stages have often been understood as one single step called "asceticism": striving for Christian perfection. The term indicates that one wants to change. I have not found a suitable collective term for this ascetic stage, the via purgativa and the via illuminativa together. I shall call it pre-contemplative prayer.

The third part of the way is the Unitive Way. In contrast to asceticism, this part of the way has been called "mysticism," for which "contemplation" is a synonym. In this stage the biggest and most radical change in the spiritual life is brought about. During the two first phases, human effort was called for to effect change, to overcome sinful tendencies, to work through psychological complexes and build up character. In the way of union something completely different takes place. God takes the initiative, and all we must do is yield ourselves completely to him. In prayer, we direct our attention solely to God. God acts. We become a tool in his hands. We live, but more than we ourselves, Christ lives in us (see Gal 2:20).

Such a change does not happen within days. It is clear that we cannot bring it about ourselves. We are totally powerless and too awkward for such an achievement. Either this oneness with Jesus Christ is given us by grace or we do not reach it. Just because the turnaround is so radical, there is a transitional passage—a no man's land—in which the change is coming, but we are not yet at the stage where God takes over in a perceptible way. During this initial stage, we have to make an effort. Paradoxically, we have to try hard not to try at all.

This means that we direct ourselves to God and trust that God will give us everything. The sign of trust is to let go of the intense effort to bring about change in our character and psyche. Our sole work consists merely in orienting ourselves toward God. The kingdom of God is within us. If we orient ourselves toward our center, the core of our being, to the indwelling Trinity, there will gradually come an incredibly strong power from deep within us which slowly gives us everything and introduces us into the state of contemplation. Sometimes this state is simply given by God. The usual way, however, is by consciously preparing ourselves to hold fast to God, to let go of all logical thinking and focusing on our own psychological progress. This transitional phase is also called *active contemplation*, because we still do actively fix our attention. Once grace grows stronger, this human activity also ceases. Our attention to God is held from within.

In this book we occupy ourselves with this great transition. We traverse the "no man's land" and change from the active striving for perfection to the state of contemplation. Our duty during this process is to cease from discursive thought and occupation with our feelings by concentrating purely and simply on God (Endnote 3).

It is not the goal of this book to lead to stages of higher contemplation. We confine ourselves exclusively to the transition from pre-contemplative to contemplative prayer.

There are many paths to contemplation. I show you just one of them. I'm conscious of the fact that God leads many people to contemplation without any external help. Frequently he uses natural circumstances. A simple life of love, some years on a sickbed, a brush with death, the leaving of one's homeland in order to live among the poor, and other events can lead to contemplation. I also deeply respect the non-Christian ways of contemplation. And there are in the Catholic Church itself many other introductions into contemplation. I do not want to exalt my way above others. On the contrary, I am very happy that they exist and I appreciate them. I myself have walked the way I describe: Should it help someone else to find his or her way, I am satisfied.

2. The difficulty of the task

The task I have undertaken in this book has one great difficulty: that is, paradoxically, its simplicity.

God is simple, and the way to the Father that Jesus Christ showed us is a very simple way. It is not always an easy, but a plain and uncomplicated path. It consists in the modest, humble, and unceasing orientation towards God. There is nothing more to say than to draw attention to this orientation towards God. And this is the enormous difficulty of this book, which has nothing to tell you but to turn you to God. Anything more would distract from the essential. It is a contradiction to write many words in order to say that you do not need any words at all. It also seems paradoxical to argue discursively (logically) that discursive thinking is useless on this journey. Or to illustrate with images that images are of no help here. Or to offer texts only to say that written documents are distractions. Or to publish a book which shows that books are hindrances on this path.

The more interesting this book might be, the more it would distract from the essential. I would really hope that the reading of this book becomes boring so that the retreatant would finally get to the essential! On the other hand, there is just this fear that the book might become boring because I say the same things over and over again. Then the retreatant might reject the way as not interesting. I can't but repeat myself constantly because I have nothing new to say. And I can't say anything new without betraying my original intention.

I feel like the Hungarian parish priest in the story: he was very much beloved in his parish. The bishop had several times wanted to move him to another parish, but because of the repeated requests of his parishioners, he was left there for thirty years and was still very popular. There was only one criticism against him, which grew louder and louder. After much hesitation a group of his lay leaders in the parish presented their concern: "Dear Father, you are such a splendid person. . . ." The priest, who had prepared each of them for their First Holy Communion years before, knew immediately that they had a complaint. "What do you want, my children?" he asked. "Well, Father," they hesitantly answered, "You have a sermon for every Sunday of the year and repeat it every year. By now we have heard them more than thirty times. Could you not prepare a new sermon for once?" "My dear children," the old man replied, "Week by week I sit in the confessional for hours, and for the last thirty years you have told me the same sins over and over again. If you invent a new sin, I'll draw up a new sermon for you." This is how I feel with my retreatants. If their problems were not always the same I could say something new. But as long as this is not the case, I am obliged to repeat myself constantly.

3. The fruit of experience

I admire the authors of the Old Testament Scriptures, who did not sign their work. They wrote under inspiration and knew they were not the real authors of the books. Everything was imparted to them. They experienced that everything is grace. I would dearly love to do the same. Unfortunately this is not possible in our culture. We always ask for the author first. It is important to know who has written the book before we consider taking it into our hands. So I must acknowledge myself as the author.

To give a retreat means to guide someone down a stretch of road. This happens in a framework of revelation. The retreat master doesn't use any specific technique. He shows the way he himself has walked and is still living. Personal testimony plays an important role. Without such testimony, the message becomes pale, powerless, and abstract; worse, it might give the impression of unrealistic theory. I was aware of this especially when I wrote Parts Four, Five, Eight, and Nine of this book; so it seemed important to me to use my own faith experience to elucidate what I wanted to say. In doing so, I do not wish to put myself in the center, but to serve the cause.

I should also mention that I learned a lot from my retreatants. In the more than 400 retreats I have conducted during my life, I listened to the participants for hours and came to share their joy and their sorrow, their fears and their trust, their despair and their closeness to God.

This book really is the fruit of experience, and it therefore aims to be a practical handbook and not a theoretical treatise. My foundation is the Catholic faith. All statements in this book should be interpreted with this in mind.

4. The Retreat Master

Ignatius calls the person who gives the retreat a "retreat master." In so-called "preached retreats" this person is correctly called "preacher," because he preaches to and has almost no other contact with his listeners. In "conducted retreats," the leaders are called "companions," emphasizing that they accompany the retreatants throughout a process. I call this person "retreat master" because he points out a specific path. He or she must be a "master" in knowing the way that leads into the presence of God and must also be a "master" in discerning where the retreatants are and in respecting their individual steps. At first, I was reluctant to use this term. But, in the simple and humble sense of House Master, or Master Carpenter, or Novice Master, I find it suitable.

5. A workbook as Retreat Master

This book is a practical handbook. While you may read it as a spiritual book or even as a novel, you should not expect that the mere reading will introduce you into contemplation. It has been written for people who want not only to understand what contemplation is, but to live it. Those who reflect on the theory of swimming will not learn how to swim unless they jump into the water. Reading this book is like studying swimming. But to learn how to swim requires a lot of persistence. We make mistakes and allow ourselves to be corrected. We lose courage and start again from scratch. Above all, it takes a lot of time.

The aim of this book—to replace the retreat master—is an almost impossible undertaking. While writing it, I kept hearing such remarks. But there are many people who do not have the opportunity to make a contemplative retreat; the book could be of good service to them. There are many priests and religious people who make retreats on their own. When they go to a quiet place, they usually take a spiritual book along to help guide them through their retreat; this book could also help them. Other people are naturally led by grace to contemplation; this book could help them as a source of checks and balances for their natural, inner processes. Young retreat masters who set out to give contemplative retreats could also find helpful support in this book. Therefore I have tried the impossible!

I also try in this book to remain constantly in touch and in dialogue with my readers, the "retreatants," to correct and encourage them. The description of concrete experiences, the Instructions for Meditation, the Review after each phase, and, especially the Dialogues, will—I hope—enable my readers to come to contemplation.

A workbook must present exercises and set up standards to show when a task has been satisfactorily fulfilled. On the other hand, contemplation requires precisely that we should not try to achieve anything. I had to face this contradiction squarely. Retreatants will realize that they will not follow the way of contemplation if they give in to the pressure of getting through the book. I shall frequently draw attention to such pressure.

Because of all these demands, the reader may well find this book very authoritarian. But the demands are linked to one condition: I show only what is necessary for the way of contemplation. The retreatants themselves authorize me. They even expect from me that I show them frankly the conditions and demands of this way.

6. Sacred Scripture

A frequent prejudice against contemplative prayer lies in its relationship to Sacred Scripture. The prejudice is mostly expressed by people and groups who can think of serious prayer only as Scripture meditation. Their criticism is that people whose prayer is contemplative neglect the Bible.

This book and its way of praying springs completely from revelation and is immersed in it. What could be more Christian than to dwell constantly, with full attention, in the presence of the risen Christ! Not only of his words, but of himself! Scripture leads us to this. It is the foundation of, and it creates the environment for, contemplation. Other than love of neighbor, I can't recommend anything more useful and necessary to prepare for and sustain contemplative prayer than to enter deeply into Sacred Scripture. "Ignorantia scripturarum ignorantia Christi est," St. Jerome said: Ignorance of the Scriptures is ignorance of Christ.

Yet, Sacred Scripture is an announcement which, like an arrow, points beyond itself. At the moment of prayer, a direct turning to Christ excludes simultaneous preoccupation with Scripture.

7. An active spirituality

Another prejudice claims that contemplative prayer leads to passivity and lack of responsibility toward others. Let us make a distinction between *contemplation* and *contemplative prayer*. Contemplation is a state in which God's action is very intense and can be felt. It relates to the third (Unitive) phase of the spiritual life. It is not a way of praying, but a state that exists or can exist at any moment of our life, during prayer and at other times. Introduction into contemplative prayer leads to contemplation's increasingly invading the whole of our life. Contemplation is not limited to the times of quiet. Contemplative people are usually more active and effective than those who are not contemplative. They pursue similar activities and responsibilities with greater ease and less effort, but without getting tired out. The examples of great contemplatives such as St. Paul, St. Augustine, St. Ignatius of Loyola, Mother Teresa, and many others prove this paradox.

History shows that the state of contemplation is not given without quiet times free from activities. Exceptions to this rule are an extraordinary grace. A sign of its authenticity is that someone graced in this way seeks out times for silence in his active life, and—in fact—makes provision for them.

This book is written for people active in everyday life. It is consistent with an ideal of the active life: there is time for daily contemplative prayer and for a contemplative retreat once a year. Working people should be able to practice contemplation in this manner.

8. Meditation or contemplation?

We have to explain the word *meditation*. In medieval use it meant discursive, thoughtful reflection: to let the text speak to oneself, to think it through, understand and integrate it, apply it to oneself, and change one's attitudes in consequence. In this sense we use the word in the Church today in relation to meditation focused on picture, scripture, painting, or music. In the Middle Ages one spoke of a trilogy: *lectio* was the reading of a text from Scripture, *meditatio* reflection on the text, and *contemplatio* resting in it, which is what we call contemplation.

Some decades ago *meditation* began to be used in a completely different sense under the influence of Eastern spirituality. The Eastern contemplative traditions received the name "meditation," which in Western medieval tradition did not mean contemplation at all, but discursive reflection. So the word arouses discussions, passions, and tensions today between representatives of different groups. I do not want to become part of this controversy. Therefore I call the prayer I teach in this book not "meditation," but contemplative prayer. The word *meditation* I use exclusively for *the time that is devoted to contemplative prayer*. I speak of half an hour of meditation, or ask what someone has done during the time of meditation. My goal, however, is not to lead retreatants to meditation but to contemplative prayer.

9. A request for understanding

This book is concerned with the difficult and radical transition from pre-contemplative to contemplative prayer. I compare it with the transformation St. Paul experienced in meeting Jesus Christ. He was a virtuous and learned Pharisee. The Old Testament, so to speak, flowed in his veins; it was his homeland. Then he encountered Christ. From this moment he had a conflicting relationship with the Old Testament. On the one hand, he considered it to be the true revelation of God and the preparation for the New Testament. On the other hand, he occasionally experienced the Old Testament *in contrast to* the light of Christ. He speaks of it in derogatory terms, particularly in connection with the law and the attempt to achieve redemption by human endeavor.

The comparison with Paul fits so well also because within him and within us there is taking place this change from "doing" to the direct impact of "grace." He calls virtues *works*, and life with Christ *grace*. In our case, we're also moving from our own efforts to the radical cessation of all human "doing." In this sense the comparison is applicable.

Of course, in another sense the comparison is not exact. In our case, we're not converting from pre-Christian to Christian life. The Purgative and Illuminative Ways are part of the Christian way, though the orientation to Christ becomes more radical with the beginning of contemplation. But grace is no less at work in the pre-contemplative sphere.

To emphasize the change from works to grace, St. Paul cannot help but refer to the Old Testament sometimes in a negative way. So he occasionally speaks about the Law in derogatory language. I see myself in a similar position with regard to the transition from pre-contemplative to contemplative prayer. The pre-contemplative way is a positive and necessary stage in the spiritual life. But I am speaking to people who are in the no man's land between the way of the virtues and the way of contemplation. I show them where their path should lead. They are still attached to the way of thinking and doing. I have to emphasize that this way does not lead them any further, and I must show what they have to let go of completely in order to enter into the new. So it can frequently happen that I refer to the pre-contemplative way somewhat negatively, with partiality, in order to show the transition to contemplative prayer more clearly. This could be the case when I am explaining how to deal with thoughts, feelings, psychological processes, and attempts to change one's character. So I ask for your understanding if, in this book, pre-contemplative prayer occasionally appears in a seemingly negative light.

10. For whom has this book been written?

For the last forty-five years, I have felt that the most important task for the renewal of the Catholic Church is the spiritual renewal of priests and pastoral workers. For more than thirty-five years, I have been working in the field of formation of priests and other men and women engaged in pastoral work, both paid professionals and volunteers. Thus I had primarily these teachers of the Gospel in mind. I dedicate this book especially to them.

This book has been written for those whose home is Christianity. I do not want, however, to exclude anybody who considers himself "non-Christian" or "not religious." This retreat, however is anchored so much in Christianity, in Sacred Scripture, and in particular in the Catholic Church, that non-Christians could have difficulty with the expressions and views in the book. Believers of other Christian Churches, however, will rarely have any problems.

Naturally, everybody interested in this book can read it. However I do not recommend that every reader make a retreat based on its instructions. I would recommend the retreat only for those who have a deep yearning for God and are therefore determined enough to fulfil the requirements of the way. I ask in this book for a regular amount of time to be given to meditation. The path I trace is a rather steep one. I expect the retreatant to do certain things which acquire meaning only during the course of the exercises. At times, participants may feel a sense of meaninglessness, and they must be prepared to experience frustration. Those who do not want or are not able to undertake these exertions had better not start at all.

Nor is this book recommended for those who are content with vocal prayer, discursive meditation of Scripture, or colloquies with God in prayer. If they do not feel the longing for a more simplified approach to God, they should continue with their way of praying. Everything has its time. Once there is the desire for a more direct entering into God's presence, that is the time to be interested in contemplation. If someone has practiced Scripture meditation for a longer period with satisfaction, and feels increasingly frustrated with the possibility of continuing to do so, this is a signal that the time to go further is probably overdue. Teresa of Avila suffered greatly from the fact that she had been forced to continue with discursive meditation, and John of the Cross also expressed himself clearly on this point (Endnote 4).

I feel obliged to express an emphatic warning. In times of silence and longer periods of solitude, much from the unconscious will surface in everyone. If you keep to the rules which I explicitly describe in this book, all will go well. If, however, the pressure from the unconscious becomes too strong, keeping the rules will be difficult if not impossible. Brooding over this conflict may have very unpleasant consequences.

I would like to give you some signs which would alert you if the exercises overtax you. In any case, I would ask you to discuss the issue with a priest or counselor. One's social behavior is a reliable guide as to whether the retreat on one's own can be recommended. If your relations with other people are blocked, you will circle around yourself in solitude and not find the way to God. I strongly advise against undertaking this retreat if you have severe communication problems in the family or at work, strong feelings of anxiety, inner tension, or frequent psychosomatic disorders. Also, if you are in an acute crisis: at least there should be counseling before you proceed.

11. The format of the retreat

You can follow this introduction into contemplation during a "Closed Retreat," by withdrawing completely into silence with no other activities for ten to thirty days. For this, it's best to go away from home to a retreat house, a monastery, or another quiet place. It is extremely advantageous to have a retreat master or another experienced person nearby on whom to call in an emergency. The duration of the retreat can vary. Originally I had planned it for ten days, and I distribute the material over ten time units or chapters. Each unit may last for two or three days according to your own inner processes. The book offers enough material for thirty days. On the other hand, the process could be shortened by breaking off after the first units. Those who follow these instructions for the first time are well advised to dwell longer on the first units. How far you get is irrelevant. During your first retreat following this pattern, the introduction into contemplation will be so great a priority that you won't be able to go through any important decision-making at the same time. You will find some remarks about discernment processes in the dialogue with Lina (Tenth Day, Dialogue 10.15).

It is possible to use this book for repeated Closed Retreats. You will find some advice in the dialogue with Sophie (Tenth Day, Dialogue 10.8). If you have previously meditated regularly before in the way this book describes, you may shorten the early units—or even skip them—and extend the last five.

This book is also suitable for a Retreat in Everyday Life. Those who choose this way could continue with their daily activities and every day dedicate a certain time—one hour or one and a half—to the exercises. In this case, you would linger over each unit for about two weeks. When a group gets together for such a Retreat in Daily Life, participants could share their experience in weekly group meetings and would find great mutual support.

Daily participation in the Eucharist is integral to the Closed Retreat as well as to the Retreat in Daily Life. I would strongly recommend organizing your time so that this is possible.

12. The structure of this book

The single chapters or days all have the same structure. Each day begins with an Introductory Talk. These correspond to the sermon or talk given by a retreat master during quiet days. In the first days, they deal with a topic that gives insight into the meaning of the retreat. As the days progress, the retreat process becomes more and more clear. If you allow these talks to have an effect on you, they will help you to basic understanding and strengthen you. If, however, you read them in a dissociated and critical spirit, there is danger of getting caught in abstract problems. Then you end up in inner confrontations which block the retreat process. Instead of being in retreat you're suddenly in the middle of a theological debate or controversy.

After the talk come the Instructions for Meditation. In the first six days these sections provide a gradual introduction to the Jesus prayer. The Instructions are meant to set a standard. Often people try contemplative prayer on their own, and they often sit in silence two or three times and discover that they are unable to pray in this manner. Contemplation is a way of life; it requires a lot of time. The Instructions for meditation will clarify how much time must be invested for a serious attempt. In addition, they give concrete guidelines for contemplation.

During the Instructions, and later in the Review, we will clarify who has decided to *make the retreat* and who just wants to *read the book.* To make this distinction more concrete, I address you as Readers on the one hand and Retreatants on the other. While the book has actually been written for retreatants, readers are welcome. A few things in this book may interest them, though they may not feel comfortable with the many repetitions. I apologize for this, but the repetitions are necessary for those who undertake the retreat . I expect that some who start by being readers will later on be stimulated to make the retreat.

The Dialogues follow the Instructions. In each dialogue between the retreat master and a retreatant, a participant speaks first about his or her experience during the preceding meditation. The retreat master listens with empathy. Dialogues are quite typical, representing thousands of real ones, though the specific conversations and the retreatants' names are not real. The dialogues differ from actual conversations especially in that the first section of empathic listening has been substantially shortened, while the second part of the conversation, in which the retreat master speaks, is more developed (Endnote 5).

If you read the dialogues carefully, you will discover many of the participants' experiences in yourself. Then the retreat master's words will enrich and clarify the exchange. The dialogues will not have this effect if you just skim through them or read them with purely intellectual interest. It is important, therefore, not to read more than two or three dialogues at a time! You don't even have to read them all. Small doses (like homeopathic cures) will suffice. If a certain dialogue does not speak to you, just skip it.

Each day ends with a Review and Transition, looking back over the Day just completed and ahead to the next chapter. Questions help the retreatant decide whether to go further or to stay longer with the same Day.

NOTES TO THE INTRODUCTION

1. The Latin word *exercitium* means *practice*. Catholic use of the technical term "exercises" (German *Exerzitien)* for *days of quiet* comes from St. Ignatius of Loyola's book, *Exercitia Spiritualia* or "Spiritual Practice," written as an introduction to the fully engaged Christian life.

2. Note for the American edition: "Discursive thought" is an important concept in this discussion. Throughout the book, *discursive* retains its scholarly meaning, "proceeding to a conclusion through reason rather than intuition" *(American Heritage Dictionary)*. American readers should not be confused by the word's looser if more familiar connotations of "rambling" or "wide-ranging," and I have often paired it with a word like *rational, thoughtful,* or *analytical* in order to keep us focused on the author's meaning.

3. Along with Tanquery, see also Charles Baumgartner's article "Le seuil inférieur de la contemplation mystique," col. 2177 ff. under "Contemplation," *Dictionnaire de Spiritualité*, Paris, 1953.

4. See St. John's *Ascent of Mt. Carmel,* Book 2, chapter 13; *The Dark Night,* Book I, chapter 9; and *The Living Flame of Love*, stanza 3, verse 3 ff.

5. See my book *Aprendiendo a compartir la fe,* Buenos Aires, 1988; German edition, *Miteinander im Glauben wachsen,* Munich, 1982.

FIRST DAY

I. INTRODUCTORY TALK: WHAT IS A RETREAT?

1. The power of nature

Toward the end of the Second World War, I was stationed in Germany as a Hungarian officer cadet in training for tank warfare. With the end of the war, I had suddenly become a refugee. Millions of foreigners were living in refugee camps, awaiting repatriation or an opportunity for immigration. I was one of them. We were provided with food and were allowed to go for walks in the surrounding countryside. But there was no work. I asked to be admitted to high school, but refugees were turned away since not even all Germans were able to attain a place. There were no books to read, much less radio or TV or other occupations. I was not preoccupied with my future, I was simply waiting for what was going to happen. I could not do anything, anyway. We were endlessly recounting war stories to each other.

After a while I got tired of talking and began to go out for long walks for several hours every day. The country around was very beautiful. I was stationed first in Kloster Polling near Weilheim and later in Floss in the Oberpfalz. Every day I walked for three, four, or even five hours. Nature was doing me good. I felt I was being purified, I found stillness, and I always returned refreshed. I often looked up to the sky and prayed spontaneously. I felt the presence of Jesus Christ, in whom all things are created, in nature, in the meadows and woods, in the light of the stars and the warmth of the sun. I enjoyed being there, but did not notice how much I was being transformed internally by nature.

After a year, when I was able to return to Hungary in March 1946, a contemplative foundation had been laid in me. I was aware of it as inner calmness and clarity. My priestly vocation became gradually clear to me at this time. I recognized only much later that nature, and—as I discovered in the Bible, especially the desert—is a place of encounter with God. In the early Seventies I spent a longer time in the Atacama Desert in Chile and made a retreat in Mechillones just north of Antofagasta. From the coastal village I usually walked out into the desert. There was a mountain nearby. I often thought of Moses in Sinai and Jesus Christ in the desert region of Jericho. My conviction was strengthened that the desert is a place of encounter with God.

2. Encountering God and self

What is a retreat? We see in the Old and New Testaments and in the history of the Church, that whenever God intended to intervene in history, he prepared a human being for the task. He usually called this person out of his normal environment and led him into the desert. He kept him there for a long period before drawing him to an encounter with himself.

This happened to ABRAHAM. God invited Abraham to leave his country and to be on his way as a stranger. He granted him various personal encounters about which we know little, but two elements clearly stand out: Abraham recognized God more and more as his God, and he experienced his own identity as father-to-be of a great tribe. Naturally, this had to happen, for every encounter is a meeting between two poles in which one gets to know the other and at the same time oneself.

Similarly with MOSES. He grew up in Pharaoh's city in a religious setting where temple, priests, sacred writings, and cult were part of everyday life. But God did not speak to Moses there. Moses had to flee and look after sheep for many years in Sinai—a monotonous and uneventful occupation. He became empty. The busy-ness of the city was gone. He found more and more his own self. The time came when God granted him an encounter in the burning bush. God revealed himself as "I AM" (Ex 3:14), and Moses found his own identity as one sent on the mission of leading the Jews out of Egypt.

An encounter with God always leads to a recognition of God and oneself. To recognize God in oneself, and oneself in God, are two sides of the same coin. They cannot be separated. There is no encounter with God which is not also an encounter with oneself. And there is no encounter with one's true self which does not imply a growing knowledge of God.

The same can be seen on the social level. When Moses led the Israelites out of Egypt, they were not yet a *people,* a unity, they did not have a national identity. They became a people through their various encounters with God, which reached their climax on Mount Sinai. From this moment they were aware of themselves as a nation, a unity, rooted in a common law, a land, a hope, and—very specially—a God to whom they had promised fidelity and on whose protection they could rely.

JOHN THE BAPTIST lived in the desert. The people of Jerusalem streamed out to him because they felt that he spoke in a way different from their priests and scribes in Jerusalem. John preached in the power of the Holy Spirit. The priests in the temple also talked of God, but indirectly, without power. They spoke of laws, morals, and customs and the strict performance of the liturgy. John spoke out of his direct encounter with God. This made his words impressive.

JESUS CHRIST also went into the desert. What was he doing there? He did not study or prepare sermons, he sought an encounter with his Father in the mountain solitude. On returning from the desert, he knew what he had to proclaim.

ST. PAUL, too, spent time in the desert. He himself described his conversion. We are not surprised to find a new element in the development of his encounter with God. Jesus Christ appeared to him on the road to Damascus. This encounter transformed him into a person totally dedicated to Christ, living solely for him. He was baptized upon his arrival in Damascus. The astonishing fact is that after his baptism, he does not feel drawn to Jerusalem to meet those who had known Jesus. No, he immediately goes to Arabia:

the desert. Presumably he stayed there for some time, probably some years. When he returned from the desert, he became a great apostle to the Gentiles. He went up to Jerusalem only ten years later to speak with the other apostles. It is remarkable how Paul's encounter with Christ and his stay in the desert are related to each other. The Damascus event—his complete orientation to Christ—leads him directly into the desert.

ST. AUGUSTINE made a similar journey. He was converted in Milan through the preaching of St. Ambrose. Shortly after, he set out for North Africa and remained a few years in the desert. As with Paul, we see a conversion to Christ and the immediate impulse to go into the desert.

Finally, I should mention IGNATIUS, the originator of the *Spiritual Exercises*. He was a Spanish officer who was wounded during the siege of Pamplona and taken home to his father's house, where he spent several weeks on a sickbed. Being bored, he began to read the Bible and a collection of Lives of the Saints, the only reading matter available there. Gradually his eyes were opened. Some weeks later, he was converted to Jesus Christ so completely that he wished to shape his whole life after that of Jesus. He planned to travel to the Holy Land and live there as Jesus himself had lived. He set out from Loyola and, before boarding a ship in Barcelona, spent a night in prayer on Montserrat before the image of Our Lady. During the night he changed his mind about continuing his journey to Barcelona. He settled down a few kilometers from Montserrat and stayed in a cave near Manresa for a year. During this time he received those amazing graces which Abraham, Moses, Paul, and many other saints had received before him.

Later he wanted to pass on the graces of his desert experience to others, and, with reflection, he worked out the plan of the *Spiritual Exercises,* a thirty-day retreat. Going into the desert alone often means that one takes roundabout routes before being led to the essential, a process which might take thirty, even forty, years. Ignatius wanted to make such circuitous paths shorter by means of experienced guidance. During the short time of retreat, retreatants may not often find the great grace of Moses and Abraham, but they can find the direction in which to go.

As we have seen in these examples, when God calls someone to be a light and compass for others on the way to God, that person has to be prepared through his own encounter with God. In decisive moments of salvation history, such purifying preparation took place during a prolonged stay in the desert, until all that is unessential had been shed, and the essential reality stood out clearly. One found during this time both the encounter with God and the experience of one's own identity, inseparable from each other. The desert is a place of encounter with God and oneself. A retreat is a limited and guided desert experience.

3. Awareness, thinking, and doing

Let us examine more closely what takes place in the desert.

One does not need to be a great spiritual master to know that the way to God opens up through awareness rather than discursive thinking. God is present, but we are not aware of him. Rational thought plays an important part in the development of religious faith, especially at the beginning. But to move on to contemplation, a change from discursive thought to passive perception is absolutely necessary. Our human nature is constituted in such a way that our behavior is the result of three steps: awareness, thinking, doing.

At the beginning there is always *awareness*. There are the sense perceptions, like hearing, touching, tasting, seeing, smelling. Spiritual perceptions are called insight, becoming aware, becoming conscious. The Latin word *perceptio* means that we perceive something of reality.

Awareness is followed by *thought,* reflection; it is our first reaction to things perceived. We integrate the perception. This is done by the work of reason: reflecting, comparing, analyzing, planning, and choosing or deciding.

The third step is *execution*, putting into practice. We act on our insight. We take action and do something.

These three steps follow each other of necessity; no one can change the process. Yet in our hectic modern world, the process has lost its equilibrium. The second and third steps are overemphasized, while perception is cut short. No sooner have we perceived something than we begin to think and reflect, weigh and judge, and often begin to brood over things. The end of the process usually is that we find ourselves in conflict and want to change everything.

The great Doer, the Frantic Reactor, awakens in us. The time for awareness is cut short.

But it is perception that leads us to God. Contemplation is seeing. The Latin word *contemplari* means seeing, looking. In eternal life we shall not think about God, we shall see God. We shall not be engaged with God in outward activity but contemplate and love him. This will be our only occupation in heaven, and it begins already on earth. But, because our restless mind and our hectic activity distract us from perception, we do not perceive God. To prepare for the grace of contemplation we must first learn to become aware.

Awareness means becoming fully conscious. It is a matter of the spirit, an activity of consciousness. The sense organs bring information to our consciousness: we perceive by looking with the eyes, hearing with the ears, smelling with the nose, touching with the fingers, and tasting with the tongue. So our exercises begin with these sense perceptions because they are concrete and easily accessible. We shall then, gradually, proceed to more spiritual perceptions.

To be aware also means to live in the present. In our thoughts and desires we tend to live in the past and in the future. What is here and now is the present. The past has gone. The future is not yet here. To live in reality means to live in the present. God is accessible in the present moment. The goal of the spiritual journey in Benedictine spirituality is to walk in the presence of God. But since we live so much in the past and the future, we have to learn to stay in the present. Constant attention to the present moment will lead us into the presence of God.

Awareness, perception, being conscious, being present: these are practically synonymous.

Awareness does not tire. Thinking and doing does. After working with our hands or heads we need a pause to recover. Awareness is recovery par excellence, its highest form. If this were not the case we would have to plan for regular holidays in eternal life, in order to recover from the contemplation of God. No, awareness refreshes and regenerates us. Every true recreation gradually leads us to contemplation, which refreshes us.

Therefore, we are going to learn how to become aware by trying to stay in the present moment, without passing on to thinking and doing. That is the difficulty of our learning process. Everyone necessarily perceives, but after a fraction of a second our mind begins to work; our attention turns from perception to our ideas. We have to learn to stay with perception.

This task implies an important change in direction. We are invited to let go of thinking and doing in order to turn wholly to awareness. As soon as we notice that we have become distracted and are busy in the world of our thoughts, we must promptly return to our perception. This demands a continuous laborious effort involving our whole being and lasting to the end of our retreat. It is our permanent task, deepening more and more on our journey together.

4. The first teacher is nature

We have reached the first concrete step of this learning process. Nature is the great teacher of contemplation. Here we set out on our way. We go out for walks as we normally do. Then we walk more and more slowly and stand still. For example, we look at a tree. We allow the tree to have an effect on us. We have hardly begun to really look, when we'll start to think about how old this tree might be. That question comes from our heads. We find ourselves on the mental level and are no longer in pure awareness. When we realize this, we return at once to our sense perception and continue to let the tree make an impression on us. Within a moment perhaps, the issue of our dying forests, and specifically the state of this tree, forces itself upon us. We are again busy with our mind and must return to awareness.

Then we listen to a bird. Not in order to know where it is sitting or what bird it is, but simply to let its voice speak to us. We give our attention to a little soil we have taken up from the ground. We remain with this sense impression. When we become distracted, we return to seeing and feeling the soil.

We must not let ourselves be led astray by our minds, for the question that will then easily arise is: when did I become distracted, why, and by which thought. This doesn't interest us. The only important thing is to continue giving our attention to being aware. The fact that we get distracted is of no consequence. As soon as we notice it, we return to perception without reflecting on how long or why we were distracted.

With awareness comes a completely new experience: we do not have to achieve any result.

Ordinarily, the pressure to do well, to produce something, causes fear and tension. In contemplation we need not achieve anything! We are liberated from the urge for efficiency. We remain in contact with nature. We can look at the blue sky, listen to the murmur of a brook, look at the busy ants, wonder at the beauty of a flower, feel the wind on our face, or let the clouds speak to us. If we hear from afar the noise of a car, we can be aware of that, too. It is important not to make a judgment or want to change something. We perceive everything just as it presents itself.

It can happen that we feel bored. Boredom is a feeling we can look at. How do I feel it? This question can direct our attention inside and lead us to the awareness of the boredom. And so we have returned to our perception. After a short time we return to our perception of nature.

The contemplative attitude leads us to an astonishing serenity. Everything that is, is allowed to be. We do not need to change anything. We leave everything as it stands. We seek no knowledge and do not observe. We just look. What is the difference between observing and looking? Observation seeks something for itself; looking is selfless. We know the difference very well. We would never ask God to observe us. But we are happy when he looks at us kindly. In eternal life we shall not be observing God, but shall live in the vision of God.

II. INSTRUCTIONS FOR MEDITATION

Dear Reader, now comes the parting of the ways. If you want to remain a reader, you may continue reading this book. But you will not join in the retreat. I ask you to make a choice. Decide whether you want to read this book or make a contemplative retreat. If you look at this book like any other reading material, read as the mood takes you. But if you want to take part in the contemplative retreat, I will show you the way. It is a long, steep, and difficult way which will make demands on your precious time. It is a way through beautiful country, but also through desert. Step by step I will set you laborious tasks. You will often ask yourself why you ever entered on this path. At such moments you must just persevere without bothering about the "why?" question. The question of its meaning will naturally arise, and I cannot explain the meaningfulness of the steps beforehand. You are following an instruction and I depend on your trust. If you're prepared to make the retreat under these conditions, I shall call you no longer Reader, but Retreatant.

Dear Retreatant, go out into nature and begin with the conscious effort to be aware.

If you're making a Closed Retreat—that is, if you want to devote some days exclusively to this retreat—spend at least one whole day in the open. Do not read, or write letters, or phone anyone; do not do handiwork; and do not listen to music. Devote yourself wholly to awareness.

If you're making a Retreat in Daily Life, take the time and remain outside in nature for an hour daily for at least a couple of weeks. It doesn't matter if you live in a town. You will find a garden or a park, and you can apply yourself to perceiving what is around you even in the streets.

If you want to make the retreat, stop reading now. The book will not run away. If you have already spent some hours in nature, you may, between such times, read one or two of the following dialogues in order to orient yourself through the experience of others. Do not read all the dialogues at one sitting. Stop after the third dialogue or even earlier and go out again into nature.

III. DIALOGUES

[In all the Dialogues, "RM" will indicate the Retreat Master's words.]

1.1 BARBARA

RM. Barbara, you have been outside in nature for some hours now. How did you find it?

BARBARA. I haven't arrived yet! All of last week is still turning round in my head. I feel very restless. I've run around outside, but have not seen or heard anything. I was quarrelling inside myself with other people.

RM. You're still agitated inside.

BARBARA. Yes, that's it.

RM. Have you tried to come to awareness?

BARBARA. No, not yet.

RM. Try to walk a little more slowly, and then still more slowly. If you find that difficult, have a good run, take a shower, and then you will quiet down. If you still can't stand still and stick with something particular, try as a first step to look around you while walking, taking a fleeting notice of something. Go back out into nature.

1.2 ANDREW

RM. Andrew, how did it go with you?

ANDREW. I enjoyed going out. I went into the woods and chose a place to sit. I closed my eyes and listened. There were so many different sounds I'd never noticed before. Once I was startled, but soon realized it was only the wind blowing through a birch tree. I listened to the birds. I've never noticed so many different bird sounds. I tried to listen, and listen again, not to miss the slightest sound.

RM. The birdsong impressed you.

ANDREW. It was an experience.

RM. This experience must have had an effect on your feelings.

ANDREW. An effect? . . . I didn't pay attention to that . . . *[pause]*. Yes, refreshing: I was full of joy.

RM. Be fully aware of this refreshing feeling and joy. You experienced it but hadn't taken notice. Center your attention on it.

1.3 JENNIFER

JENNIFER. I was out for a long time. First I really marched. Later I slowed down and stood still. I went a few paces and made contact with the environment. I looked into the sky and stared at the wandering clouds. Then I looked for quite a time at a rare flower. It was simply beautiful. After awhile, thoughts came. It got noisy inside me, and the hectic pace of the last

weeks returned. I found myself making plans. I had a few
good ideas for my work.

RM. You got caught up in your ideas.

JENNIFER. Yes, they seemed important to me. I wanted to think
them through and then return to awareness.

RM. . . . to think them through. . . .

JENNIFER. Yes, to think them through. Or are thoughts such a bad
thing?

RM. Whether bad or good, that's of no interest to us. An answer
would lead us into more thought; we would react with thinking. Learn to come back at once. Don't finish thinking your
thoughts through—they won't ever stop anyway.

The important change we have to make in this retreat is to
come to the inner conviction that thoughts compared to
awareness are neither important nor interesting on the way to
God. Feel your way into yourself and let this plant or that
stone have an effect on you. Become aware of what is coming
to you from the flower. What you can work out or invent isn't
interesting, but only what you receive and become aware of.
Feel what is really there. Pay attention to what concrete reality says to you. That is more interesting than the most beautiful thoughts. Turn from the world of thoughts to the awareness of immediate reality. Then return to what you feel
spontaneously, right away.

1.4 FELIX

FELIX. I went out and looked at many things. After a while I became furious. I have come here to learn how to pray, instead
of which I'm told to look at flowers. I have heavy responsibilities in daily life, and my time is precious. Piles of letters
are waiting on my desk. I could do thousands of useful things.
But I am told to look at flowers. I'm still raging and regret
having come here.

RM. You see no meaning in what we are doing here.

FELIX. How can I? I am not a flower gardener.

RM. You're angry.

FELIX. That's right.

RM. At the moment we aren't interested in whether we seeing meaning or not in what we're doing. Look, the retreat is like mountain climbing. Imagine a guide who knows the high mountains—their pathways and their dangers. A group entrusts itself to him. In their own interest those who want to participate have to follow his instructions. After their return from the mountains, each person can go where he or she likes. We don't need guides in the valley where the roads are well marked.

It's similar in this retreat. You have come trusting that I can show you the way you seek. So we came to an agreement. I'll show you a way and you'll walk with me for a stretch of ten days. I did ask you explicitly what you expect from me, and whether you are clear in your mind about what I can show you. If you've changed your mind, I am ready at any time to change the contract we agreed on. I don't want to pressure you. I keep asking from you only what you yourself have authorized me to ask. It's too early to make judgments before the end of the time we agreed on, because you can't assess what is important on this journey. We can't say whether a soup is tasty or not if we haven't tried it.

I lead you on a new and steep path. Practically speaking, each of you will ask yourself at some stage whether the path makes any sense at all. That question can arise, and it's in order. But don't follow it up. If you ponder it, you're back in your head and have already left the path of awareness. What's on the stage is of no interest to us. If you're furious with me, study your rage.

FELIX. I shall think about that.

RM. Feel perfectly free, Felix.

1.5 CLAUDIA

CLAUDIA. I went outside with mixed feelings. I didn't have a book with me, and then I remembered that I wasn't supposed to read.

RM. This made you feel uncomfortable.

CLAUDIA. Yes, without a book I feel unprotected, as if I'm then more confronted with just me. But I did go out all the same. I had a lot of thoughts. When I saw a dying tree a few yards in front of me, I was deeply moved.

RM. You identified yourself with that lifeless tree.

CLAUDIA. Oh, yes. Then came sadness, a great deal of sadness. I saw myself in the tree. I felt like the dried up stump, without life—dead and finished. I then returned to a way of praying which I haven't practiced for a long time, which is that I just let it be and look at it as it is.

RM. And then you became more peaceful.

CLAUDIA. Yes, the sadness remained for a while. It even intensified. I cried a little. Later came more peace. Looking more closely, I saw more life around the dead tree, and I stood there for a long time in peace.

RM. That is contemplation. You see, you discovered it quite naturally, without anyone telling you. Love says, "It is as it is." To look at it and leave it as it is—that's what contemplation is all about.

1.6 JACK

JACK. I was outside a long time and tried to get into awareness. What you say about awareness as a way to God makes sense to me. I tried to remain totally in the present, but I noticed how often I became distracted. I decided to observe when and why I become distracted, and tried to find the cause and become conscious of the when and why. A few times I managed to reconstruct my train of thought quite well.

RM. You hoped to avoid the distractions by finding their cause?

JACK. Yes, that was my intention.

RM. And did you succeed?

JACK. I can't trace all my distractions back.

RM. Look, Jack, I can predict that you won't get far in this way. To seek causes is a mental process, leading you to reflect and analyze. It's a contradiction in itself, to want to get away from the mental level by mental activity. Give it up, this seeking for the causes of your distractions, and return to awareness.

1.7 SABRINA

SABRINA. When I was outside, I saw trees in the distance. I decided to go there and ran across the meadows. I wanted so much to reach the woods. Suddenly I came upon a barbed wire fence blocking the way. I got really angry, but that didn't make the fence disappear. I was furious. Then I realized that there was something fishy about my reaction: why did I want to reach the woods at any cost? Nonetheless, I couldn't dismiss my anger against the fence.

RM. Do you know what the barbed wire fence symbolizes?

SABRINA. Yes, I do. It's my limitations.

RM. You see it clearly. May I offer a recommendation?

SABRINA. Of course.

RM. Go back to the wire fence and make friends with it. Try to give it gentle strokes, or a hug!

SABRINA *[with an amused smile]:* That's funny! I'll try.

[The next day.]

RM. So how did it go?

SABRINA. I went out there. I couldn't hug the fence! But I walked quietly along it, back and forth. After awhile I could put up with its being there. Perhaps I can now also allow some of my limitations to exist. I grew a lot calmer today.

RM. Sabrina, we're going to learn something else. I said that we don't want to "achieve" anything in this retreat. I sent you out into nature with the task of giving your whole attention to awareness. You went out, but set yourself the goal of reaching the wood. You were determined to get there—so much so, that you became angry when you didn't succeed. I understand you very well. We live like that most of the time. We can't stand our own company. Does that sound familiar to you?

SABRINA. Yes, I've often noticed how many people waste their holidays by making plans which they're determined to carry out during their free time, instead of giving themselves the time and the rest. They must drive as far as possible, see many cities, and invent countless pastimes—all in order not to come to themselves, not to stay with themselves. The thought of putting up with themselves fills them with panic.

RM. Exactly! Go out again and make no plans beyond walking slowly and looking at what you find around you. Try to look and listen without any other intention. That's the beginning of a new way that leads to God. God is everywhere, but we run past him without seeing him. Try to remain with a feeling instead of setting a goal for yourself.

1.8 DAVID

DAVID. I was outside and tried to get into awareness. There were moments when I could identify strongly with a tree and really felt its gentle murmur in myself. When a breeze danced through the leaves, I felt it in myself. Gradually, I became conscious of the many thoughts that swarmed around inside my head. First I was astonished, then increasingly shocked by this beehive of thoughts. Though awareness hadn't completely stopped, my world of thoughts was right up front: ideas, reflections, images, memories, commentaries. I couldn't switch off. I never would have believed that I'm so helplessly overwhelmed by thinking!

RM. You were surprised.

DAVID. Unpleasantly so.

RM. It was a very important experience. Many people come to the beginning of the retreat who truly think they don't have this problem. Yet shortly, they're amazed at the multitude of thoughts that swirl around inside their heads. It's the same in everyday life: thoughts run right alongside us in the everyday race of our occupations. But we're not conscious of the thinking. When external activities cease, and we could quiet down, we find we can't stop thinking because our brains keep on working without a break!

DAVID. That's exactly what happened to me. I wanted to switch my thoughts off, but found I couldn't because I can only replace my thoughts with other thoughts. I can't get out of this vicious circle.

RM. A real vicious circle.

DAVID. Exactly.

RM. Well, you don't need to switch off your thoughts. Turn to the awareness of a flower. As long as you're in wonder about a flower, there aren't any thoughts. Leave them behind not by rejecting or fighting them, but by simply turning to awareness. As long as your attention is given more to the flower than the thoughts, they'll retire to the outskirts of your consciousness and no longer disturb you. Later, you'll hardly notice them, even though they might never stop completely. What is important is to direct your attention to something concrete.

1.9 ANDREA

ANDREA. This morning, after working in the kitchen, I went outside and sat down on a bench. Pretty soon I noticed that I was tired. I first allowed myself to feel this tiredness. It wasn't exactly uplifting, but I was able to stay there. When I said to myself, "I may now be tired," I got quite joyful that it was okay to feel tired, that I didn't have to overcome the tiredness: I may feel tired and be tired. So the time passed quickly.

The experience was important to me: I don't have to do anything, achieve anything, change anything, have anything to show or prove. I may now be just as I am. For a time I kept returning to this awareness and remained with it. I became quiet in myself, and suddenly I had the impression, "I am here." This feeling was very simple and filled everything. I remained in this awareness for a good while. Later, thoughts again came closer, but the experience with tiredness and being here was more telling. I feel I'll often be drawn back to that awareness.

RM. Yes, you're on the right track.

1.10 VERA

VERA. I went out early in the morning and saw a wonderful sunrise. Long before the sun appeared, I saw the dawn brightening, painted pink above the horizon. Shortly before sunrise I saw the full moon just setting in the opposite side of the sky. Then the horizon turned a bright red. The few clouds were beautiful, as if in a painting. I stood there until I saw the first glimpse of the sun. I remained there a long time in wonder. The birds sang so beautifully, and I told myself: "Now you have seen something marvelous and can lift up your spirit to God."

I began to pray, to praise God, and began to converse with him. I spoke to him for a long time in prayers of praise. I told him much of my life and kept repeating the prayer of Brother Klaus of Flueli. I prayed for people—for the sick and suffering, for the Third World, for my parents and my grandmother who died a few months ago. I prayed for a long time. It was beautiful, I felt deep devotion and gratitude.

RM. You had not prayed this deeply for a long time.

VERA. For a long time. I could tell God many things from the depth of my heart.

RM. I'm happy that you were able to pray in that way. But now I want to lead you a step further. I tell you about contemplative prayer, which is different. Words, thoughts, and feelings gradually ebb away. In eternal life we shall not be speaking to God or using words to ask God to help other people. In eternal life we shall remain in loving amazement.

VERA. I was *in* loving amazement.

RM. Yes, that is why I want to set you straight.

VERA. I don't understand.

RM. You *were* in amazement, and that leads to contemplation. That's the reason why I sent you out into nature. When you had the impression that you had remained in wonder long enough, you passed on to vocal prayer and many words, which is a step backwards in contemplation. You unconsciously believed that your prayer in words was more of a prayer than the wonder itself.

VERA. Shouldn't I pray?

RM. No, you should not pray like this right now. Remain in wonder; it will lead you to contemplation, which consists in remaining in wonder. God touched you there and led you to wonder. But since you returned to vocal and affective prayer, it's clear that, on your scale of values, the formulated prayers rank higher than the simple amazement.

I invite you to change your understanding of prayer. Wonder is the final step on the way to prayer. In eternal life we shall be in eternal wonder. So I ask you to drop the formulated prayers and remain in awareness. I show you how the path continues. Remain in awareness or—when it happens—in wonder.

1.11 MARCELLA

MARCELLA. Yes, I was outside and found it very beautiful. I felt intense joy in living and clearly experienced it: I don't have to be aware, to taste, to hear, or to see. Things themselves directly offer themselves to awareness. It was a beautiful experience. By simply being there these things offer themselves to our awareness.

RM. You didn't feel any pressure that you had to be aware?

MARCELLA. No, it was a pure joy to be aware.

RM. Be fully aware of this joy. It comes to you spontaneously and offers itself to you.

1.12 KEVIN

KEVIN. I walked around outside and devoted myself totally to awareness. I wasn't conscious of individual things so much as of the whole of creation: the sky, the wind, the earth, and everything together. I felt its fullness and an incredible breadth. It impressed me as a whole, not so much the details.

RM. The all-embracing cosmos.

KEVIN. Yes, but after a while I became very tired.

RM. You felt tired?

KEVIN. Yes, but the tiredness wasn't caused by my little walk. I brought it with me into the retreat. Before that, activities had blocked it out. And now, when I am beginning to become quiet, it shows up again. I had to move faster so that this tiredness couldn't get the upper hand.

RM. You automatically wanted to overcome tiredness by movement.

KEVIN. Yes, that is true.

RM. Look, Kevin, we're only on the first day of the retreat. Let's handle your tiredness differently from what you're used to. First, look at your tiredness. Tolerate it. Don't fight it. Ask yourself how you feel it. Tiredness is something we can be aware of. It's even closer to you than the tree. Have a good sleep and then go out again into nature. Try to stay with awareness.

1.13 MARY

MARY. On my little walk I looked at the barley, corn, and potato fields. Later I found an anthill in the wood. I was occupied a long time with the thought of how these creatures live and what they do. I touched the anthill with a stick and saw how they carried their eggs away in a panic. I watched carefully how they interacted with each other. I could have stayed there for hours.

RM. You were interested.

MARY. They live in a way still unknown to us.

RM. It was a good step to enter into something quite different. We forget our problems; we get new perspectives on our difficulties. This can lead to greater quiet. Do you see a difference between observing and seeing?

MARY. No, so far they are both the same to me.

RM. But there's a great difference. Through observation we want to know and have information. We want to attain something, like knowledge. In contrast, mere looking doesn't want to reach anything. From looking comes love for what one sees. Looking is selfless and disinterested. We would never wish God to observe us, but we are glad when he looks on us with love. In eternal life we shall not observe God, but see him and therefore love him.

MARY. I see—I observed the ants; I didn't contemplate them.

1.14 LISETTE

LISETTE. Today, on my walk, I felt great joy. At first I saw a corn-field and touched tassels on the ears; then I went down a little path . . . *[thoughtfully]*. And what then? Oh, I came to the chapel in the woods and lay down on a bench and felt simply happy. I heard many sounds. I let the sun shine on me and enjoyed being there like a child. That was the strongest impression in my joy. Just to be—I could have skipped and hopped about. I know this feeling. I often calm down this way, just being there without doing anything.

RM. Simply being there.

LISETTE. Yes, the sense of being there was the main thing.

RM. Were you able to stick with the awareness of your being there?

LISETTE. Yes, spontaneously. I stayed with this awareness. I became quite still inside. The awareness of simple, plain existence fascinated me—or better, filled me. It was so interesting that for a while, I'm sure, I had no thoughts. Or at least, I don't know whether I had thoughts, I don't think so.

RM. That is the way. To be present, to be there, is already the first step into the presence of God. Direct your attention often, and as long as you can, to this being there. It will become more and more interesting and lead you into the joy of the present moment. But don't try to achieve the joy; remain in the wonder of being there.

1.15 MARTIN

MARTIN. I thought a lot about the future and the past. As soon as I become aware of anything, I automatically begin to analyze. I question everything, want to understand and integrate everything. I can't be satisfied until everything is perfectly clear. I find it very hard to stay in awareness.

RM. Your mind stays in control.

MARTIN. Yes, I would say it has to put everything in order, so that ... *[thoughtfully]* everything is clear.

RM. Clarity gives you security.

MARTIN. I don't like to link clarity with security.

RM. Hm, you don't like it?

MARTIN. *[After a while, reflecting.]* There's something true in that; I do feel more secure when I see clearly.

RM. You're more relaxed and carefree when you see everything clearly.

MARTIN. Yes, that's right. ... *[After a pause]* ... Yes, it's also true that if I can't see the whole of something, I feel insecure ... *[pause]*. When I don't understand something I get restless and begin to look into it.

RM. Look deeply into it, so that you can stop worrying and feel secure again.

[Pause.]

MARTIN. I recognize how much insecurity lies behind my urge to categorize everything. *[Long pause.]* I think I'm more insecure than I'd realized.

RM. Hm. . . . *[Pause.]* Let's leave it at that for now.

1.16 VIVIAN

VIVIAN. I didn't get on well with awareness this morning. I had so many thoughts—very negative ones. I'm preoccupied with my cold. In fact, I'm wondering how I can persevere in this retreat with such a cold. . . .

RM. Your cold worries you.

VIVIAN. Yes, it takes a lot of my attention. It's there now and really annoys me. I can't help paying attention to constantly blowing my nose.

RM. You see that as a necessity.

VIVIAN. I can't see it any other way. I just have a cold.

RM. You'd like to be rid of it so that you could begin to meditate.

VIVIAN. Yes, I'm afraid that it will last all ten days, that this stupid cold will ruin my retreat and the days will all be lost. I don't want that. I want to make the retreat and learn contemplative prayer.

RM. You want to learn it, but can't wholly enter into it.

VIVIAN. Not enter into it? I'm trying hard.

RM. I don't question your effort, only the object of your effort.

VIVIAN. Why?

RM. Contemplative prayer doesn't consist in achieving something, but in becoming aware of what is there. You want to get rid of your cold in order not to lose these ten days and learn contemplative prayer: you want a great deal! I'll show you another way. Look at your cold and allow it to be there. You don't need to want to be rid of it. Allow yourself to lose ten days. And you don't need to learn contemplative prayer. Your cold is your present. God is present for you at the moment in your cold. God is also present in your fear of loss. Learn to look at what is there without wishing to change it.

VIVIAN. Good. I shall try to occupy myself with my cold.

RM. No, Vivian. I didn't mean that. There's a great difference between looking at your cold and being occupied with it. Looking brings rest. Rest brings tolerance. Occupation with your cold would set your mind and will in motion and lead to restlessness. Simply direct your attention for a time to how your cold feels. If you can remain attentive in just looking, but without thoughts, you will find rest.

After having looked at your cold—the fear, the misery of it—for a moment, return at once to awareness of nature and remain with that. If you can't go out because of your cold, sit down in your room, or walk slowly up and down the corridor, or stand still in front of the window and look out. Becoming aware of what is there leads you into contemplation.

1.17 RALPH

RALPH. I asked myself this morning what would help me most at the moment, and felt it was going for a walk. So I went into the garden. But I'd hardly put one foot out the door when I felt so restless that I returned straight away to my room. I saw my briefcase beside my bed, full of papers and work which still had to be done. I put my briefcase into the closet and left my work alone. I felt better after that. I went out again and felt contentment and joy. The pressure to work was gone. I was glad to be here. But almost immediately, negative thoughts, aggressive thoughts arose in me. I'm still shocked to find how much space these aggressions take up in me and how they rob me of so much strength.

RM. How did you handle the aggressions?

RALPH. I thought, damn it!—do they have to come just now when I have such beautiful feelings and everything is well with me? Why do they return to me just now?

RM. You reject these aggressions.

RALPH. Totally!

RM. Accept them. Allow them to be there. Look, God makes his sun to rise upon good and bad alike. Everything can remain before God. Remember the temptations of Job in the Old Testament. When Job was prosperous, Lucifer asked God to be allowed to test him, to see whether he really was as good as he appeared to be in his prosperity. We would most likely have thought that this mustn't happen on any account. According to our ideas, evil shouldn't touch Job. But God allowed it. He had no fear.

As far as God is concerned, evil may exist. As long as we try to suppress one part (the evil part) of reality, we have to live with tension and conflict. We have to reintegrate the suppressed part of ourselves with the whole. If what we call "evil" can be reintegrated into the universe, it will be good in itself. Only then can the tension between good and evil cease. In God there is no duality between good and evil. In him flows only the living stream, eternal love. Don't fight against your aggressions. Accept them in love, and they will dissolve.

1.18 TONI

TONI. For a very long time I was focused exclusively on my future. I'm very concerned about how to continue after this retreat. It took a good while before I even noticed that I was in the woods. I looked at a tree, and senselessness arose in me: what is the use of looking at a tree? What good does it do me? Suddenly, almost without my noticing, the question magically answered itself: it brings me nothing and takes nothing away. It's simply there as a gift. It's free of charge. When I realized this grace, my heart became lighter. I went on trying to remain in awareness without any other end.

RM. Yes, contemplation has no other purpose. When we stop expecting something, a new world opens.

IV. REVIEW & TRANSITION TO THE SECOND DAY

Dear Reader, I hope this part of the book has been useful to you. You may have found some inspiration or recognition in the thoughts on these pages. I can also understand if there was too much repetition for you. In any case, I wish you much pleasure in further reading. Perhaps you'll like the book and decide to try out the retreat at a later date.

Dear Retreatant, you have reached the end of the first day. If you're making a Closed Retreat you will have spent at least one day outside in the awareness of nature. However, the first day is usually needed for settling in, and it's possible that you were exhausted and needed more sleep at first. If you haven't rested, do it now. We can't meditate in a tired state. Maybe the time you spent in nature on the first day was actually very short. Don't hesitate to take one or two days longer. The time will not be lost. Nature is an excellent teacher of contemplation. I hope that you have discovered already that the best recreation is remaining in awareness.

If you aren't spending the whole time in retreat but practicing a Retreat in Daily Life, you've been outside in nature for an hour a day for two weeks.

Quite apart from the question of the kind of retreat you are making, look back on what took place. I'll help you with a few questions:

- Are you able to take part in daily Eucharist?

- Have you been able to experience what it means to remain in awareness of nature?

- Do you find joy or rest in nature? Were you able to remain sometimes fully attentive without thinking of anything specific or expecting something? Do you perhaps feel that a new relationship with nature is growing?

- Are you more aware of your thoughts? Have you begun to handle them?

- How do you get on with the Dialogues? I hope you're staying with some and not reading on impatiently. They are only interesting when we allow one at a time to have an effect on us, without passing on immediately to the next one.

- Are you determined to continue the retreat? It demands a lot. If you have determination, it will be easier.

If you have not yet spent all the time in nature we agreed on, don't go further. If you feel the urge to go further, test yourself by becoming aware of your impatience and desire to achieve—and let it be. We can't accelerate the retreat faster than the time needed for the inner process. Inner development in the retreat is like the blossoming of a flower: It doesn't open more quickly just because we stand by impatiently, waiting to pick it.

If you've really finished the first day, I wish you good progress on the second. What follows is meant to place before you the solid earthiness of this contemplative retreat, its central relationship to reality. We shall also take a further step in our exercises, progressing from awareness of the exterior world to awareness of our own bodies. We begin by quietly sitting or kneeling. Nature has prepared us for this and will continue to accompany us.

SECOND DAY

I. INTRODUCTORY TALK:
THE THREEFOLD RELATIONSHIP

1. I was sick and you visited me

In the Gospel, Jesus Christ speaks of the parallel relationship with God and neighbor (Mt 25:3-44). When we visit the sick, we visit Christ. When we feed the hungry, we feed the Lord. When we welcome the homeless, we welcome God. When we visit a prisoner, we meet Jesus Christ. He identifies the relationships we have with others with the relationship we have with him. He tells us that everything we experience in dealing with our neighbor takes place at the same time between God and us. If we want to know how we relate to Jesus Christ, we can learn from our human relationships. Everyone acts with God the same way as with his neighbor.

Quite often, our relationship with God suffers from illusions because we think it depends only on our intentions. When we want to love God, we think we are doing it already. We think much the same at the beginning of our human relationships. Perhaps we are impatient with another person, but we think that this was just an accident, and we can easily convince ourselves that this won't happen again.

Contrary to our intentions, it happens again and again. It occurs so often that—faced with the reality—we finally accept that our subconscious influences us in our relationship with people. And in fact, the subconscious affects our relationship with God also, even if we tend to believe that the subconscious has nothing to do with it. We abandon ourselves to the illusion that our free will determines our relations with God. The intention to love him makes us think that we already do love him. But if we believe the Gospel passage just referred to, we must admit that it is not so.

Our subconscious affects our relationship with God in the same way as it does our relationship with our neighbor. The only way of knowing with certainty where we stand with regard to God, is to take all our human relationships together and look at them. What happens in these relationships also happens in our relationship with God.

A concrete example: if I have human relationships with a hundred people, and really love twenty of them, reject twenty, and have a fairly "normal" (but also superficial) relationship with sixty, then I must conclude that my love for God is 20% real love, 20% rejection, and 60% superficiality. This 60% means that God exists for me at such a distance that he is practically absent from my life.

As long as I look down on a single human being, I also look down on God. The extent of my contempt depends on the place this person has among all my relationships. A child's relationship to its mother can, for example, make up 40%, 50%, or even more of its relationships. As long as I'm angry with one person, I am also angry with God. As long as I ignore or envy a single person, I also ignore or envy God. As long as I fear one single person, I am also afraid of God. If I am jealous, I am jealous also of God. This identification of love for God and love for other human beings provides the only chance of anchoring faith fully in life.

Many people gauge their love of God to be worth more than their human relationships. That is a clear delusion. They regard themselves as having more faith than they really have. I have often been asked, "How can I integrate my faith in my life?" This question is prompted by the idea that while these people have great faith, they just can't make it concrete in their actions. So I have always answered, "You don't need to translate your faith into daily living. You can read from your daily living how great your faith really is."

Before translating our supposed faith into daily life, we should read from our love of neighbor how great our faith really is. Only then do we stand on the firm ground of reality. From there, we can make the effort to have both relationships—which really are one—grow together. It will not make the way easier, but at least it excludes the delusion that one lives one's faith already, but not yet one's love for one's neighbor.

2. The way out of a crisis

The fundamental truth about relationships became a decisive experience for me through a seemingly everyday occurrence. I was professor of theology and spiritual director at a theological college of our Order in Argentina, when I went through a crisis of faith. It was during the time of great changes after the Vatican Council in the early 1960s. I found I could no longer believe in God. I had the feeling that there was nothing outside the visible world. The atheistic worldview seemed to me the only possible one. I had the impression that I had made a fatal mistake when I entered the Jesuit Order and became a priest. My whole life was brought into question. This crisis lasted a long time, and I was prepared to give up my faith and my priesthood, but I didn't yet have the inner certainty that God really didn't exist. Three years passed, without any decisive alteration in my state of mind. Every day my crisis confronted me. I was teaching dogmatic theology. As spiritual director, I had to clarify the vocation of my fellow Jesuits to the priesthood and the Order. I preached every week at Sunday Mass and heard confessions for hours. It was often oppressive. I didn't feel dishonest because I was truly searching, but everything I did was accompanied by great inner tension and doubt.

A seemingly banal occurrence led me onto the right path. There were about thirty professors of theology and philosophy living in our community. We had a common room where every day after dinner we had coffee, which we prepared ourselves in a small tea kitchen. Before we went back to work, the cups had to be washed, always by an older retired professor who had less work than most of us had. One day he protested indignantly that we always left the cups sitting around and took no notice at all what happened about them. To emphasize his discontent, he told us off quite angrily. I heard him, but returned to my work and forgot the whole thing within minutes.

In the afternoon, I went for a walk during a break. Suddenly, I had the insight that this fellow Jesuit had brought a problem to our notice and that I had not opened myself to it at all. I was painfully stunned by my attitude. And as I went on with my thoughts, I had a still more disagreeable insight. My crisis in faith rose up in front of me. I became conscious of the parallel between this everyday event and my crisis. I had heard my brother's problem, but didn't take it seriously. I had not really listened. I asked myself whether something similar was happening in my relationship with God. Had I perhaps been so busied with my thoughts and activities that I kept God at a distance and therefore felt unable to believe in his existence? The parallel fit, and it shook me deeply.

But I soon recognized that this insight had opened a door to allow me to emerge from my crisis of faith. If I tried to open myself to people, a change might take place in my crisis of faith. I tried for a year to be more open to others and allow them to come closer to me. In a year, the crisis was over. Once and for ever the connection between human relationships and relationship with God had dawned on me, and it became a guideline for my whole life. I was so struck by this discovery that it appeared to me like a theory of Einstein, something unheard of. After a short time I recognized how old my "new discovery" was! It has been clearly expressed in the Gospel for 2000 years.

Since then I have become firmly convinced that the main task of religious education is to teach that loving God and loving our neighbor as ourselves is one and the same. Christian faith remains a lifeless theory as long as this understanding has not become flesh and blood in us.

We treat God the same way we treat other people. The parallel is mathematically exact, without exception. But to be really precise, we have to speak of a further component. Our relationship with God, which is the same as that with our neighbor, runs parallel also to the relationship we have with ourselves. If we reject our neighbor, we also reject God, and so also ourselves. If we do not love ourselves, we cannot love the God who gives us his life. If we don't love ourselves, where would we get our love of neighbor? We can't hate ourselves and at the same time love God and our neighbor wholeheartedly. These relationships are inseparably intertwined. We have only one heart with which to love God and our neighbor and ourselves.

3. *The best training for interaction with people*

Why do I write about this theme at the beginning of the retreat? Contemplative prayer demands time and silence. In providing for silence, we soon ask whether silence does not make us egotistical and estranged from the world, or even from ourselves. Would it not be better to devote these precious days to demonstrable service of others, instead of wasting them in doing nothing?

Let's look more closely at what truly keeps us from loving others. In my opinion, our love of neighbor suffers most from our not listening to each other, not paying attention to one another, because of our need to achieve. The first problem in dealing with others is that we don't listen to them. To listen to someone means not just hearing the words but accepting what lies behind those words. Still more, it means to be with him with all our senses so that he feels entirely understood and accepted.

Real listening is difficult for us. In our normal interactions, we only listen long enough to understand roughly what our partner in conversation wanted to express. Then we continue to follow our own thoughts and interests. The other person may go on talking, but we are no longer with him. For example, someone tells somebody else about a beautiful trip he made last week. Hearing the words, "beautiful trip," the "listener" immediately thinks about one of his own recent excursions, and he says, "Yes, I also had a wonderful trip." What happened? The first speaker wasn't listened to, though he was probably still full of his experience and wanted to share it. The word "trip" brought the hearer back to his own trip, which brought him immediately back to himself. He appeared to be continuing to participate in the conversation, but in his mind and words he was already with himself, far away from the other. He was no longer listening.

Another example: someone tells us his problem. Immediately, we give him a piece of good advice. We believe we know what the person needs in this situation. He probably didn't want our advice, he only wanted to be listened to. He wanted to pour out his heart, and had looked for someone who would listen to him. We, however, can't bear seeing someone suffer. We immediately feel the urge to offer help. The urge doesn't allow us to listen to the end, but forces us to give good advice. We console a sick person by whispering to him to trust in God, or we tell him of a medication that we think will surely help him. There is no need for this. The medical care will be the doctor's business. The sick man merely wants to be listened to and accepted. To listen demands inner calm and the courage to stay with suffering.

Something similar happens in a discussion involving world-views. Each person sees only his own ideas, begins to expound them, and forgets to see the other human being who wants to be listened to. It isn't the human being that counts, but ideological opinions. How quickly we forget the human being and put our ideas or interests in the center of everything! We need a great deal of inner detachment to have different opinions and interests, and yet place the other person at the center of our attention.

What does contemplative prayer teach us? It teaches us to hear. It teaches us to listen to God and so also to listen to people, for they are one and the same thing. Or to put it the other way around: If we can give an ear to other people, we can give an ear to God. No technique, no group dynamics, no training in self-awareness seems to me as helpful in relating to others as learning to hear.

What does a contemplative retreat lead us to? Learning to hear. We learn to listen, to receive, to allow things to be as they are, to allow them to have an effect on us. As soon as we have learned this, we shall be able to be attentive to God and to our neighbor, for our relationship to both is the same.

The second obstacle in dealing with people is the pressure to *achieve something*. Modern society exerts pressure on us, wants us to show what we can achieve. Everyone is judged according to his achievements, whether these are valued or despised. That is the law that rules not only in the material world but also in human relationships. Massive pressure is exerted on us to achieve something.

Some simple examples: Imagine a student, nearing her exams, who doesn't manage to cover all the material quickly enough. Or imagine a manager who discovers that his firm is in the red and threatened with bankruptcy. In either case, pressure intensifies and works on the nerves. The person becomes stressed, the body gets tense, the first symptoms of a breakdown appear. These people can't think of anything but problems. The pressures cause them to fixate on what they want to reach. The goal becomes all-important, ever bigger, all-absorbing. More and more, everything else loses importance until it disappears from consciousness and is no longer seen. Gradually, other people are seen only for their usefulness. Like it or not, respect and love for other people are eclipsed, even totally suffocated, under the pressure to achieve. Aren't many families suffering because one partner comes home stressed and no longer sees members of the family as people?

Call to mind the Good Samaritan (Lk 10:30-37). A half-dead man lay in the gutter. A priest passed by. He was under pressure to get to Jericho quickly. He saw the wounded man only with physical eyes, but could not visualize or get involved with the suffering human being. Maybe he had a conference to lead or a funeral to preside over, and he had to be on time. Under pressure, he wasn't able to be aware of the other person *as a person*. The second passerby must have been in a similar situation. The third man to go by was the Samaritan. He probably was a merchant travelling on business. He was also under pressure. But he was able to disengage himself for a moment and become aware of the other person's need for help. He stopped and cared for him. Next morning he returned to his business affairs. The difference between the three men does not lie in the differing degrees of pressure they were under. The difference lies in the fact that the first two couldn't disengage themselves from this pressure. The Samaritan was able to distance himself from the pressure of his pursuits for the time that was needed to respond to the wounded man.

Under pressure, we aren't really able to be aware of our neighbor. In order to love people we must let go of the forces that drive us. Even if a stranger just says hello in the street, we must be able to let go of everything for two or three minutes, so that we are one hundred percent present to this person alone and have no other concern. We should let go of all other thoughts to be able to be open to this person. This is very difficult for us. The problem isn't the demand for achievement; the exterior world around us must demand results. The challenge is to free ourselves from external pressures at the right moment. Can we turn off the road, or are we slaves of our drive to get on? That is what matters.

What does contemplative prayer teach us? It teaches us to turn off the road. We learn to be simply there for God, without plans, cares, aims, and intentions, free from all other thoughts and activities. If we can be like that, we can be there for God and for our neighbor, for they are the same. But if we can't disengage ourselves from our desires, pursuits, problems, opinions, and urge to be active, we encounter neither God nor other people. On this point also, contemplation is the best training for human encounters.

II. INSTRUCTIONS FOR MEDITATION

1. Sitting

Dear Retreatant, since you have come to awareness and stillness in nature, we now begin our first exercises while sitting still or kneeling. Choose, if possible, a quiet place for meditation where you will not be disturbed by the telephone, books, or visitors. It can be a meditation room or a corner to which you retire for prayer. This solitary place will help your recollection.

Your body is best brought to recollection by sitting still or kneeling. The correct body posture is a help to inner stillness and attentiveness, and that's why I'm telling you how to sit. Books could be written about correct sitting. Many meditation methods place great emphasis on the exact, correct way of sitting. Such emphasis could distract us from the essential, however, and I describe here some basic rules that are sufficient for the long term.

The important thing is the upright body posture. In order to become quiet, the body has to take a posture that will not require movement for some time. Sitting in a crouched position demands heavy muscle work to keep the body straight. But if you sit upright, the spine rests one disc above the other, an effortless position which you can maintain comfortably and motionlessly for some time.

The body is an expression of the soul. When depressed, a person allows the upper part of the body to slump down, while the happy, vigorous person lifts his chest up, which allows the strength of the body to flow and to lift up the soul. Body attitude, on the other hand, can have an effect on the soul. That's one reason why the upright position is important for meditation.

There are different ways of sitting or kneeling. You might sit on a chair. Place your feet with both soles on the floor in such a way that the distance between them corresponds to the breadth of your hips. The chair should be high enough that your thighs are horizontal. Don't lean back, or at least only at the hips. From the thigh upward, the body should be erect and unencumbered.

You might sit on a prayer stool. If so, pay attention to the upper body's erect posture. You can also make a saddle from folded blankets and sit on that. Adjust for height according to your own requirements.

Through Eastern meditation, the various lotus positions have become well known: I can recommend them if you already know them. But I wouldn't advise you to begin learning them now, for that would take up too much precious time. The ways of sitting I've described are sufficient to start with. It's good to be able to change position now and then, since the introduction to contemplative prayer leads to several hours of quiet sitting or kneeling. Changing your way of sitting between exercises will lead to painless body posture.

2. Breathing exercises

Sit down. Be aware of your body. Ask yourself how you feel your body. (You don't need to answer this. This question and those that follow serve only to call your attention to a present sense of awareness.) Take two or three minutes to go through your body and pay attention to its different parts for about half a minute: your feet or legs in contact with the ground, the lower part, the upper part, the hands, the face. Then ask yourself whether you are fully present and ready to begin.

Pay attention to your respiratory tract. You might try to become aware of these things in order: First, direct attention to your breathing. The air comes and goes. Don't try to influence it (we're not going to do anything with it; we just want to be aware). Whether your breathing is calm, fast, shallow or deep, regular or irregular—this is of no importance. Just perceive how breathing takes its course in you. Breathe through your nose. Then turn your attention to the nostrils through which the air enters and try to feel the movement of the air along the inside passages of the nose. Don't breathe more heavily in order to feel more; instead, cause your inner ears to perceive what is happening in the nose. Remain for half a minute with this awareness.

Now you can move on. Ask or remind yourself:

- How do I feel the inside surfaces in this lower part of the nose?

- Move a little higher: how do I feel them in the middle section?

- The air that comes in is cooler, the air that goes out is warmer: am I aware of this difference in temperature?

- How do I feel the movement of the air in the upper part of the nose?

- Follow the breathing tract. First it goes up, and then almost between the eyes the path turns to the back. Can I feel this?

- Listen inside yourself, asking whether you feel the movement of the air along this stretch. It doesn't matter if you lose the thread. Our priority is not to feel these particular places, but rather to learn to listen.

- Feel and try to follow your breath millimeter by millimeter.

- The path then turns downward and slowly reaches the mouth from behind. The space widens and becomes more familiar.

- Does any air enter the mouth?

- Listen into your throat. How do you feel the movement of air in the throat?

- Pay attention to the larynx. It's a long stretch. Feel your way forward by tiny increments.

- How does the air pass the larynx?

- Follow the way through the windpipe toward the bronchial tubes.

- Air imparts itself to the lungs through the bronchial tubes. How do I feel the bronchial tubes?

- We are now in the lungs. How do I feel them?

- Direct your attention to the ribs. The ribs move with the breathing. How do I feel the movement of the ribs?

- The diaphragm is the lower limit of the chest. It is the motor of the breathing process and moves up and down. How do I feel it?

- Go further still. Try to feel, directly beneath the diaphragm, how the organs are pressed down through breathing and then return to their normal position.

- Direct your awareness even deeper into the abdominal cavity and try to be aware of the air pressing the abdomen forward, and how it swings back again. Remain fully alert and present.

- Remain with lively interest in awareness: what is taking place there?

- Remain in this awareness without interruption.

These are the qualities of meditation: to remain wide awake, present—present because of interest, present with determination.

This exercise is to last for twenty to twenty-five minutes. The best way would be to read through this list a few times until all the places mentioned are clear to you. When the real exercise starts, please leave the text aside. Even without reading and with your eyes closed, you'll be able to be aware of the areas of your body. Remain in awareness of these different places until you no longer feel the urge to move on, but remain peaceful, in the present. (Another way to proceed would be to read the list of questions and observations onto a cassette, leaving half a minute's time after each one. You could then play the cassette during the exercise.)

If you are making a Closed Retreat, practice this exercise at least eight times during a whole day. You can do it once before breakfast, three times in the course of the morning, three times in the afternoon, and once in the evening. Besides these exercises, I recommend spending the rest of the day in the open, as you have been used to during the first day. Don't read. Don't write (except perhaps a short entry in your journal, if that is your habit). Don't talk on the phone, don't look at TV. Put aside any hobby, like painting or crafts. But for recreation, you can run or do gymnastics or other physical exercise.

If you are making a Retreat in Daily Life and so have two hours daily for the exercises, you need to do it twice as often, sixteen times total. You must judge for yourself when you are fully relaxed, without the urge or impatience to go on, perhaps even until it is pleasant for you to remain at the individual stages. You won't spend this time in vain. In between the exercises, it's advisable to go into nature or into the open, even if you're in town.

III. DIALOGUES

2.1 MICHAEL

RM. Michael, how did you get on?

MICHAEL. So far I've done the breathing exercises four times. I didn't experience some of the stages, and I was also distracted, but on the whole I'm content, for I always finished well before the 20 minutes.

RM. You finished earlier.

MICHAEL. Everything goes fast with me.

RM. And what kind of feeling did you have throughout?

MICHAEL. Feeling?. . . It seems to have been just like my work. I fulfill my responsibilities quickly and efficiently. Then I can move on to the next task.

RM. This readiness and ease in fulfilling your duties gives you a good feeling. Isn't that true?

MICHAEL. Yes, it is.

RM. Now, Michael, we can learn something new! We aren't going to complete a task as quickly as possible as in your professional work. If you move on quickly, you may not fully arrive at awareness. When we live wholly in the present, we don't want to hurry; we are learning now how to hold on and linger.

At first, this may seem like a waste of time, but it will eventually lead us into a new world still unknown to you. We need to experience pausing and becoming aware. We will come to feel that it isn't necessary to hurry, but simply to rest in the present and be alert, and see what comes from this. Go on repeating the exercise and try to stay with each step of the way, as long as nothing urges you to move on. Remaining with the same thing, fully awake and interested, is characteristic of contemplative prayer.

2.2 ESTHER

ESTHER. To begin with I was wholly there. Then I came to the points about the nose and the mouth and felt nothing. I began again. Again I didn't feel anything.

RM. You were disappointed.

ESTHER. Yes, I was even annoyed.

RM. You wanted to feel that area of breathing.

ESTHER. Yes, I didn't want to pass on before I had felt it.

RM. You wanted to *achieve* being aware of it.

ESTHER. That was the task.

RM. Not exactly. You wanted to achieve something. When you didn't succeed you got annoyed. We don't need to achieve anything here. Just to continue being attentive will suffice You can listen for something even when you don't perceive anything about it.

ESTHER. Should I go ahead even when I don't feel anything?

RM. You could also remain listening for a while, without becoming aware of anything, and then move on. The important thing isn't so much the object we are aware of. To find your way into wide awake awareness is the essential. The ultimate goal is the presence of God. He is present without our being aware of it. That's why we are learning to be aware.

2.3 HUGH

HUGH. I didn't get on well at all. I feel incapable of this exercise. Thousands of thoughts came to me, memories of the past. Then I remembered that I'd forgotten to make a phone call. I tried frantically to keep it in mind and not forget it again. Then the constant thoughts about my work—how I could do some things differently. A swarm of thoughts! I didn't get into the exercise.

RM. You gave up.

HUGH *[with a smile]*. Not wholly . . . perhaps I got a little impatient.

RM. How did you handle the flow of thoughts?

HUGH. I wanted to be rid of them. I didn't want them. I wanted to be present to the exercise.

RM. You fought them.

HUGH. I had to, they kept me from my task.

RM. Look, Hugh. I'll show you another way. There is no need to fight our thoughts; they'll only increase. Resisting and rejecting creates a duality between what we want and what is real. This contest causes tension, which produces more and more thoughts.

Turn to awareness without fighting your thoughts. They're welcome guests allowed to come into the house. They're permitted to come and go. The homeowner can tell them, "Make yourselves comfortable. Feel at home! I have work to do and shall return to you when I am free again." Try to devote yourself totally to awareness and the thoughts will gradually retire. You'll be able to feel less and less disturbed by them.

HUGH. I am not to pay attention to my thoughts, then?

RM. That's right, pay no attention to them, but look for a moment at your feelings.

HUGH. I had no feelings.

RM. You didn't feel anything during all this time?

HUGH. No.

RM. You weren't discontented with your exercise?

HUGH. Well, yes, I was exasperated. How couldn't I have been when nothing went right?

RM. Didn't you say just now that you also became impatient?

HUGH. Yes, I did.

RM. You see. This discontent and impatience have nurtured your thoughts. When you feel many thoughts coming, you can always *listen into* yourself to become aware of which feelings gave rise to them. You'll accept them when you can say to yourself, "I feel impatient. I don't rejoice in it, but I allow the impatience to be there." By admitting impatience, you let the tension subside. The impatience is accepted and can dissolve.

This is how we handle thoughts and feelings. We don't need to look at thoughts, but simply return to awareness. Feelings, however, we can look at briefly—for just as long as we need to allow them to be there.

2.4 VERONICA

VERONICA. I've tried this exercise twice already. The first time it went very well. I felt everything quite intensely. I thought it was very helpful when, at the end, many tensions eased in my abdomen, and I could feel my breath right down into my belly. Perhaps I've never felt it before so deeply and calmly. I enjoyed it and would have liked to stay there. The second time I didn't succeed as well. When I reached the lungs my breathing became very shallow and I couldn't continue. Everything below my lungs was blocked. I tried, but nothing went well! Then I gave up and just sat there for the rest of the time.

RM. You're disappointed that you didn't succeed as you expected the second time.

VERONICA. Yes, exactly.

RM. You were expecting something and wanted to achieve it. Reach into yourself: Could you let go of the results of your meditation? Devote yourself to awareness, and let whatever will happen, happen?

VERONICA. Yes, But I wanted it to continue as it had begun.

RM. You'd find it liberating to renounce this desire to achieve. We can accumulate material possessions, but the spirit works differently. In the spiritual realm we can neither possess anything nor manipulate processes. When we can let go—give away possessions and move on—we experience the circle of love. Whenever we try to hold on to something, it escapes from between our fingers.

2.5 KEN

KEN. I got on amazingly well. Because of my cold, the air could only pass through one nostril, but it functioned! Then the second time I didn't finish. I felt nothing, or almost nothing, in my chest. But I was able to let it be so, and felt it moving in me. It was very nice.

RM. You were fully in the present.

KEN. Yes, I found what it means to stay, to remain.

RM. It's a good sign that you didn't reach the end of the exercise at the right time. What impression were you left with?

KEN. Impression?. . . I don't know exactly. I became more quiet and calm. It would probably be too much to say I felt securely at home, but contentment was there. I'm only now becoming conscious of that, while I am telling you.

RM. The exercise left an impression with you.

KEN. Yes, it did, but, as I said, I'm only aware of it now.

RM. That's why I asked you. If you look at your contentment for a moment, you'll become even closer with yourself. The path leads there.

2.6 SANDRA

SANDRA. Something interesting happened to me. I could hardly believe it. As I devoted myself to the exercise I came to a point—I don't know whether in the throat or further down—which I felt very distinctly. For a while I was there wide awake, and the awareness caught my whole attention. I didn't really feel anything more that was special, but even without anything happening it became so interesting that I did not want to pass on. I don't know whether thoughts came or not. If they did, I didn't notice. I was simply in the present, in the feeling of that particular spot. I don't even know how long I stayed with it. Possibly it was only a matter of moments, but it left a strong impression on me.

RM. Not eventful, but interesting.

SANDRA. Strange.

RM. You were given an important experience. As with any grace, one can never know if and when you will experience the same again. That does not matter. Gratitude for it is more important. And something else. This moment became a pointer to you. That's where the way continues. You will be led more and more into the present moment. Go on single-mindedly. Then everything will be given to you.

2.7 RUDOLF

RUDOLF. I'm dissatisfied. My breathing went too quickly and I wanted to breathe more slowly. But it didn't happen—I became quite breathless. Then I remembered your recommendation not to influence the breathing. It wasn't easy, and I wasn't successful in letting it "breathe in me" naturally. I ended up manipulating my breathing without wanting to. When I pay attention to my breathing, I automatically control it.

RM. This desire to control is uppermost in you.

RUDOLF. Yes, I noticed it now.

RM. Can you remember similar ways of acting in your daily life?

RUDOLF. If I'm honest, yes. I like to organize, notice quickly what's wrong, and take care of everything. I'm active. Whatever I put my hand to gets done. But it isn't easy for me to let something run on its own steam.

RM. Or let it run differently from the way you think it should.

RUDOLF. Both could be true.

RM. During meditation we are the same as we are in daily life. Quiet meditation is like daily life under the microscope. Here, however, we become more easily aware of what is taking place, because exterior activities are absent. You have now been offered an opportunity to learn how to let things happen. For the greater part of our life our breathing is unconscious. It is breathing in us. The body knows exactly how much air it needs. When we have taken less breath for a few seconds, a deep breath comes spontaneously and the balance is restored. When we pay conscious attention to our breathing, we suppose the body does not know how much oxygen it needs.

This exercise is a very favorable opportunity to learn that we do not need to manipulate everything. We pay attention to our breathing, but don't interfere. If you learn that, you'll find it easier not to interfere in everything in daily life. Learn to be attentive without manipulating. We are here concerned with the change from doing to seeing. But remember, not even this change needs to be a success.

2.8 CLARENCE

CLARENCE. Your talk about the parallel between the relationship with God and other people has hit home strongly. I got an insight into many things. I was shaken to realize how I treat God. There is a lot of criticism, rejection, indifference, jealousy and anger against people in me. I am filled with consternation to know that I treat God in the same way.

RM. You feel shocked.

CLARENCE. I've often talked to others about the love of God and took it for granted that I love him unconditionally.

RM. It was true of your intention. Now you have been able to look more deeply. This insight you received is sufficient. Are you able to let that stand without wanting to alter your love for God?

CLARENCE. It saddens me.

RM. Allow yourself to be sad. Do not be afraid of your sadness. Accept it. It wants to come out and be liberated. Look kindly on your sadness. Let it come and it will dissolve in time. After some time, return to awareness. See what comes to you from being aware of your breathing. Engage yourself totally in that.

2.9 JACOB

JACOB. I began with the breathing exercise, but felt nothing for long stretches. This changed when I discovered that it goes more easily when I recall a picture of the individual organs. I could stay with that. It went quite well.

RM. You form a picture of what it looks like inside you.

JACOB. Yes, then I can stay with it.

RM. You are visually gifted.

JACOB. It certainly is my stronger side.

RM. Pictures hinder our effort to become aware. That's why we don't work with the imagination. There is a great difference between awareness and images. Images are our own product, they can exist without relation to reality. They are in our head and are independent from reality. Awareness however is pure perception of reality. The thing we are aware of does not depend on us. We only open ourselves to receive what is really there. In awareness we are turned to what is real and so rooted in the earth. Awareness leads us to immediate experience. Neither concepts, thoughts, nor images stand between us and reality.

JACOB. You mean, reality is direct.

RM. Yes, and that's important for our way. Today we talk a lot about the image of God. We are counseled to examine our image of God and change into a more positive one. Someone who had a strict father, it's said, suffers under a strict God. His image of God does not correspond to the real God. He is advised to try and change his image of God. The image of God is a concept, a representation.

JACOB. The image of God is not God himself. That's what you mean, isn't it?

RM. Yes, we don't work with the image of God. I haven't even asked you whether you believe in God or not. We are going a much more concrete way. We direct our attention to what is real and contemplate what comes from there. We learn awareness of reality. At present we are still trying to become aware of our breathing process. But we are more and more coming to the awareness of the present moment. It's of no interest to us to have (or not to have) a clear picture of it; we experience it directly.

Awareness of the present is a first step to awareness of the presence of God. God is there. We aren't aware of him because we are still beginners in awareness. We do not need to form concepts, ideas, images of God, because we go the way of experience. We are aware of the present, and when we become more sensitized and receptive, the presence of God will open to us. In eternal life we shall not imagine God but remain gazing at him. Eternal life already begins here. Our way is therefore very concrete, rooted in the earth. It leads to immediate encounter, a thing images and representations cannot produce.

JACOB. That means I must not imagine the various parts of the breathing channel.

RM. No, don't try. To make it easier for you to leave images aside, I began with questions: what do I feel in such and such a place? You can answer yourself that you feel nothing, and yet continue listening. You can go on paying attention, in case at some time perhaps something will reveal itself. The question, "What do I feel here or there," isn't a question to be answered.

2.10 GRETA

GRETA. I think I had a very important experience. At the beginning I could feel everything very clearly and distinctly. I suddenly felt nothing between the upper part of the nose and the area at the back of the mouth. I wanted to feel it and concentrated intensely on it in order to become aware. So for quite a while I was fully engaged in wanting to feel something. Then suddenly I discovered the difference between concentration and listening. I noticed how the desire to concentrate created a lot of tension which was blown away as soon as I became conscious of this desire. I became all ear. I didn't need to make anything happen: it seemed unimportant whether I felt something or not. I had nothing to achieve and was present—fully awake. It was given in some way, and was a completely new state for me. I didn't manipulate anything; I was simply there. I even believe I had no thoughts at this moment. But I am not sure about this.

RM. As you say, we cannot achieve such a state at any time. But we are given such moments to help us find the way to the one necessary thing.

2.11 JAMES

JAMES. For a long time I could follow the breathing and remain with the successive impressions. That was beautiful. Then something began to disturb me. I have no idea what it was! Gradually, I became very tense, and I felt irritated at the same time. But suddenly I had an insight. In a flash I saw that I was a perfectionist, wanting to do everything well. I simply cannot bear anything that is not quite perfect. After this first insight, images rose up in me from the past, in which I wanted to do excellently in everything.

RM. This was a shock for you.

JAMES. Yes, and it mobilized me within. I asked myself how I could change. I didn't know what to do about it.

RM. And you began to explore that instead of returning to your breathing.

JAMES. It was important for me to find out.

RM. Exactly *because* it is important to you and you don't know how to go about it, allow yourself to be guided. I show you the way to change.

JAMES. What is the way?

RM. Not the way of thought, of planning and doing, but the way of stillness and awareness. The Gospel says that if we seek first the kingdom of heaven, everything else will be given to us (Mt 6:33). To seek the kingdom of God means at the moment, remaining in awareness. Contemplate what is there, attend to the present. That is already a foretaste of the presence of God. God is there. He himself will change you.

JAMES. I can see that.

RM. As long as an insight is pure awareness, you can stay with it. You can also be aware of the feelings that arise from the insight. But allow yourself to be as you are and return to breathing. The desire for change is understandable, but it leads you completely away from contemplation.

2.12 PAULA

PAULA. I'm often distracted. Someone said he had returned his attention to the exercise and then immediately had gone off again. I see myself in that category; the same happens to me—Really! I come back, and the next moment I am elsewhere. I only notice it after it's happened. I can't do anything about it. I am not succeeding in remaining present there.

RM. You feel helpless against distractions.

PAULA. Yes, I'm not recollected and have no influence on my state of attention.

RM. And what about your determination?

PAULA. At the beginning I felt something like determination, but I only tensed up. I constantly suggested to myself, "You must succeed. It just can't be that you are not able to be present even for a minute." Instead of being there, I blocked myself and was wholly exhausted at the end.

RM. There is a great difference between wanting to achieve something and determination. The desire to achieve is directed to results, determination is independent from the result. You wanted to fight through to awareness. You were intent on the result. But you do not need to reach a result. It isn't essential whether you can remain with it for only a minute or for half an hour.

Determination is the spiritual attitude to give yourself totally, to surrender to it. Less important is whether you are crowned with success or not. To want to arrive at something demands will power, which controls the whole body, makes it tense, and blocks and exhausts it when success constantly fails to occur. Determination in contrast is a spiritual attitude which doesn't produce tension. It leaves the body relaxed. It doesn't make one tired. Free yourself from seeking the results and try to give yourself to the exercise with more determination.

2.13 GERARD

GERARD. It started right away getting up this morning: one failure after another. I'm a flop! The pain wasn't in my body, but in the deep insights into myself. I found it unbearable to be as I am, with all my incapacity, my weakness of concentration, the inability to feel anything, with the uninterrupted flow of my thoughts—and on top of that the impatience in having to bear all this. I couldn't stand myself anymore.

RM. You find it difficult to bear with yourself.

GERARD. I do not want to be a failure.

RM. You feel you are a failure.

GERARD. Yes, and I feel powerless before this fact.

RM. Powerless.

GERARD. Yes, that's it.

RM. You feel a tremendous tension between what you want to be and what you actually are.

GERARD. Yes, and I see no way out of the inner conflict.

RM. May I show you a way? Try for a moment to leave your will alone and look at yourself simply as you are. Allow yourself to have thoughts. Allow yourself to feel nothing. Allow yourself to be powerless. Allow yourself to be "as you should not be." Allow yourself to be unable to change anything. With this, one pressure will already subside and you'll no longer need to be something you are not. You will be more at one with yourself. Learn to look at yourself as you are with acceptance and serenity. We must first accept the starting point before we can change anything. See how breathing happens in you. First be reconciled with yourself and your feelings and with the way you are now. Everything may remain as it is. You need not change anything.

GERARD. But, I want to change.

RM. That's the problem. Try to let go of your desire to change. Before adapting reality to your will, try to adapt yourself to present reality.

2.14 TINA

TINA. I could easily follow my breathing. I distinctly felt the difference between warm and cold air breathing in and out. I was totally with it down to the bronchioles and the chest area. But then suddenly I wasn't there. I didn't notice that I was wandering off, but I was very interested in how and when it happened. I was drawn away from awareness, but I soon realized that this, too, leads only to reflection. So I dropped my investigations. In the abdomen, and parallel to it in the back, I felt strong warmth streaming through me. It was a sense of well-being. I remained longer in the exercise than I'd planned and could have stayed even longer.

RM. Keep going in just this way.

2.15 PETER

PETER. I found it difficult to concentrate on the points in my head. Especially the area behind the nose. Whew! that was hard work! It was easier with the abdomen. I didn't have to concentrate so much on it there.

RM. In the head area you felt very much under strain.

PETER. Yes, concentration there took quite a bit out of me.

RM. There's a difference between concentrating and attentive listening which seems very important. *Concentration* implies making an effort. If we say that somebody concentrates, we imagine the person with wrinkled forehead, tense and even exerting himself. But when *listening attentively,* one is fully relaxed. We can only pay attention when we open ourselves and are ready to receive what comes. When we are attentive we don't decide what will come. We are like an open antenna which receives what comes. Try to feel in yourself this difference, and change from concentrating to attentive listening.

2.16 REGINA

REGIINA. I feel a lot along the breathing passages and am able to stay with it. But I noticed that I watch myself all the time. It's as if I am doing something and afterwards I go through everything again in order to check whether it was right.

RM. You need to be certain that you do it correctly.

REGIINA. To be certain? . . . I don't know . . . yes, it could be that I feel a little uncertain. Perhaps it's the fear of doing it incorrectly.

RM. Hm. . . .

REGIINA. Yes, I feel this fear *[long pause]* . . . now I feel it less.

RM. Could you allow yourself to do something incorrectly?

REGIINA. Not easily!

RM. You don't need to show results. It is sufficient to enter into the exercise with inner determination. If something has really gone wrong, it will show, and then you can change it. But to double-check everything after you've done it—that's very strenuous and leads to exhaustion.

REGIINA. Yes, I can see that, but I don't know whether I can let go of it.

RM. Even shutting off this need to control doesn't have to be successful. It is sufficient to keep trying.

REGIINA. But how do I know that I am really not making a mistake?

RM. You are afraid of making a mistake without being aware of it. Look at this fear and permit yourself to feel it. The fear could then dissolve.

REGIINA. Yes, but how shall I know that I am not making a mistake?

RM. There is no need to know. It is much better to make a mistake for a time than to go through everything a second time. Real mistakes show up at the proper time with all clarity.

REGIINA. I see it more clearly. On one side, I only have to accept my fear, and on the other, I must have the courage to make a mistake.

2.17 EDITH

EDITH. I am quite present during the meditation. Thoughts and distractions come in between, but I can return to the exercise. During one of the exercises, I felt a very severe pain in my neck. When it got more intense, I concentrated on it. I felt myself into the pains until they dissolved. Then it got better again.

RM. You took hold of them and removed them.

EDITH. Yes, I did.

RM. It is possible to get rid of pain by concentration. Not a bad solution, but it's "making it happen." There is such a thing as autogenous training—auto-hypnosis. We give commands to the unconscious. For example: I become quiet, I am quiet. These commands are received by the unconscious, and the person quiets down. This isn't bad, but it's in the very nature of a command that I am involved in making it happen. Contemplative prayer in contrast is not *making*, but *allowing* things to happen. Pain must not be vanquished, removed, overcome, or manipulated. On the contrary, it must be admitted and allowed to hurt, until it dissolves of its own accord. It's a renunciation, a surrender, of active doing. Contemplation is looking. Beyond this, we're convinced that, in the human spirit, there is a healing force which becomes active in stillness and dissolves the pains. The power of nature brings it about. Everything happens through grace.

2.18 DAMIAN

DAMIAN. I felt my breathing consciously for the first time. But I didn't feel anything in my chest, and was also distracted. In the abdomen I was again present. It really was like a new discovery of my breathing. I've never felt it so distinctly before, how breathing takes place in me. I had the feeling of well-being and didn't really want to finish the exercise. *[Pause. . . .* and something else: I realized that before this I had always partly directed my breathing myself. This time I had the certain experience of just looking on without manipulating anything. I'm very grateful to you that you didn't ask me to breathe deeply but to leave the breath as it is. That was beneficial for me.

RM. This experience of not influencing shows you the direction to contemplation. Our way continues by following this track.

2.19 TRAVIS

TRAVIS. Most of the time I got on well with this exercise. Once, at the beginning, I felt a cramp in my foot and ankle and asked myself, "Oh, how will this go; I'm only at the beginning of the meditation." Then the thought came, "Well, I let it come as it comes, and pay attention to my breathing." The cramp gradually disappeared. I even had the impression that these pains helped me to retain awareness. They strengthened my recollected attention.

RM. What you describe is indeed possible. It can happen. There are bodily pains that come from sitting badly, and in that case we must change our posture. There are also pains we cannot easily identify. If we turn our full attention to breathing, it often happens that we no longer feel the pain and it ceases. In this case, as you have just experienced, it helps us to recollect. If the discomfort becomes too great, you can change your position once, but this shouldn't be done continuously. In meditation the body normally becomes quiet in such a way that the need for change isn't felt. During meditation, many different pains can occur which don't arise from the position or from bodily infirmity, but rather from a psychological cause. These, you should just endure.

2.20 DORIS

DORIS. I begin the exercises with interest, but after a few minutes tiredness forces me to yawn and doze. And soon after, I really fall asleep. I fight it, but in vain—I just fall asleep.

RM. You fight sleepiness.

DORIS. Yes, I try. But it doesn't disappear. I have no idea what I should do.

RM. Haven't you had enough sleep lately?

DORIS. I've come from an extremely stressful situation and have overworked myself. So far I haven't been able to recover.

RM. You're still exhausted.

DORIS. Yes, I am overworked and don't have any energy.

RM. Sleep it off. Give your body what it rightfully deserves. Of course, it's better to begin the retreat rested and relaxed. But since this wasn't possible for you because of the work situation, you have to sleep during the first days. Later, tiredness and sleepiness can arise that signal an unconscious escape from oneself. It isn't always pleasant to face up to oneself. Resistance against such encounters can lead to sleepiness. Fighting against sleepiness doesn't help much. It is great wisdom to see one's bodily limits realistically and give the body what it rightfully demands. We accept ourselves as we are.

2.21 WILLIE

WILLIE. I was very capable of being present. When I got to the abdomen, I felt pressure which then extended to the chest area. Shortly after, I felt tension in my back—above the shoulder blades, in the middle, everything was cramped. I thought I couldn't bear it any longer. I got hot and cold and was tempted to stop. Suddenly I remembered your words, not to take notice of the pains and tensions and return to awareness. I tried it. At first it wasn't successful, but I tried to stay with the task with all my senses. Suddenly—I don't know how it was possible—I was really engaged and no longer felt the tension. It disappeared in an instant. I've never experienced anything like that before.

RM. Yes, a very helpful experience. That's the way it is. If we try to be present with all our senses, pains and tensions disappear. But we can't go back to see whether the tensions are still there. Otherwise we are not with our breathing, but with the tensions. And then they often return.

2.22 TED

TED. Yesterday I was terribly angry. I was with you for a talk and wanted to move on to the next day. You told me not to, and to keep to the breathing exercises. That got on my nerves. I wanted to go on. I don't have many days at my disposal, and if I take these free days, I want to use them well and get as far as possible. And now you demand that I stay in this place! Time is racing on. The others are allowed to go ahead to the next exercises, but I am left behind like a kid in primary school.

RM. You felt left behind.

TED *[still irritated]*. Of course. Excuse me for saying this, but I said to myself in my anger: "This idiot doesn't notice that I want to keep going."

RM. Thank you for your trust and honesty in expressing what you feel. You wanted to march on before you had come to rest, remaining still. Progress isn't measured by the quantity or difficulty of the exercises, but by your inner calm. You can't yet stay with one area when doing the breathing exercise. You may have "sat" for eight or ten hours, but if you haven't yet discovered the taste for remaining in one particular place, there isn't any point in going further. You can give your time to God in this repeated exercise. Change your attitude. Learn to remain in awareness through this one exercise and rest there. When you are in the present moment, you won't any longer compare yourself with others.

IV. REVIEW & TRANSITION TO THE THIRD DAY

Dear Reader, you have now read many dialogues. It could be that you found them interesting. Have you noticed how these dialogues enrich your understanding of contemplation? Perhaps they have also given you new insights, or something has struck you as important.

Dear Retreatant, you have now finished the second period (or Second Day). Possibly you already find the retreat fun. It could also be that you found it difficult to repeat the exercise eight times. Let's look back over things; I'll help you with some questions.

- If you are making a Closed Retreat: Have you repeated the exercise eight times? If you are making a Retreat in Daily Life, the question is: Did you spend two weeks with it?

- Each time, did you go through all or nearly all the areas of the breathing passage mentioned? Did the exercises last twenty minutes and not less? If you haven't completed them, I advise you not to go further. It isn't important to get on with the book, but to get down to the inward way. The exercises help us in this.

- You can also examine yourself in another way. If you are able to stay with the exercises and felt the tendency to remain a longer rather than a shorter time with the individual areas, you can go ahead to the third day with a good conscience. The inclination to prolong the exercise beyond the stipulated time is a positive sign. If you stayed a shorter time with the individual parts and finished the exercise early, it would be better not to go forward at the moment.

- If you've read more than three dialogues in between the exercises, it could be that your interest is more intellectual than spiritual. You want to know something about contemplation rather than make the journey.

If you have now finished the second day, I wish you God's blessing for the third. In the Introductory Talk of the third day I show you the correct basic attitude in contemplative prayer. We also take a new step forward in this practice. During the first day, we tried to come to awareness while walking. Relaxed body movement and the variety of nature helped us to remain attentively in the present.

On this second day, we came closer to ourselves, and more delicate perceptions helped us come to recollection. But, like bees, we flew from one flower to another and so proceeded by steps along a path toward awareness. Now we will no longer need to pass from here to there. We'll stay in the same place with our awareness. The breathing exercises have provided the necessary stillness.

THIRD DAY

I. INTRODUCTORY TALK:
SELF-CENTEREDNESS & GOD-CENTEREDNESS

1. *The original human condition and the Fall*

In the creation narrative, in the form of a story, Sacred Scripture explains to us humankind's present condition between wholeness and brokenness. The story's purpose is to describe the essential orientation of human nature. Let's look at it closely.

The first human beings were created wholly oriented toward God. That was their nature, their original condition, and also their happiness. It placed them in harmony with all creation, in peace with one another, and at one with themselves. The Fall meant that human beings fell from this orientation to God and became oriented toward themselves. They became their own standard. Instead of living focused on their center, God, they became caught up in their own selfish viewpoints, self-will, selfish desires, plans, and goals. From being God-centered, they fell back to self-centeredness.

This led to chaos. We were separated from our beginnings. Harmony with nature was shattered. We experienced our environment with pain and with thorns. War began among us. Each one placed him or herself, personal interests, advantages, and desires, at the center. The worst was that, henceforth, we had to experience di-

videdness inside ourselves. In our self-centeredness, we lived in
stark contradiction to the universal love for which we were created.
We no longer could accept ourselves as we were. We could only
accept part of ourselves. We were divided into two selves: one we
could accept, another we had to ignore, fight against, and suppress.
Fragmented and torn, we could not find our own identity and no
longer knew who we were. We began to run away and flee from
ourselves, making a place for ourselves in other things and external
distractions, far away from our own inner self. This chaos brought
sickness, suffering, and death, a state which continues until today
and can be found in every human being in need of redemption. Redemption consists in Jesus Christ leading us from self-centeredness
back to God-centeredness.

2. The experience of self-centeredness

How do we experience our self-centeredness? One indicator is our
feelings, which throw us back on ourselves. We can easily recognize this in the influence on us of what we call, in a simplified
way, our negative feelings. If we have fear, we only think of our
threatened self. If we're enraged, we feel our helplessness in es-
tablishing our position. If we despise others, we can only see that
we're better or know more than they do. Each of our negative
feelings can be seen in this manner.

Another indicator of self-centeredness is the world of fantasy in
which we live. Let's imagine a typical dreamer. He lives within a
self-centered cosmos of which he is the creator, from whom everything that exists in his world originates. He is also the redeemer
who alone is able to put right what does not function in his universe. He is all-knowing, because there is nothing existing or happening in his dream-world that he would not know. He is
all-powerful, because he can do absolutely everything he wants in
his dream-castle. In one word, he is the god of his dream-world.
And in this consists his self-centeredness.

We think we aren't such dreamers. But when we begin contemplative prayer we find out how much we live in our thoughts.
Thoughts are necessary, but we experience a flood of them that is
neither necessary nor useful for our life. For example, a retreatant
goes for an hour's walk. But she has nothing to reflect; she only
wants to be aware. Yet most of the time she spends thinking. Her

thoughts become independent and stream on incessantly even though she does not want them. It's a world of thoughts comparable to the world of dreams. It makes us self-centered. In this world we're all-knowing, all powerful; we're creator and redeemer.

Worries also make us self-centered. Worries are always *my* worries, *my* burdens which *only I* have to carry. We create for ourselves a world of worries in which our ego is god, in the same way as in the world of dreams and thoughts.

It's similar with our desires: they nourish our self-centeredness. In today's consumer society we are enticed every day to hoard up more and more possessions. Desires increase like the sand on the seashore and form a wishing-world as self-centered as the dream-world, worry-world, or other worlds already mentioned.

Self-centeredness is also recognized in self-will. The self-willed person judges everything from his or her egotistical viewpoint and tries to force his or her own interests without regard for anyone else. Even if these tendencies don't go as far as tyranny, fanaticism, or paranoia, they can conceal deep-seated self-centeredness.

Sacred Scripture and theology divide self-centeredness into three categories: Thirst for possessions, lust for power, drive for prestige.

Thirst for possessions—avarice—presents the fundamental form of self-centeredness. The Bible treats this problem unceasingly under the theme of poverty and wealth. The prodigal son wanted to possess his heritage. He only remembered his father after losing all his possessions. The rich young man went away sad, unable to give up his many possessions. Avarice drives anyone setting his or her heart on possessions, whether they actually belong to him or whether she only craves them.

Lust for power drives us to force our will on others and set ourselves and our plans in the center of things. The disciples often sought power for themselves. The Pharisees always wanted to be in charge.

Drive for honor, pride, and ambition also recur in Sacred Scripture. It is imaged as the thirst for approval, admiration, and praise. The poor widow in the Gospel, unnoticed, humbly cast her two coins into the treasury (see Lk 21:1-4). She gave her last penny. The Pharisees ostentatiously gave their large sums of money in the public eye. They sought publicity and human attention: This was their self-centeredness.

3. *From self-centeredness to God-centeredness*

How can self-centeredness—that is, avarice or wishing for possessions, striving for power, lust for honor and prestige—be changed into God-centeredness?

Not recognizing others as persons is the foundation of self-centeredness. The self-centered person sees only the self endowed with the dignity of personhood. All others are objects for use. But objects can have neither possessions, nor power, nor prestige. At the moment a person in the distance is recognized and accepted internally as a person, avarice will change into readiness to give and share. Power-striving will change into readiness to serve. Grasping for honor gives way to respect for and recognition of others. The *self-centered* person is able to become *other-centered.* Then it is no longer the ego that takes precedence, but the encounter with the other.

Since our relationships with fellow human beings run parallel to that with God, other-centeredness is mirrored in our attentiveness to God. Avarice that has changed into the ability to share with others becomes *surrender* in our relationship with God. Power-striving, having given way to willingness to serve our neighbor, then becomes *worship and service* in our relationship with God. Desire for prestige, turned into respect for others, becomes *adoration and praise* in our relationship with God.

The following three pairs show the poles between self-centeredness and other-centeredness:

> Avarice   >   to be able to give
> (surrender to God)
>
> Thirst for power   >   to be ready to serve
> (service of God)
>
> Lust for prestige   >   to respect others
> (praise and adoration of God).

Redemption consists in the fact that Jesus Christ has lifted us out of the bondage of avarice, power-striving, and lust for honor, into giving of ourselves and to service and praise of God.

We find a clear illustration of this in the Our Father (Mt 6:9-13). The petitions begin with the attitudes just mentioned. Jesus Christ makes us avaricious human beings say, "Your kingdom come"—as we should say, "Not my kingdom, O Lord, but yours must come among us." We force our will on our fellow human beings, so Jesus teaches us to say, "Not my will, but yours be done!" Above all, we pray, "Not my name, O Lord, but your name be hallowed!" We pray that our own honor will be replaced by the honor of God. As if this were not enough, we repeat these three elements of God-centeredness once again, "For yours is the kingdom (possessions), the power (strength), and the glory (honor)."

I am struck by the way the Mother of God is described for us in the Gospel. At the Annunciation, the Angel speaks to Mary. The conversation ends with her *gift of self,* "I am the handmaid of the Lord. May it be done to me according to your word" (Lk 1:38). Mary at once sets out *to serve* Elizabeth (vs. 43), and then sings the Magnificat, the most beautiful *hymn of praise* (vss. 46-55).

4. The pious egoist

The three elements of our encounter with others determine our relationship with God. They are even the essence of everything religious. Religion, the relationship with God, of necessity expresses itself in surrender to, service for, and praise of God.

Let us go a step further and look at this relationship in a seemingly paradoxical case. We imagine the pious egoist.

The avaricious pious person prays often and long. But since he is avaricious, the structure and content of his prayer remain self-centered. He prays in order to get something from God, be it material possessions, health, or knowledge. It is central for him to get something, to improve his lot. He is unaware of how much he is concerned with himself and not with God. His prayer and his human relationships are really self-centered. Instead of surrendering himself to God, he demands that God be occupied with him.

But the essential in prayer is self-surrender. Are our prayers selfishly greedy? Are they demands we make on God? Desires to make our life more comfortable? The Our Father teaches us what God-centered petitions can be like. Other prayers of petition are not bad, if they are first of all praise of God's sovereignty rather than a demand for something.

There is another pious egoist who in a veiled way engages in a power struggle with God. He has an all too clear picture of God's will. God wants justice, peace, harmony, love. Knowing this, he comes before God and asks him to carry it out: Evil must be overcome, the sick child must not die, people must come to faith, war must end, peace shall reign in families. He does not notice at all how much these petitions express his own will. As long as God hears them, he is the faithful servant of God's will. But if God doesn't hear them—or not at once—then disappointment, discontent, and sometimes rebellion against God rise up in him. "How can God allow such misery and injustice?" he asks himself. The more he rebels against God, the clearer it becomes whose will he wants to see done—his own.

Similarly with prestige. The "pious" Christian who also seeks honor is both fervent and virtuous. She wants to earn recognition from God and looks for rewards. She constantly needs to justify herself before God and to prove her righteousness, for she wants to win the kingdom through her own goodness. She seeks redemption through her own good deeds. St. Paul says of such people that they want to gain salvation through their works: They are really seeking, not God, but the gifts of God. Religion doesn't consist in asking for God's gifts, but in making God the center of our entire search. That is what matters, and I can't sufficiently stress this. As long as we seek God's gifts, we're self-centered.

5. Self-centeredness in the Eucharist

In the Eucharist we experience Christ's self-surrender and make his attitude—pure surrender, obedience, and praise of the Father—our own. The prayers used in the celebration of the Eucharist are prayers of self-giving and praise. We call the Mass a *service* because we serve Jesus Christ and the Father. But if we come to Mass with a self-centered attitude, we feel distant from the liturgy inside ourselves. This is often why Christians do not fully enter into the celebration of the Eucharist and become bored. If all we want is to hear a sermon, enjoy hymns, or satisfy our "religious needs," we miss the essential. At the beginning of Mass we have the Liturgy of the Word, to help us enter gradually into Christ's self-gift and praise, and into his attitude of doing the will of the Father. In the liturgy, God is the center. If we place our own desires, problems, and needs—and so ourselves—at the center, we shall feel out of place.

6. Self-centeredness in meditation

Why am I writing about self-centeredness in the midst of the retreat? Because there's a very real danger of going into meditation with a self-centered attitude, or of falling into one. If we listen closely to why most people meditate, we have to shake our heads. Their statements are ambiguous, for their intention of seeking God is always indirect, or at least it often seems that the intention is so hidden that it's difficult to believe in its genuineness.

Many of those we ask say that they want to become quiet. Tired of the world's hectic pace, they want to distance themselves from it. Others claim that meditation improves the quality of their work. Others again seek clear thoughts and right decisions. Some want healing. Often the reason is to revivify smoldering or dead religious feelings. Many want to integrate the past, change their behavior patterns, or think about their future. Some are looking for a kind of therapy in meditation. All these answers reveal that it is *God's gifts* that are being sought, not *God himself.* Contemplation is to seek God alone and to trust that he will add everything else that is necessary (Mt 6:3).

Surrender to God is often made in words. It can also be expressed in deeds. But we can also give ourselves to God with our being. To be simply there for God: This is the deepest and purest surrender. This is our way.

We can *serve* God with words, with actions, and with our very being as a servant—present to God as one who serves. Our service is directed to this goal.

We can *praise* God with words and hymns, with actions, and with our being. We say of birds and plants that they praise God simply through their existence. This kind of praise and adoration of God is the purpose of human life. Contemplative prayer is surrender, service, and praise of God with our whole being. To be there, to exist for God.

7. *The practice of being there for God*

And so I plead with you, dear Retreatant. Each time you begin contemplative prayer, please renew your intention to give your time to God. "I give you this hour. That is my surrender. I am here for you." Or you can say that you want to serve or adore God. I set this plea in your heart. Never omit it. I recommend that you connect your renewal of intention with something specific, so that you are always reminded of it. With this in mind, say an Our Father before beginning, or renew the intention when you enter the room in which you meditate or at the moment when you sit down.

At the end of the meditation, evaluate whether or not you were there for God. It's a simple test: If the meditation didn't go well, you can nonetheless get up wholly content and can say, "Lord, this was a very miserable hour, but I did what I could, and so I am content." Then your meditation was a time given to God. But if you feel discontented and frustrated, you were looking for something for yourself, and you'll feel irritated because you didn't get it.

You clearly seek God in meditation if you feel independent of the results rather than focusing on yourself and your spiritual progress. If we really give the time of meditation to God, we're content, and it doesn't matter whether this time was "useful" for us or not. I ask you to make this test after each meditation in order to learn by degrees to be there for God without any other purpose. It doesn't matter if you don't immediately succeed. Not even this freedom from an agenda needs to be achieved. We are only trying to direct our intention constantly to God and remain in that attitude. The more the attitude becomes real for us, the more we shall expressly *be there for God* during our everyday life, whatever we may be doing.

II. INSTRUCTIONS FOR MEDITATION

When we work with our hands, great strength passes through them. This is even more true when we deal with our neighbor. When we help the dying, we touch them with our hands. Through this bodily contact, new energy flows over from us into them. We stroke children; for babies this is the most important way of making contact. When friends meet they shake hands; their strengths come together. Others embrace in a still stronger sign of the union of their vital power.

Jesus Christ also used his hands. He often worked his miracles by touch and laying on of hands. This knowledge has come down to us and is visible in the sacraments. Most sacraments are effected by touch. The clearest sign of empowering is the laying on of hands. Through the hands, the vital power of a person flows over to another. Sacramentally, the hands carry the power of the Holy Spirit. The strength of hands flows intensely through the centers of the palms. These form an energy center through which vital life energy is dispensed outward. When we join hands, we place palm on palm in a sign of genuine exchange and combination of vital energy.

There seems to be historical proof for the belief that Jesus was nailed to the cross through the wrists. But all pictures of the resurrection nevertheless show the wounds in the center of the palms. His grace seems to have been transmitted through the palms of the hands.

When we want to gather strength and not scatter it, we join both palms together. The power is then passed not outward, but into an internal circuit where it strengthens our vital energy. The conscious presence of the person intensifies. We are more recollected in ourselves. That is why the Christian recollects himself in prayer with folded hands. When I learned the Mass rite before my ordination (which was before the Vatican Council), I had to be very exact in practicing the liturgical rubrics. One rubric called on me to hold the hands at shoulder height, a hand's width away from the shoulder, and with the palms facing each other. I was surprised at so detailed a prescription. But when I prayed the Eucharistic Prayer for the first time in this bodily attitude, I felt intense recollection. I was aware that a power circuit coursed through the palms and caused vital recollection. Since that time, I know that one may not only *pass on* inner vitality, but also *collect* it. Folding our hands leads to deep recollection. I could say a lot more, but it's better to show you.

Sit down. Fold your hands. Among the many positions for the hands, choose the one most comfortable for you. All that is important is that your two palms be in as close contact as possible. You don't need to press them, but merely place them gently together. They won't touch. You can place the folded hands loosely in your lap. If the hands pull your shoulders forward, put a folded blanket or something similar under them.

Renew your intention to give this time to God as surrender, service, or adoration. Start by becoming aware of some parts of your body, until after a few minutes you are ready to begin. Only then feel your way into the center of your palms. If you don't succeed in this, begin with trying to feel your hands as a whole. From there you can approach the center until you also feel your palms. Direct your attention to the center of your palms as if to ask, "What do I feel in the center of my hands?" Remain twenty minutes in this awareness. You can use an alarm clock, an egg timer, or something similar. When you're distracted, return to the awareness of your hands and try to remain in awareness.

During the first day of our retreat, we came to the awareness of nature. We still needed much exterior and inner movement and change. During the second day, we tried to come nearer to ourselves and direct our attention to an inner process. Now we need still less exterior motion. We try to remain with our attention in the same place.

Take two time periods of twenty minutes each. Between these, pause for five minutes. You may get up and move about, but don't lose your recollection, so that your body will more easily become quiet for the second period.

If you're making a Closed Retreat, meditate in this way eight times each day (or four sessions of two periods, with a five-minute pause in between. For example, do two times twenty minutes in the morning and another two times twenty minutes in the afternoon, taking five-minute breaks in each period. Don't forget to spend your free time after the meditations relaxing in nature.

For a Retreat in Daily Life, I recommend doing this meditation twice daily in succession for at least two weeks. You are giving one to one-and-a-half hours daily to your retreat. During that time, you can sit for two periods of twenty minutes each. Take the rest of the time for gradual preparation before each exercise, and also allow the exercise to end gradually.

I must emphasize that this is not an optional exercise which one might choose to skip. No, it is a fundamental step, important for all that follows. This is the core of our journey.

III. DIALOGUES

3.1 CATHERINE

CATHERINE. I have already tried several times to experience my hands. After awhile I felt calm. Many thoughts came, but I always returned again to my hands.

RM. You felt them.

CATHERINE. Yes, at first I felt them as a whole; I felt their presence, and they gradually became warm. It felt pleasant, and I remained aware relatively easily.

RM. You probably also felt the center of your palms.

CATHERINE. More the hands as a whole. I was gratified to feel my hands at all. I paid no attention to the center of the palms.

RM. Continue starting out as you have done so far, but then come more and more to the center of the palms.

CATHERINE. Where the wounds of Jesus were?

RM. Yes, exactly there! We aren't conscious of the power flowing there as long as we don't quietly turn our full attention to it. It may take time before we become aware of the power. If we don't feel it, it's equally effective to remain in simple awareness.

CATHERINE. Does it then become very still inside?

RM. Open yourself to it, and we'll see.

3.2 JOHN

JOHN. I didn't get on well. I felt nothing and don't know what I'm supposed to feel. So I was scarcely present at all—everywhere and nowhere and annoyed—because I don't know what this is all about.

RM. You feel resistance to the exercise.

JOHN. Yes, I feel lost. That doesn't satisfy me.

RM. It isn't that you must feel something special, something I thought up, that you have to look for until you find it. Simply listen to what comes to you from your hands.

JOHN. But I don't feel anything.

RM. You don't feel your hands at all?

JOHN. What am I supposed to feel in my hands?

RM. The hands themselves. Do you feel that you have hands?

JOHN. Yes, I know that I have hands.

RM. We are not concerned here with "knowing" but with present awareness. Are you aware of your hands? Do you feel just now, at this moment, that you have hands? *[Pause]* Rub your hands as you do when washing them . . . yes, just like that. Do you feel your hands now?

JOHN. Yes, now I feel them.

RM. Now touch your left palm with your right third finger. Do you feel your left palm?

JOHN. . . . . Perhaps a little. . . .

RM. Remain with that a while. . . . You see? That's all there is to it. Now join your palms and listen into them. Remain with them. Try to stay with this awareness.

3.3 MARIA

MARIA. During the last meditations, I had many more thoughts than before. I listened into my hands. I felt something in the solar plexus at the same time. Then later, during my walk outside, I felt a lot of resistance, which isn't usual with me.

RM. You felt resistance.

MARIA. Yes, resistance against the thoughts. And generally, that things will come which I don't like much. And so on.

RM. And how did you deal with the resistance?

MARIA. I wanted to overcome it.

RM. If you feel resistance to the thoughts, you want to be rid of them, and if you don't want the resistance itself, you will suppress it. Try to allow what is there to be there. If you have more thoughts than before, it's a sign that worries, feelings, or tensions are still hiding behind them. Allow them to be there. Don't stay with your thoughts. Turn your whole attention to the palms of your hands. In this way, you disengage yourself from your thoughts without fighting them.

MARIA. And how do I get rid of my feelings?

RM. In the first place, by accepting them. You say that you don't want "these things." But these things are *in you.* If you don't accept them, you can't come to yourself. They stand between you and your deepest self, between you and God.

MARIA. How do I know which feelings lie behind my thoughts?

RM. You've already mentioned the first: the resistance to and defensiveness against having these feelings.

MARIA. How do I go about accepting my feelings?

RM. You learn to turn your attention for a short while to your resistance and, without thinking about it, simply to look at how it feels. You permit your resistance to be there. Then you return to your hands. The resistance will remain, but you don't need to be preoccupied with it. You treat it as you would a wound: When it has been disinfected and bandaged, it may still hurt, but you no longer think about it. You can go about your work and continue to feel pain, but you needn't think about the wound any more; you know it will continue to hurt until it is healed. You aren't fighting against the wound, but giving it the time it needs to heal.

3.4 OLIVER

OLIVER. I frequently tried to "listen into" my hands. I felt the palms and the back of my hands. Then I tried to become aware of every finger and was often able to stay with it for a while.

RM. You went for a little walk through the different parts of your hands.

OLIVER. It helped me to remain present.

RM. That's good that you're able to stay with it for awhile. Now come slowly to the center of your hands. To go along your fingers isn't bad. Now, however, we're going further by staying in one place, the center of your hands. Listen into it and become aware of what comes to you from there. Always return to the same place.

3.5 STEFFI

STEFFI. I don't feel my hands, and then I get restless! I get frustrated and think, "Yes, the others are getting on well. They can do it already, but not me."

RM. You feel competitive pressure.

STEFFI. Not intentionally, but it just comes. What should I do?

RM. Hm. . . .

STEFFI. I don't want to compare myself with others. How can I switch that off?

RM. You don't need to switch it off. Be aware that you compare yourself, and then return to the awareness of your hands. Even if you compare yourself with others a hundred times, return to your hands and try to remain in awareness of them. It doesn't matter if you don't succeed. Just keep trying.

3.6 CHRISTINE

CHRISTINE. I got along astonishingly well. I had two different experiences. I was able to remain in awareness, and I found it very interesting. The listening was something alive and attractive. It was beautiful to rest in the simple awareness of the center of my hands.

The second experience was that my hands brought me back from my thoughts. Without noticing it, I often followed my thoughts. Then, suddenly, I felt my hands again and was intensely present. I didn't come back by my own doing; the awareness of my hands called me back.

RM. This is really encouraging! Open yourself still more to this awareness of your hands. Remain present with all your senses. You'll see how much more you'll receive from them. May I ask a question?

CHRISTINE. Of course.

RM. Before the quiet times, did you renew your intention of surrendering, of serving, of praising?

CHRISTINE. I did this consciously the first time and told myself that I meant it for the whole day.

RM. It's good to renew the intention before every meditation. The first cup of coffee in the morning isn't enough for the whole day. You have to keep replenishing.

3.7 RICHARD

RICHARD. I was quite capable of being aware of my hands. They got warm. Then I felt how the circulation flowed through my whole body. It was very enjoyable. But during my walk in the middle of the day, I got very sad. I became conscious that I'm constantly thinking. I'm caught up in my thoughts, almost imprisoned by them.

RM. You were sad about it.

RICHARD. Yes, I didn't know how to escape from this prison. I know during meditation where to come back to, but I felt lost outside. I couldn't escape from my thoughts.

RM. You can escape through awareness. Thinking and doing fills a small space in this world, which we do occasionally experience as a prison. From this narrow space we can escape by a secret staircase. It's awareness. It leads to your true self and to God. Through awareness we come to being, to the absolute.

RICHARD. That's still doubletalk to me. It's too high for me to grasp.

RM. We can't possibly escape from our world of thoughts through more thought. As long as you are lost in thoughts, there's no way out. Suddenly you notice that you are caught up in your thoughts. You become sad. The first step is to look at your sadness by telling yourself, "Yes, I'm sad." Looking at your sadness like this, you're already in awareness. But don't stay there too long, or you'll fall back into thoughts without noticing it. From awareness of your sadness go on to awareness of what's outside you. Take notice of what is there: a tree, a flower, a sound. If you direct your awareness to your own being in that context, you've come a good step further.

3.8 SHARON

SHARON. At the beginning of meditation I'm wide awake, but then I gradually begin to doze off.

RM. You fall asleep.

SHARON. Yes, and I don't know whether it is physical tiredness or whether I do something wrong. After a while, I feel the way you do reading a boring book. My eyes get heavy. I can hardly keep them open.

RM. Aren't you too passive?

SHARON. How is that "too passive"?

RM. We usually sit with passive attention in front of the TV set. It's entertainment. The director takes care of our attention. But if we sit passively in front of a book when we're studying, we don't get anywhere. We need active attention. In meditation, we become dull if we're only passively present. Bring a lively interest to the exercise: What am I discovering? What reveals itself to me? What sensation comes to me from the palms of my hands? Listen into your hands with engagement and interest. When we remain in awareness like that, it's thrilling!

Or do you think we'll fall asleep in eternal life? The presence we're only now becoming aware of is the first sign of the presence of God. It captures our attention. So be present with all your senses, and you won't fall asleep.

3.9 LUKE

LUKE. I could feel into my hands very well. It was as though they melted into each other. I didn't feel them as separate, but rather as a globe. Then I became conscious that I told myself everything: "Now feel your hands, what do you feel?" "Just now you got distracted; come back, remain present." There was constantly this voice, and the meditation went on two tracks: my effort and my judgment on it.

RM. This disturbed you.

LUKE. Yes, it disturbed me at first. But then, when I didn't succeed in turning the voice off, it became very annoying.

RM. It annoyed you . . .

LUKE. Of course, I didn't want to hear it anymore.

RM. Here we can learn something very important. There isn't any fighting in contemplation. A warlike attitude brings division. *We are here* and *the enemy is there*. The duality builds walls and creates tension. There isn't any duality in God. In God everything is one. Everything is contained in him.

This is what Jesus wanted to say in the parable of the growing weeds (Mt 13:24-30). The workers thought the weeds would overrun the crops and wanted to pull them out at once. The farmer told them to let the weeds grow. At harvest, the weeds would be integrated back into the universe by fire. In the material world, there's always opposition between good and evil. Evil fights against Good, and Good attacks Evil. But in contemplation, we discover a new perspective: unity, harmony, reconciliation, love.

LUKE. That sounds very beautiful, but what can I do when, against my will, a voice inside me comments on everything? I have to fight against it.

RM. Free yourself from the commentator, but don't reject him.

LUKE. How?

RM. Allow the commentator to stay. Turn your attention to your hands and take no further notice of him. Leave him alone.

Compare it with what happens when you're studying. You sit down to study. Loud noises from the street irritate you. You can't concentrate on your book. Even if you try hard, you won't succeed at first. But if you try to be present to your task with every bit of your attention, you'll gradually succeed. The noise is a nuisance, but you're already concentrated on your reading. You keep on, and even though you're still aware of the noise, it no longer irritates you. After awhile, you become so engrossed that you hear the noise only marginally in your consciousness. It no longer disturbs you. Later, you don't even hear it anymore. Only afterwards do you realize that it was there all the time. A disturbing factor can thus gradually retreat into the background simply by our turning to the task at hand.

This attitude is also very important in daily life. No need to smash the darkness. It's sufficient to kindle a light. Then all darkness disappears.

3.10 HANNAH

HANNAH. When I became aware of my hands today for the first time, deep gratitude welled up in me and showed itself in tears. Then at midday, I felt pain in my knees. I tried to come back to awareness, but in spite of my effort, the pain got worse.

RM. You had a lot to endure.

HANNAH. I was about to run away.

RM. Enduring a lot of pain isn't the goal of meditation. Change your position. It's good to have two different ways of sitting and to change them periodically. Pains can come from bad posture; we have to sit properly and try various ways of sitting. Or, there can be pains in the knees originating from internal tensions. One shouldn't take notice of these.

HANNAH. How do I know what causes the pain?

RM. When you sit upright in a way that doesn't strain your knees beyond what you can easily bear, you should be able to sit for half an hour without pain. If pain arises again in later meditations, it's probably caused by inner tensions. If the pain isn't too great and you're resolved to go on with the meditation, recollection often deepens. Consequently, if you stay with the meditation, the pain often disappears suddenly. Note whether or not the pain in your knees remains after your meditation. Pains coming from tension or from reasonable effort will cease within two or three minutes. If you still feel the pains after half an hour, they're an organic condition. In that case, don't strain them much more; that might cause lasting damage.

3.11 HELMA

HELMA. I felt my hands as if they were in a magnetic field, as though a power held them together. I felt something in the solar plexus—or maybe in the region of the heart, I don't know—like a connection to this magnetic field. It spread over my whole body.

RM. You were able to stay with it.

HELMA. Yes, but after a while it was gone. I wanted to experience it again, and tried to do it for awhile. Then I noticed how tense

I became. All at once I realized how I want to interfere in everything, manipulate everything. I felt rather painfully how this need to make things happen keeps me from actual awareness. I saw scenes from my life in which I wanted frantically to reach something. I was so disconcerted, actually frightened of myself!

During the following meditation, I experienced something central. Since early afternoon, I felt joy in knowing that I didn't need to make anything or reach any goal. It was an incredible liberation, and I still feel it. I felt secure in just existing and not needing to achieve anything. I *may just simply be*. I find I'm carried by my being. I don't need to struggle for security. I don't have to show anything and feel much more free of the opinions of others. My security rests in my being. I'm at home in my being, and so I can let go of my need to achieve. After that, thoughts came again. When I became conscious of distractions, I returned to my feeling. I was astonished to have felt no guilt or sadness at all. I simply said to myself, "It was like this and it simply is like this."

RM. Keep on with this practice.

3.12 OSWALD

OSWALD. I've been trying for two days to get into my hands. Unfortunately it doesn't happen. I don't feel them and I don't get into them. They're far away and I can't reach them.

RM. You can't reach them.

OSWALD. No, I don't get there, I don't find them.

RM. You don't need to get there. You want to get into awareness of your hands for all you're worth. You want to achieve it. But you don't need to go there; instead, let your hands come to you. Be interested in whatever does come to you from your palms. That's a 180-degree turnaround, a change in your fundamental attitude. You are a priest, and we priests too often act this way when we proclaim the Good News: we think that in every case we have to go out to others to bring the Gospel to them. If we don't succeed and are rejected, we think the world is bad and unbelieving.

OSWALD. Yes, exactly. I often feel like that.

RM. There's an essentially different approach to people that comes from turning around your attitude.

OSWALD. . . . but how?

RM. We can see what comes from the people themselves and learn from that. Listen to what they want to tell us, how they understand the Gospel; find out how they experience Jesus Christ in their life. It's possible to listen to the message the people have for us. If we're open to that, a relationship develops, a deep contact, leading us ultimately to a better awareness of how God works in us human beings. Certainly all their suffering comes to confront us, but we are closer to reality.

This turning to reality is also necessary in our relationship with God. We want to come to God. We want to come closer to Jesus Christ. He's there. He reveals himself. We only need to listen. He speaks in the quiet, but not in human words. He speaks through reality. He reveals himself in our deepest being, in our own consciousness. All we have to do is listen without preconceived ideas. Awareness of our hands is important. More important still is the receptivity that brings that awareness about: It relates us to reality.

3.13 ANNE

[Anne has been offered an important job, a great challenge to her. There are many pros and cons about accepting the offer. She's been thinking about it for some time, but the decision isn't due right away after the retreat. At the beginning of the retreat, she discussed everything and then agreed with the Retreat Master to allow the problem to rest during the retreat.]

ANNE. I try to feel into my hands. The whole day I'm weighed down by oppressive tiredness. Today I already had a nap, but the tiredness is still there. In between, I also felt impatient.

RM. You feel heavy, as if you've been knocked out.

ANNE. Yes, that's right, really knocked out.

RM. Anne, you must have been occupied with your problem.

ANNE. Yes, but I don't need to make a decision now during the retreat.

RM. That's why I asked you to leave your worry alone and not lose time over it. Did you succeed in this?

ANNE. The truth is that I couldn't really let go of it.

RM. As long as you hold on to this worry and keep thinking about it, you won't get any further. You can't solve it by thinking about it. Otherwise you would have solved it long ago. You have already reflected long enough. Don't you think so?

ANNE *[smiling nervously]*. Yes, it's true.

RM. Your problem isn't a mental one. Your heart and your unconscious are deeply involved. Problems in our emotions or unconscious need to be solved there, not in our head. Through quietness, we can descend into this depth. But under one condition: that you stop thinking about it, leave your problem alone, and devote yourself with determination to awareness. It's for this reason that awareness is important. Feel attentively and exclusively into your hands. Clarity can come from deep within only this way. It won't come as an idea, but as a kind of conviction, already well thought through. A clarity coming from deep within. Whenever your problem surfaces in meditation, let go of it.

ANNE. I'll try.

3.14 FRANCES

FRANCES. I'm still very tired. The heat here is terrible. I can't feel anything because of it.

RM. The heat keeps you from awareness.

FRANCES. It gets on my nerves. I can't bear much heat.

RM. Look, Frances, there are two different things here. On the one hand, the oppressive and suffocating air. It is unpleasant, I can see that. On the other hand there is your dislike of this heat, which makes up more than half of your discomfort. Once you're prepared to endure the heat and suffer it, most of your discomfort will be gone. But if you work yourself up into aggravation of your dislike, your irritation and impatience will also increase.

3.15 LOUIS

LOUIS. Today I had fewer distractions and thoughts than yesterday. I can remain in the center of my palms. But it's so dead and dry, without any highpoints.

RM. You're disappointed that you experience no highs.

LOUIS. Yes, I remember from past experiences how very interesting it could be.

RM. You long for a repetition.

LOUIS. Yes, that's what I'd like.

RM. With this desire, you unconsciously block awareness. You want something for yourself. Try to be there for God, less for your own advancement or the experience of something interesting. Do you renew the intention to give this time to God before every meditation?

LOUIS. Not always.

RM. Get used to doing it each time. It's an essential, a really fundamental attitude for this retreat. Without it, our search for God can easily become striving for self-realization in the egotistical sense.

LOUIS. Hmm.

RM. Examine your desire to experience special highpoints during the retreat. Look at it explicitly. Return to awareness of your hands.

3.16 ADRIAN

ADRIAN. The meditation would go better if I didn't have this back pain that causes me to change positions constantly. Unfortunately, moving doesn't help; I only get more restless. So I can never really settle down. The pain gets worse and tortures me.

RM. You sit restlessly.

ADRIAN. Restless is too mild a word. I'm tormented.

RM. Could it be caused by the way you sit?

ADRIAN. What is the right way?

RM. The human body is a wonderful organism, harmoniously built. The spinal column has a central role. It carries the body. When sitting, you must remain straight so that the vertebrae are resting on each other with even pressure on both sides. The spinal column can easily carry a heavy weight. But if we sit like the Tower of Pisa we're in difficulty after a short time. If the Tower of Pisa were the human spinal column, don't you think it would be in great pain? The tower was built straight, and now it is near to toppling over. One side of it carries the weight of the whole tower.

Between the vertebrae are the discs, which ensure the spine's resilience. If they are constantly under uneven pressure, they begin to hurt. If the pressure is even, one can sit endlessly without pain. If we sit crooked like a question-mark, the discs and also the spinal muscles are loaded on one side. They get cramped, and it hurts.

ADRIAN. How do I sit correctly?

RM. Sit with your center of gravity on your stool and not bent forward. You can find your center by placing your hands under your seat. Find out where it is by moving slowly forward and backward, until you feel where the weight is greatest. Most often we sit bent forward, so that your body's weight doesn't rest on your chair, but on your upper legs. Correct this. Sit straight and avoid a hollow back, which also causes pain. We create a hollow back when we push the belly out in front, and the sacrum forms a hollow curve. Sit on your pelvis without sagging. To illustrate: imagine yourself pulled up by the hair on the top of your head. You automatically have to straighten up so that your spine is straight. That's the right way to sit.

ADRIAN. I'd really prefer to straighten myself up rather than allow myself to be pulled up.

RM. No one will pull you, but the image works. There's another possibility: Sit down and let yourself sag. This is the so-called driver's posture. Then make your back hollow. Thus you experience two extreme, wrong positions. The right posture is in between, in the middle. To avoid a hollow back, be sure your upper legs are in a horizontal position. If they hang down, as if from a very high stool, they can cause a hollow back.

Avoid letting your shoulders fall forward. Push them back and then down. This relieves back tension. The posture should be relaxed. As the spine is built up, vertebra on top of vertebra, the muscles can relax. One can then sit for long stretches of time loosely, effortlessly, and without pain. If, however, you suffer from a curvature of the spine, you must have an orthopedic doctor or therapist show you the proper therapeutic exercises. At the beginning of the retreat, it's best to pay attention to a correct posture. As we come closer to

ourselves, pains can arise which don't result from sitting incorrectly, but from darknesses deep within.

3.17 GREGORY

GREGORY. I never know whether to keep my eyes open or shut.
When they're open I look at an icon or a light. When they're
shut, images and pictures appear.

RM. If you're able to stay wholly in awareness, it's better to close
your eyes, because this leads to fewer distractions. But if you
aren't fully present, closed eyes may let the dream images,
representations, memories, and so on, increase. So open eyes
can contribute to a better link with reality. In this case, it's
good to look on the ground one or two yards away. Only
lower your eyes, not your head. In order to come back to reality from dreams, it's often sufficient just to open your eyes for
a short time. Then you can close them again.

3.18 WALTER

WALTER. Before meditation, I often tried to give the time to God or
to tell him that I'm there for him. I also make the "test" after
meditation and find regularly that I'm not fully satisfied. It's
clear to me that I can't be present for him without other intentions: I have self-interests that I can't deny. I'd like to become
quiet, let go of psychic ballast, become free, make progress in
recollection, and so on. I could go on listing more things. So
repeating the prayer to be there for God—as far as I'm concerned—is a joke. It carries no weight. I can see theoretically
how good it would be just to be there for God. But I'm also
selfish and have to live with that fact. I can't honestly tell myself that I'm there for God. Neither can I reach the point of
getting up from my blanket satisfied. Can I stop this prayer?

RM. You don't feel that the intention to be there just for God is
truly your own prayer.

WALTER. I don't feel genuine.

RM. Not genuine?

WALTER. I can't be there without any other intention. I'm an egocentric person. But I must say, your talk helped me. It showed
me the self-centered abysses in myself and opened my eyes to

my life. I was struck by my bottomless egoism. I never saw my weaknesses so clearly. I came to the conclusion, almost with despair, that I can't change them.

RM. This filled you with dismay.

WALTER. Yes, and in this state I should tell God that I'm there for him? I can't.

RM. You don't need to.

WALTER. What?

RM. I only asked you to renew your *intention* to be there for God. You don't need to achieve it, to make yourself truly there for him.

WALTER. I shall only renew my *will* to be there?

RM. Look, Walter, we're hitting something fundamental here. I take from you the burden of having to change yourself. We place this burden into the hands of Jesus Christ. You occupy yourself with him; he will take care of you. Tell him, "Lord, I'd like to be there for you. But I can't. You, Lord, can do everything; you can give me this singleness of intention at every moment." If you pray in this way, you have renewed your intention of serving him. You are freed from the pressure of having to change. That's precisely the difference between pre-contemplative forms of prayer and contemplation. *We* don't need to bring something about. It suffices to trust that God will give us everything as a gift.

WALTER. I think I'm beginning to understand.

RM. Let's go a step further. You made the mistake of being much too occupied with yourself. You wanted to destroy your self-centeredness first before you would come to God. This fixated you completely on yourself. Be occupied with God. Look at him. He takes care of you.

WALTER *[humorously]*. That's what I want, but you hold me back with paying attention to my hands.

RM. You're still too much in your thoughts. In order to free yourself from them, you must come to awareness first. May I show you once more what truly matters?

WALTER. Certainly.

RM. Jesus Christ describes the attitude of a person in meditation perfectly in the Gospel (Lk 12:35-38). He calls the servant who is ready waiting for his master, "blessed." The master is at the wedding. The servant is blessed when the master finds him awake at whatever moment he might come. Imagine that the servant is awake, but is only thinking of himself and grumbles, "Where is that fellow all this time? After all, I need my sleep too. I've worked the whole day and I'm tired." In this case the servant's heart and attention remain solely within the self. But if he says, "I'm happy that my master can celebrate together with his friends. If he is content, let him remain there. I am always here." In this case his heart is wholly with the master. It is the same with us. If we aim at fighting self-centeredness, we shall find ourselves immediately in a vicious circle. We'll remain with ourselves. But if our heart and attention are with him, we're oriented toward him. Your self-centeredness is his problem.

3.19 LEO

LEO. I'm getting on fairly well. I listen into my hands. I became conscious of how much I'm expecting something to happen, that I might see God in some way, or be given light. At other times, I'm hoping to feel consolation or love. I don't know why, but this desire for something to happen is always there.

RM. You aren't quite satisfied with your attitude.

LEO. That's right—I'm becoming slowly aware that I have been waiting a long time for an encounter with Jesus Christ. I have a great longing for God. It gives a special color to my meditation. During meditation, I feel impatient and, really, slightly disappointed.

RM. You long for God; that is good and important. From this, you begin to expect a new experience of God that isn't quite part of the longing. Try to let go of your desire for an encounter with God. It's absolutely *not* necessary that anything happen. The only necessary event is your surrender, your service that looks for no reward, and your adoration, without any other motive.

If something happens, it will be like this: God will purify and deepen your surrender, your service, and your adoration—he'll make of them a whole. We don't usually notice this. The encounter with God consists in surrender, service, and adoration. If you stop expecting anything—really anything—in this world, except to give yourself freely, just to serve and adore him, then by itself the illumination, the vision of God will become apparent. But we don't normally feel surrender growing in us.

LEO. Isn't there some sign that I'm coming closer to God in meditation?

RM. A good sign is that such questions disappear. Not because you've stopped longing for God, but rather because you are no longer occupied with yourself, but only with God.

LEO. But shouldn't I know whether I'm meditating in the right way?

RM. If you turn your attention to God and are ready to suffer everything life asks of you, then you meditate the right way. You don't need to know anything more.

But there are sure signs that you're on the right path. You can become aware of them only after meditation and after the retreat, not during it. If after some time of contemplative prayer you notice that you love people a bit more without trying to do so, that you feel more patient with them; if you notice that you're more positive in your attitude toward life, that you have greater tolerance in difficult situations; and if you're able to accept yourself as you are; yes, then your contemplative prayer is moving in the right direction.

3.20 FANNY

FANNY. *[She comes in noticeably tense.]* I stick to the recommended times and try to meditate, but nothing goes right, and I have to force myself to sit there. I want to meditate. It all seems like play-acting to me. I sit down regularly, but have to force myself, and am in no way present there.

RM. You feel resistance to the meditation.

FANNY. Yes, it's like play-acting. I want to meditate, yet I don't want to. It doesn't have any meaning for me. The whole set-up here appears to me rather absurd. But now that I'm here, I tell myself, "So, get on with it and do it." But I fall into anger and inner tumult as I keep trying. The more I want to meditate, the more impossible it becomes.

RM. You force yourself in spite of your resistance.

FANNY. Yes, I force myself.

RM. Don't try to force yourself. Stop the meditation, go out into nature and listen into yourself. Listen to what you really want inside yourself. Open up to your inner self so you can find out what you'd like to do. Free yourself from the pressure.

FANNY. But that's failure.

RM. That is not failure, but a search for your genuine self. At this moment, meditation to you is something imposed. It can't reach inside, because deep within you is something else. That's why you have the impression of play-acting. We want to try together to free you from this pressure so that you can discover your inner freedom. Follow up what frees you.

Go into nature, relax, listen to what arises in you, what you enjoy. Don't go to meditation now. You don't need to come to the Eucharist either, if you don't want to. You must feel free. Come back tomorrow and tell me how it went.

FANNY *[next day]*. Yesterday when I left you, I started to cry. I cried almost the whole night. I became aware that I'm under massive pressure. I also became aware that I'm under great pressure to achieve something in the parish, and the same pressure has arisen here. I started out enthusiastic about my work and took it up eagerly, but I always feel underneath that I'm overburdened. Here the same thing happened. I arrived and wanted to make a real goal of meditation, but at the same time felt the pressure of being stressed by it. It's as if I've put on boots that are too big for me. In the parish, I work with the First Communion Class parents, who are older than I am and often criticize me behind my back. When I happen to hear some of it, I feel very hurt. Every time it hits me that I can't do this work.

[A long conversation follows; she's in her first year of work, and the parish community is difficult to handle. She's conscious that it's normal to have difficulties the first year. Before giving up her profession, she wants to learn patience or to adapt the job. She nonetheless continues to relate that she also has very good experiences and successes in the same parish.]

RM. Do you now feel happy about beginning again with meditation?

FANNY. Yes, I really do.

RM. Then begin again, but only for short periods. Don't go at it with all your energy. Try to stay in contact with your center and to feel what comes from within. If you feel pressure again, try to look at this pressure and tell yourself, "Yes, I'm now getting stressed again. It's welcome. I'll look and see what the stress is going to do in me." If the pressure doesn't stop, interrupt your meditation. Go outside until you are free of it. But don't pressure yourself to do it quickly so you can start meditating again.

FANNY. I think I get it.

RM. Something else, Fanny. Your pressure was caused by being stressed and by overtaxing yourself. You can make that tendency to stress out dissolve completely, if you treat it as I just described. With time, the tension will subside and not return. Then you'll be wholly free and can become contemplative in your everyday life.

FANNY. Thank you.

IV. REVIEW & TRANSITION TO THE FOURTH DAY

We've come to the end of the Third Day. Let's briefly summarize the format of your periods of meditation:

You listened into your hands for twenty minutes. But before each meditation, you gave your time to God or Jesus Christ, and expressed in a prayer that you wanted to give yourself to him, serve him, or praise him. (If anyone didn't do this, I ask that you pay more attention to this practice during the next day. It's the essence of every meditation.) After the prayer, you briefly directed your attention to your body, how it felt, and then into the center of your hands. Whenever you became distracted, you returned again to your hands.

At the end of twenty minutes, before leaving the meditation, you asked yourself in a short review if you were content with the meditation. This made you conscious of the degree of surrender, of readiness to serve and praise God, that animated your meditation. In this way you've gained a lot of experience. Don't give up if the exercises appear meaningless to you. You know from experience that it's often a laborious trek before something new reveals itself from within. We are seeking nothing less than a way to God. Mere curiosity, or an exclusively theoretical interest, won't provide enough nourishment on the journey. You know about the driver who used to drive at breakneck speed and was advised not to drive faster than his guardian angel can fly. We can recommend the same here: no one should go on to the next step without having given his guardian angel time to administer the help he needs.

If you're making a Closed Retreat, you meditated at least four times a day, each time for twice twenty minutes. In this way, you'll have entered slowly into the rhythm of the retreat. Did you give in to the temptation to read other things? Don't read, please! or the flow of your thoughts won't stop. The desire to read would be a sure sign that you haven't let go of your mental processes yet. Reading a few dialogues is enough. It would be splendid if you no longer feel the need for more than two or three dialogues after each meditation segment. I also hope that you've avoided all activities except one hour's housework or handiwork. You didn't telephone or write letters, prepared no sermons, and above all, didn't talk to anyone. Silence is absolutely necessary in retreat. I hope you went outside into nature in between the meditations. I hope that you found yourself strolling outside rather than ambling in the world of your thoughts.

If you're making a Retreat in Daily Life, you've practiced this exercise during two weeks. I'm sure you first took the time to quiet down from your daily activities before sitting down to meditate. So you've actually needed more than forty minutes in order to sit for two periods of twenty minutes.

I'm not asking you whether you felt the center of your hands or not, for we shall remain in the awareness of our hands for the Fourth and Fifth Day, exactly as we did on the Third. The only difference is that we'll extend the time of meditation to thirty minutes, so that every unit lasts twice thirty minutes, with a five minute break between. We'll continue with the thirty minutes throughout the retreat.

In the next Introductory Talk, we'll look at the other side of God-centeredness: The prerequisite for becoming filled with God is to become completely empty of oneself—a key theme of contemplation. I call the theme to your attention. I wish you courage and determination for the Fourth Day. You will see that your steadfastness and endurance will be rewarded.

FOURTH DAY

I. INTRODUCTORY TALK: CONTEMPLATION & SELF-EMPTYING

1. Life and death

At the age of seventeen, I once stood face to face with death. It was toward the end of the Second World War, in January or February, 1945. I was a Hungarian officer cadet and was sent to Germany to be trained in tank warfare. I was stationed with fifty comrades at Erlangen in what later became the American barracks. It was the time of the great bombardments of Nürnberg. At every air-raid warning we had to flee into the open for protection. From there, each time we could observe the hellish fire over Nürnberg. After the air raids the city was enveloped in flames. The various troop units in the area were sent to Nürnberg to save lives and fight the fire.

One day, after having watched the devilish spectacle over Nürnberg until midnight, we were awakened at four o'clock in the morning to do rescue work. We were to go by train, but got only as far as Fürth, from which point on the rails were destroyed, and we proceeded on foot. I didn't know the city at that time, but I seem to remember that our way led from Fürth to Nürnberg's principal station, and through an underpass into the southern part of the city. Some houses were still burning. Everywhere, buildings were in ruins. People were searching in the debris for their families. I recall two people carrying a corpse from a ruin. We weren't yet far from the main station, still on the march, when our officers declared that we had reached the quarter of the town where our rescue operation was to begin. It was half-past nine in the morning. We were still marching when we heard the sirens again, and after a few minutes the first bombs began to fall. We were in the center of the quarter that had been bombed the night before, and we knew that the bombing was going to resume.

We sought refuge in the cellars. We tried to get into a two-story house at first, but then decided on a four-story house across the street. After the first wave of bombs, when we went back into the open, we saw a deep hole, maybe five meters, where the first house had been. If people were living there, they couldn't have survived.

We'd hardly begun to extinguish the fire when the second bombardment began. We fled back into the cellar. I had never experienced anything like this. A rain of bombs fell in the streets. Everything in the cellar shook. When we dared to come out, the street was unrecognizable.

I want to tell you what I went through down in the cellar: We heard the detonation of the bombs and the whole cellar shook. We had the impression that it lasted for hours, but it could only have been ten or fifteen minutes. A terrible fear seized me as soon as this inferno began. Death was close and imminent. I was young and didn't want to die. In my helplessness, I was overcome with a mighty rage because I could neither defend myself nor run away, and was forced to face death. I rebelled with all my vitality against being dissolved into nothingness. It was an impotent and desperate struggle against death. While anger and fear thus raged in me, suddenly a great peace invaded me. I knew: God is present. It's of no consequence whether I die or not. It's good as it is. Nothing of real importance can happen through death. These weren't thoughts, but an immediate knowledge from which arose peace, security, and the sense of being held. The presence of God was a certainty not to be doubted, even though externally everything looked the same as before. I was conscious of God's existence without question. It would have been easier to doubt my own existence than the presence of God. It simply was like this. I was seventeen and couldn't have developed this experience through thought. I didn't know, either, whether this knowledge was given to everyone or not.

When I left the cellar, I noticed a change in myself. In the midst of ruins, rubble, and debris, in the midst of human apathy, distress, and tension, I felt joy and the desire to help. I was able to devote myself with heart and soul to the rescue work.

That experience became important for me. I remembered these moments often at first, but sporadically later on. The feelings that accompanied them disappeared after some weeks. Their overriding actuality passed. But something remained: An intuition of—a longing for—the absolute, for the risen Christ in whom everything exists, the knowledge of our real home. With this, my relationship to our passing world also changed, and that fact had a decisive influence on my life. I had been given to look death in the face and experience the nothingness of the world. And I want to speak about this now.

2. Relationship with the world

The world, human life here on earth, lost its character as "absolute" through my experience. It became unimportant to me in comparison with the presence of God. The world moved to second place. In the light of God, it is the living-space of our earthly pilgrimage where we spend a time that will pass away.

I learned to know the value of death, of renunciation, and of being poor. I understood that loss and a feeling of powerlessness aren't the worst calamities in life. I became conscious of the meaning of the cross. I understood the parable of the Prodigal Son in the Gospel (Lk 15:11-32). I saw why he had to lose everything and be confronted with nothingness and also with his abject misery. It was necessary for him in order to be able to believe in the presence of his father. Many places in Sacred Scripture took on a new meaning through this experience of mine.

- The Samaritan woman who begged for the living water had first to have insight into her miserable experience with men before she could have access to Jesus (Jn 4:27-42).

- At the moment of encountering Jesus, Zacchaeus felt the inner necessity of giving away his money (Lk 19:1-10). Nothing less was possible. His relationship to money had changed through this view of Jesus Christ.

- The criminal crucified beside Jesus had to experience and admit his total failure in life before being able to hear, "Today you will be with me in paradise" (Lk 23:43). I understood why Jesus preached that we must first lose ourselves in order to win true life (Mt 16:24-25). Indeed, it couldn't be otherwise.

Later I understood many of the poor in South America who possess almost nothing but live in inner joy. In a special way, I gained insight into the encounter of Jesus with the rich young man. That encounter calls for a closer look:

> As he was setting out on a journey, a man ran up, knelt down before him and asked him, "Good Teacher, what must I do to inherit eternal life." Jesus answered him, "Why do you call me good? No one is good but God alone. You know the commandments: 'You shall not kill; you shall not commit adultery; you shall not steal; you shall not bear false witness; you shall not defraud; honor your father and your mother.'" He replied and said to him, "Teacher, all of these I have observed from my youth." Jesus, looking at him, loved him, and said to him, "You are lacking in one thing. Go, sell what you have, and give to the poor and you will have treasure in heaven; then come, follow me." At that statement his face fell, and he went away sad, for he had many possessions.   (Mk 10: 17-22)

The man came to Jesus to ask for counsel. A deep religious hunger inspired his search for eternal life. Jesus gave him sensible norms of life which govern people's behavior in this world. They are part of the Ten Commandments. They could be summed up: Love God and neighbor. They are rules which can, rightly understood, easily be made part of one's life. In keeping them, one need not renounce oneself and the world. One can realize one's own plans and use the whole world for one's high ideals and the attainment of perfection. The human being and the development of this world can remain in the center. The Ten Commandments could be seen as the Golden Rule for the continuous endurance of this earth. They demand human effort, but only serve the reasonable development of this existing world. We can suppose that the rich young man had a similar understanding.

The young man, however, was dissatisfied with Jesus' answer. Instinctively he felt there might be deeper things. He was looking for a more radical form of love of God. Jesus took him seriously and confronted him with renunciation, with the loss of his plan for his life, and the giving up of his securities in this world. He suggested to him to sell everything and give the money to the poor. The rich young man became aware that he could not integrate this simply into his future. It would require a radical change of outlook, and the experience of letting go of everything would lead him into unknown dimensions.

He hardly, or only fleetingly, noticed that Jesus offered him a fulfillment which could only be obtained by renunciation: to live with him and be led by him from death to resurrection, from poverty to inner riches, from nothingness to fullness. This was too much for the young man. He felt unable to open himself to poverty and insecurity. His relationship with the world was still an absolute one. The world was his home. He could take small steps in the direction of the absolute within this world, but he was unable to move his life's center of gravity to the true absolute through the dialectic of nothingness. He wasn't able to place himself wholly into the hands of Jesus. The apostles had this trust. We read in the story of their call that they left all things and followed Jesus Christ (Mt 4:18-22).

When all inessential things have fallen away, the essential can reveal itself. Only a person confronted with emptiness can experience earthly life in its genuine reality. He or she is given the capacity to see the world in its right place and live in it joyfully and effectively, without *being of* this world—to use the things of this world as if not using them. Only then can the readiness grow to live with equanimity in wealth or poverty, in health or sickness, for a short or long life.

I, too, had to fight extreme fear and rage against the total destruction of my earthly life and be confronted with nothingness, before I could be given a hint of God's presence. I did not become a saint through this experience. I kept my weaknesses and faults, annoyed and hurt others, was selfish. And there were times when this experience of God's presence went into hibernation. I often tried to get myself better situated on earth. Something, however, remained in spite of my sins: I always knew in the depth of my soul that the world is relative, that we have no permanent home here, and that we go through death to resurrection. This knowledge opened my eyes to contemplation.

3. The difficulty of talking about this theme

I find it enormously difficult to speak about this "law of emptiness." If I'm honest I must say that I have found here the greatest difficulty in my ministry for the last thirty years. I don't find it difficult to preach that we have to orient ourselves toward God. All believers agree with this and no one contradicts it. But if I say that this orientation is impossible without letting go of the world, I often meet with criticism and misunderstanding. I find deaf ears. I often painfully experience my helplessness when speaking of the relativity of life, for I am reproached with pessimism, moral rigidity, blackmail, and escapism, or I become involved in endless discussions in the name of reason or psychology.

It's certainly true that confrontation with the relativity of the world isn't always the best way to take. It cannot always be understood and can be poison for some. It is easy to renounce life as long as one has not really lived. I knew people who didn't fear death. For me not to fear death was comprehensible only through the experience of the presence of God. But these people showed no longing for the absolute. Their lack of fear did not result from the experience of the light but from the rejection of life. They had not yet begun to live and build a positive relationship with the world. So the loss of life was no problem for them: When they began to become reconciled to life, I saw them suddenly begin to fear death. They learned to fear for their life. At first we have to try to live in the world, accept life, love it, and rejoice in it. Only then can the experience of our limits lead to transcendence. Until then that experience merely justifies the refusal to live.

When we affirm life, love and passion for life and the world increase. We feel at home. To speak of transcendence or the limitations of earthly life threatens us. We want to hear about God only as far as he can be fitted into our world and life plan (at least with only minor changes). Consciously or unconsciously we seek for the profit God can bring into our world. But when I speak of the transitoriness of the world and the suffering that is part of life; of the law that it's we who have to fit into God's life, not God who has to be fitted into ours; when I speak of the meaning of sacrifice and renunciation, I provoke fear and face negative reactions. Only people who are receptive to contemplative prayer can look at the limitations of life. Only they understand "the law of emptiness."

4. Renunciation in human life

Everyone has to go through diminishment. We are all led through the nothingness of the experience of death. God guides us step by step with pedagogical wisdom and gentle love to this self-emptying.

To a certain degree, every decision confronts us with renunciation. To choose something means to renounce what has not been chosen. A doctor has to renounce all other professions. When a woman marries a man, she has to renounce all other men. I have accompanied hundreds in the process of decision-making and have found that the difficulty doesn't lie in choosing, but in renouncing. Most people can't make up their minds and hesitate because they can't let go of either alternative. When we make decisions, we necessarily experience loss and emptiness until we have completed the task of mourning. We learn self-emptying in every choice we make. Our life's journey leads continuously toward emptiness.

Women and men marry. They experience in this great love, communion, security, life, and happiness. They give inner room to their partner. They renounce, however, freedom, hobbies, work opportunities, and often friendships. They receive something greater, but they have to give up, have to let go of many things. Then the children come. They need much time, attention, and space, even while bringing considerable joy and happiness to their parents. To make room in oneself for children demands letting go of plans and wishes for oneself.

It isn't long before children leave their parents' home and leave a void behind. Their rooms are empty, the coming and going, weeping and laughing of children stop. The children's friends no longer stop by or phone. The parents have to accustom themselves to be alone with their partner. The void is very hard to bear, as evidenced by the attachment with which many parents hold on to their children.

Retirement is often felt as loss. People don't feel useful any more. They try to fill this emptiness with hobbies, travels, or TV, and are often only partially successful.

Then comes the death of the spouse. It nearly always provokes a deep crisis. Long established habits come to an end, and profound loss is felt. Slowly, one's own death appears on the horizon. This is one of the biggest moments of crisis in human life. We are confronted with total annihilation.

When we have come through these phases of life step by step, accepting and suffering them, we shall find it easier to face total nothingness for a moment, until in the next moment, everything is given to us. Others without the experiences may need to catch up, during the last moments of life, with renunciation and letting go.

These moments of our life, especially the final confrontation with death, aren't chosen by us. They are imposed by life. We are free only to accept them willingly or to reject them.

5. *Voluntary self-emptying*

There are repeated calls in Sacred Scripture to let go voluntarily. The Beatitudes are the hymns of this invitation. Blessed are the poor whose hands are empty (Lk 6:20-23). Blessed are the hungry whose stomachs ache. Blessed are the persecuted who have been driven out of their community or land and face homelessness. They shall find a home in the kingdom of heaven. Each of the Beatitudes invites us in its own way to empty ourselves. As death leads to resurrection, so every Beatitude contains a promise that assures us that this emptiness will not remain empty. It will be filled by God.

Jesus recommends that we not worry about what we can say when we stand accused before tribunals and kings. Instead of filling our minds with thoughts, we are to keep them empty. Jesus himself will inspire us with the right answer at the right moment (Lk 21:12-15).

But for this to be possible, we must silence our reason. St. Paul says of Jesus himself that he did not cling to being divine (Phil 2:5-11). He voluntarily emptied himself, to be humbled by death on a cross. That is the most radical emptiness. The Father filled it by giving him the name which is above all other names.

6. *Examples of voluntary self-emptying*

I'll give a few more examples of how the law of self-emptying plays a role in everyday occurrences as well as in great events.

The first is listening. When we truly listen to another person, we become empty for the time that we do so. We leave aside our own ideologies, interests, and urgent tasks, our urge to want to help, but especially our own thoughts and feelings. We put ourselves into the shoes of the other. But take note: this is true only for the actual time of listening. Other phases of dialogue follow, but for the time of receiving, the listener must forget himself and be wholly with the other. Are we not, in our pastoral work, too occupied with organizing, arranging, demanding, correcting, and giving advice? Are we not lacking in simple, single-minded self-emptying when we listen to others?

In this pastoral sphere, self-emptying plays another special role. We might ask this central question: Do we rely on our own powers, or rather on the grace that makes us an instrument in the hands of God? Trust shows itself in the pastoral preparation we make. If we build only on ourselves, we emphasize intellectual study, research, and organization. We shall find little time for quiet stillness in God's presence. But if the pastor trusts in grace, he will stress, in his preparation, quiet openness and remaining in the presence of God. He will experience how he becomes more receptive to grace—and better disposed to be an instrument of grace—in God's hands. The pastor or pastoral counselor should not neglect the theoretical and practical preparation, but limit his own activity. That, too, is self-emptying. There is self-emptying in guiding others. The leader of a group, assembly, or organization has to set aside his own interests, personal plans, and ideas for the time being in order to identify himself with the interests of the group. If we cannot do that, we use the group for our own ends. We disappoint the trust placed in us. So Jesus Christ says that among the apostles it should not be as with kings and rulers, but the leader should be the servant of all (Lk 22:26).

The same situation is repeated in a peace-making process. When a mediator tries to reconcile two opposing groups, he or she first identifies with the position and interests of one group and then goes to the second and mediates on behalf of the first. Then he does the same in reverse. He empties himself for each group and receives in himself their mutual animosity. Many theologians describe the mediating role of Jesus Christ in this way. He came from the Father to speak in the Father's name. The people crucified him for this. He identified himself with us and appeared before the Father in order to represent us. The Father so laid on him the sins of mankind. Jesus emptied himself twice over, and thus was able to make peace. In the Catholic Church, religious life and living out the evangelical counsels has always been seen as a sign of radical self-emptying. The highest form of self-emptying is voluntary martyrdom. I think of Maximilian Kolbe [a Polish Franciscan priest during the Nazi persecution]. He had just escaped an arbitrary death sentence because the lot fell to another prisoner. Maximilian saw that this was a man who had family and children. He felt how the children would need their father. Voluntarily, he stepped out of the line and asked to take the place of the condemned. His petition was granted, and he was executed. He went freely into the deepest self-emptying. No one has greater love than one who lays down his life for his neighbor. No one can be more filled with God than one who enters this total emptiness.

7. Contemplation and self-emptying

If it is true that God fills emptiness, that every form of poverty and powerlessness attracts God's presence, that the Beatitudes proclaim the way of emptiness, and that the essential reveals itself when all accidentals have been cast off, then there is no time when we should become more empty than in prayer, where we seek nothing but to be filled wholly with God.

That is exactly what the Church teaches us about prayer. The development begins with vocal prayers, like the Our Father and the Hail Mary. During adolescence, when young people ask questions about meaning, they begin to reflect on the interconnections of the world. Reflective modes of prayer are discovered: Scripture meditation, examination of conscience, revision of life. With time, these pass over into more affective forms of prayer in which we bring before God our feelings, ranging from rebellious revolt to pure surrender.

Prayer gradually deepens, so that all our feelings become bound together in one single state of being. We can find numerous names for it: surrender, love, praise. The ecclesiastical definition of such prayer is 'loving attention to God.' Words, thoughts, the ups and downs of feelings, have ceased. Everything has become simplified in a loving, waiting gaze. That is the transition to contemplation. It is also called active contemplation, to which we want to devote ourselves.

I wish to emphasize that everything has its own time. Pre-contemplative prayer, centered in vocal prayers, reflections, and affective prayer, is in itself good and necessary until we reach the time of simplicity. At that time the law of emptiness begins to enforce itself. Only one who dies can rise. Only one who has given everything can receive. It is as in the Eucharist itself: Only what has been offered to God can be changed and given back, transformed, in Communion. Emptiness leads to contemplation. Contemplation is nothing else than that God fills us and our activities in such a way that we no longer live, but Christ in us; that we are no longer making something happen, but Christ in us. But this demands, step by step, renunciation of our vocal prayers, thoughts, and feelings.

Finally I am returning to the rich young man. Let us imagine that he asks Jesus not how to win eternal life, but how to make a retreat.

Jesus would say to him: "Meditate on your life, go through the sins of your past, and be converted to the way of the commandments. Then take the Gospel, meditate on it, and grow from virtue to virtue. Work at changing your character, and study your psyche to work through your unconscious conflicts. Should it be necessary, make a choice by considering arguments for and against, and observing the inner movements of consolation and desolation."

The rich young man would answer, "Lord, I make a retreat like that every year. Is there not something more?"

Jesus Christ could answer him, "I show you a steeper way. Sell your thoughts, your concepts and reflections, your concern about psychological health. Sell your worries about plans, decisions, and activities. Give away your wishes, your images and representations. When you have lost all the supports of your usual prayer to which you can cling, and when you feel completely helpless, then come and remain poor and naked in my presence."

May Jesus Christ find great joy in our setting out on this way.

II. INSTRUCTIONS FOR MEDITATION

We remain with the awareness of the palms of our hands. Feel into the center of the palms as we outlined before. Place your palms together. Renew the intention of giving this time of meditation to God as surrender, service, or praise. Then direct your attention for two or three minutes to your whole body, until you are truly present. Listen into your hands and remain in this way.

You have meditated so far for two sessions, each of them twice twenty minutes. Extend that time to twice thirty minutes. It won't be too long. You will soon find that the end of meditation will surprise you, or that you don't feel the need to get up after the half-hour.

You may continue to read one, two, or three dialogues between the meditations—that is, after a unit of two half-hours—and let them speak to you. Try not merely to take them in mentally, in order to know more, but let them have an effect on you. You'll succeed better in this if you feel your way each time into the experience of the particular retreatant with an open heart. Does it echo in you? Does the retreat master's answer mean something for you?

Remain some moments with this, without reading on out of curiosity.

If you are making a Closed Retreat, I recommend that you meditate for four sessions a day. Pay attention to the silence. Don't read other things, but spend all your free time out in nature.

During a Retreat in Daily Life, try to do this exercise more often and repeat a session of two half-hours every day for two weeks. This difference is necessary because in a Closed Retreat, which has more intense recollection and silence, the exclusive occupation goes deeper. For retreatants in daily life, distractions that come from daily occupations are diminished through more hours of meditation.

III. DIALOGUES

4.1 ELIAS

ELIAS. One day before the retreat I got a cold. I was annoyed because I couldn't meditate with a cold, and I really did want to. I don't have any free time in the year other than this week. I went to the doctor for antibiotics in order to have peace. The tablets didn't help much, and I'm still fighting my indisposition.

RM. You are fighting your cold.

ELIAS. I have to do that if I want to meditate.

RM. The cold doesn't fit into your picture.

ELIAS. No, I'm longing to be with God. I want to enter really into this retreat.

RM. Look, Elias, if you want something at any price, you suppress everything that stands in your way. During our first conversation I showed you how you suppress certain feelings at work because they interfere with your goals. Yesterday you told me that you have too many thoughts. Together we saw that perhaps you suppress something in your fight against thoughts. Now you tell me that you've come to the retreat blocking your cold with antibiotics, because it doesn't fit into your picture. Look, you were overworked, and your body is signaling by the cold that it is overburdened with suppressed tensions. It wanted to release them into the cold. Tiredness and tensions wanted to come out. You blocked them with antibiotics. What you don't like, you send back into your body.

If you treat your body in this repressive way, there is a danger that you are also a dictator with your fellow human beings, arresting and putting into jail all who oppose you. I'm not against antibiotics, but pay attention to what is happening behind your cold.

ELIAS. I should probably listen more to my body ... *[pause]* ... have more reverence for reality.

RM. During this retreat Jesus hastens to meet you in your cold. Receive him with love.

4.2 PATRICK

PATRICK. The meditation is going well. I concentrate on my palms and remain there consistently. I'm not plagued by many thoughts either. This is already going on for a considerable time. I'm aware of a strong resolve and surrender and have confidence that this is right. I'm calm. I can say this truly all the more because I experience the same in daily life and in my work.

RM. Patrick, I'm glad to hear it. But when I look at you a question arises in me.

PATRICK. What question?

RM. I know that you are a very consistent person, and that you really carry out what you have decided to do. And you are highly valued because of your good achievements. This is right and praiseworthy. However, the question that arises in me is whether you aren't meditating a little too consistently.

PATRICK. Too consistently?

RM. *[Is silent.]*

PATRICK. It could be that I approach the thing a bit too doggedly.

RM. *[Is silent.]*

PATRICK. I have sometimes been told—in jest, I suppose—that I'm a hard nut.

RM. Contemplative prayer is something delicate. It is like a flower that grows gently by being surrounded with love and regarded lovingly as it unfolds. One can water it and put it in the sun, but not directly urge it to grow. As the flower unfolds, so also the being reveals itself, and with it the presence of God. For all of us who are used to efficient mental processes, there's a danger that we still want to control. I'm asking myself whether you are sitting sufficiently relaxed and at ease. You just said you "concentrate" yourself into your hands. The word "concentrate" betrays that there's still something hard in you, something related to achievement and management.

PATRICK. Why?

RM. I'd like a more sensitive, delicate expression, like "listening," "hearing," or "looking." We don't have to bring God here or reach him. We need not make an effort to make him come here. He's already here, but we don't notice it. All we need to do is become more receptive. We don't need to look for an amplifier, but an antenna which will also pick up the weaker short waves.

4.3 LUCY

LUCY. I'm unsure whether or not I should continue keeping my diary during the retreat. So far I've always written down what happened each day. But now I feel a bit doubtful.

RM. You feel unsure if this is the right thing just now.

LUCY. On the one hand, I want to keep track of essential thoughts, in order to return to them later. But then I can see that "remaining in the present" means giving this up.

RM. There's nothing against writing down the events of the day in a few words. But not so much the thoughts you heard or generated, rather what happened in you. You might try to find out whether it isn't a kind of greedy possessiveness that makes you want to write everything down.

LUCY. That could well be.

RM. Everything that happens remains in you and becomes integrated into your life. It isn't necessary to possess it a second time on paper. When we have experience, we don't need to write everything down.

LUCY. It's true—I've never gone back to the many diaries I've kept!

RM. Look into yourself and ask whether you wouldn't feel freer and less burdened if you could stop writing a diary and trust instead that God will show you everything.

4.4 AGNES

AGNES. I tried to feel warmth in my hands. It didn't work. In previous meditations, I sometimes succeeded. Not anymore.

RM. You have the impression that everything is at a standstill.

AGNES. Something hinders me, but I don't know what it is.

RM. Why did you want to feel warmth?

AGNES. Because that is very pleasant, and you asked me to feel warmth in my hands.

RM. Not quite. I didn't want to determine what should come from your hands. If you want a result, you move from awareness to doing something. There is no need to achieve something. It isn't a question of feeling warmth or anything else. It's a question of the attitude of receptivity. We're learning to receive whatever comes from your hands, or better still, from reality.

AGNES. Yes, I can see that. In daily life I always want to determine how everything should be. My attitude is ruled by "must," "should," or "will." If it turns out another way I'm discontented or impatient, and I fight against or for something. . . . *[Pause]* . . . I'm beginning to see how a change of attitude is needed.

RM. Yes, attentive receptivity is enough. We learn to approach reality with reverence. That's why I keep speaking of "listening." When we're listening, we can't determine what sound "has to come" or "must come."

AGNES. But to become all ear.

RM. That's what is most lacking in our relationships with others. Each one wants to reach a result, to convince or change the other. So we can't receive others and let them be as they are. That's the problem in our relationship with God as well. We create an image of God. We think we know what he's like and what his will is. And so we expect predictable reactions from him. But God is wholly other. He is. We don't find him because we aren't unconditionally and undeterminably open to him.

4.5 SARA

SARA. I've fared very well with my meditation. I felt my hands at once. First they became warm. Soon after I felt them as a whole and at the same time became aware of the soles of my feet. Then I felt a tingling in my hands and then a feeling of well-being. I also felt something like a globe in my hands. Then they got cold and I had a strange sensation—as if they were quite separate from me. After that I felt them again very close.

RM. A rich bunch of sensations.

SARA. Yes, I'm used to practicing many body-awareness exercises. I don't find it difficult to enter into these sensations and follow whatever shows itself.

RM. Now we'll go a step further. We come from the many to the awareness of the one. It won't be important to be aware of new or strange sensations, but to remain in the awareness of one thing. Try to stay alert with the awareness of one sensation—for example, the warmth—even if nothing new occurs. Try to pay attention to one detail and remain with it, as if time were standing still, as if nothing new could therefore be expected—only the eternal being, now. Try to notice what remains always the same in all these sensations, and try to stay with this one ever-present thing.

SARA. And what is it that's always there?

RM. Try to find out.

4.6 FRANK

FRANK. This is my fourth day of retreat. So I've become quiet and am listening into my hands during the meditation. It's going well. But I question whether I shouldn't after all read something else in between. I have an interesting book beside me that has often inspired me in my life. I always go to it when I'm stuck, or when I seek deepening of faith. Wouldn't it be useful to sustain the listening with some thoughts from this book?

RM. You'd like to read.

FRANK. Yes. I would. But it isn't just the liking. The reading would complement the meditation.

RM. It would complement it with thoughts, feelings, fervor, and memories.

FRANK. You mean, with what we're trying to leave behind.

RM. We're trying to get away from the mental level, from feelings, and from preoccupations. Reading nourishes you with these elements. In themselves they are good, but we're trying to get to a deeper level—to being, even to being conscious. For this, it's better to be wholly open to the present and devote oneself to the discovery of being. It's the most direct way to the presence of God. We aren't looking for thoughts about God or for holy feelings, but for the immediate contact with God. The present itself is the open book in which we read.

4.7 GEORGE

GEORGE. I always sleep badly in retreat and have wild dreams. Last night I dreamt such a confused story that I even surprised myself. I know my dreams and recognize their message. I have a lot of practice in interpreting them. But that they're so much more restless during retreat I can only ascribe to the fact that during the day I enter more deeply into myself and stir up things in my unconscious. During the night these come to the surface.

RM. That isn't a false interpretation, but how do you go to sleep?

GEORGE. I get into bed and try to go to sleep.

RM. What we go to sleep with, that remains with us while sleeping and when waking up. Before going to sleep, try to direct yourself once again to God and fall asleep thinking of him. Where your heart is, there are your thoughts. And there also your dreams originate. You will see how effective it is to fall asleep surrendering yourself to the Lord. You will notice it when you wake up. Christian parents train their children to say their evening prayers so that they fall asleep with the thought of God, of Jesus Christ, or of the Mother of God. This helps not only children, but all children of God.

4.8 BRIDGET

BRIDGET. I'm very discouraged. I've already given up hope several times because I'm not getting anywhere. I can't stay present during meditation. I've often given up. It's useless. I don't get into my hands, and if I feel anything, it's only for a few seconds. A moment later I'm somewhere else again. I'm pestered by thoughts so much that I feel powerless to free myself from them. And it's not just now. It's been so for quite a long time. I ask myself what I'm doing wrong. And I'm also suffering from a restlessness that torments me. I'm always on the point of giving up.

RM. You want to give up because you can't meditate quietly.

BRIDGET. Yes, it isn't going well.

RM. And what should be going well?

BRIDGET. The meditation of course!

RM. That's where the trouble is. You want to reach quiet meditation.

BRIDGET. Yes, that's what I would like, but where is the trouble?

RM. Precisely in your wanting to achieve something. You don't need to get anywhere. Not even to quiet and proper meditation. You can always try with resolve to come to awareness, success or no success. The results are unimportant. We don't need to obtain anything. The serious and constant attempt is sufficient.

During the retreat something begins to move in you time and again. In your case, it's restlessness and discouragement. As long as that isn't resolved, it exerts pressure on your body, your feelings, your thoughts, and then you can't meditate calmly. But that doesn't mean that the meditation is without effect. May I ask something?

BRIDGET. Certainly.

RM. Do you renew your intention of giving every half-hour to God, and do you make the test afterwards to see whether you have really done this?

BRIDGET *[with hesitation].* Not really. I did it on the first day after you asked for it, but not since then.

RM. Begin again and be faithful to it. That means every day, and before every meditation.

4.9 TIMOTHY

TIMOTHY. I meditate calmly, but when a noise disturbs me, I become unreasonably annoyed. I become more and more restless and am not able to disengage myself from the noise. A short time ago there was a construction area in front of our house. Someone was using the pneumatic hammer for hours, frequently turning it off and on. I got really angry! Or if someone talks in front of my door, I can't get away from it. I grow more and more annoyed at the other person's lack of consideration—more than at the voices themselves. People ought to be aware of the nuisance they are. Even slight noises distract my attention. My neighbor breathes so loudly during meditation that I get worked up and can't meditate at all.

RM. You get annoyed at noises.

TIMOTHY. They distract my attention.

RM. It isn't the noises that do that, but your annoyance. Turn from the disturbing factors to your present feeling. Remain for a moment with your ill humor. Then return with all your senses to the awareness of your hands. Don't pay any attention to the noises and interest yourself in your task. The man with the pneumatic hammer is doing his work, and you devote yourself to yours. If this doesn't help, try to become aware of individual parts of your body to bind your attention more easily to your meditation. For example, notice your feet in contact with the floor, after a few seconds, notice your pelvis and the way you sit. Then pass on to the upper part of your body and then to your face. After such an excursion through your body you are already more in awareness and can return to your hands. But don't stop to observe whether the pneumatic hammer is still working and disturbing you, or everything else will come back. Remain in awareness. Devote yourself wholly to it.

The best place for meditation is certainly not next door to a pneumatic hammer. If the noise overwhelms you, seek another place. With the noises you get along in the same way as you did in your studies. If you sit down to read a book, the noise can annoy you. If you concentrate on your book in spite of that, the noise can still disturb you, but you find a moment when you're with your subject. If you go on patiently concentrating, the noise gradually recedes to the edge of consciousness. The work draws your attention more and more. Later you don't even hear the noise anymore. You only become aware that the noise never stopped after you're finished reading. We can direct our attention and also ignore disturbing factors in such a way that they fade from consciousness. But this requires that we consistently pay attention to what we want to hear.

4.10 JON

JON. During meditation, I start doubting after a few minutes whether I'm properly oriented or just circling around myself. I ask myself whether I'm doing something wrong. I don't succeed very well at letting go of these doubts. As long as I'm uncertain I can't rest. Of course, I'm by nature the controlling type, needing to know whether I'm doing the right thing.

RM. You feel uncertainty.

JON. Yes, I do in fact feel uncertain. . . . I don't know whether that's the only reason for my doubt.

RM. You want to know whether you are meditating properly.

JON. Yes, I do.

RM. You don't need to know. Look at your feeling of uncertainty. It's better to take the risk of doing it wrong than to neglect looking at the feelings that occur. The whole problem starts there.

JON. Okay, let's take it that I've looked at my uncertainty. Does that mean that I'm now properly oriented, or have I only been circling around myself?

RM. "Circling around oneself" means moving into thought patterns. Thoughts aren't "I myself," but satellites of our true self. With thoughts, you're with your satellites and not with the sun of yourself. These planets circle around the self: Am I good enough? Do I make a good enough effort? Is it right how I'm going about it? Shouldn't I be able to be better at meditation by now? All these questions and attempts to answer them are "circling around oneself"—activities of the mind related to the self, but not the true self.

"To come to oneself" is something quite different. Looking at the true self is being in awareness. Looking exclusively at yourself, you're led on to the awareness of being, as immersed with awareness as someone else is lost in work. He forgets himself. You experience that you are, and this is no longer the experience of your "own" being, but of being itself. You're led to the presence of God. The Gospel says that the kingdom of heaven is within us. In the same way, God is with and in us. We are one with God, but don't yet experience it. We can't imagine this oneness, either, but we know that in coming to ourselves, we come nearer to him. The mystics said that we can never see God, but we can experience in the core of our being how we are children of God. That's why we direct our whole attention to the self. When we look at the self without any thoughts, we shall slowly approach our true being. There are no more questions, answers, doubts, or thoughts in this sphere. It is here that the presence of God can reveal itself.

The way to ourselves starts concretely with the awareness of our hands. We cannot yet look at the pure presence of God. We would be losing ourselves at once in "circling around ourselves." First, we learn to come to awareness without thoughts. Everything has its own time.

4.11 JEROME

JEROME. It's going well and also not going well. I get into my hands and try to remain there. I mean, I keep coming back. But I'm still very tired, and something doesn't function, and I don't know the cause. Last year, when I made this retreat for the first time, I felt a freedom I'd never known before. My relationship with my parents also improved a lot. The retreat gave me greater inner security and was a decisive event in my life.

RM. You're looking for a similar success this time.

JEROME. Yes, that's why I came.

RM. Now you're under pressure to make a retreat similar to last year's.

JEROME. Yes, I feel I'm somehow under pressure.

RM. That is the pressure to succeed. You planned to bring something about during this retreat. Would it be possible for you to alter your attitude and let go of your expectation? Wouldn't it be liberating for you to abandon the comparison with last year's retreat? Nothing has to happen here. You don't have to declare any success. Write this time off. Look at this time as completely lost, as something from which you don't need to profit. Drop all your expectations and give this time to God for nothing. That's sufficient. Learn to be there simply for God, undemanding, to remain quietly in the awareness of your hands. We don't come here to have something, but to give ourselves to God without any other expectation. It's unimportant whether you receive something or not in doing so. Don't worry about it.

4.12 RONALD

RONALD. I meditated calmly and with recollection during these last few days. Today, however, many thoughts and images came. I grew restless. I remembered the TV news: War and injustice and misery everywhere. It got me down. I had a happy childhood myself, and don't feel burdened by my past. I was engaged in youth groups and so learned how to take responsibility. I also was politically active in Third World groups. The injustices in the world weigh heavily on me. It's clear to me that I have a certain responsibility for other human beings. This realization came to me with such violence, that I could no longer feel into my hands. How can I sit like that when so many people die of hunger, are persecuted, driven out, treated unjustly, and murdered? Can I sit like that as if all this didn't concern me? Shouldn't I instead work for justice and structural change? This torments me. I can't become quiet again.

RM. You feel tension between your responsibility for others and your passive sitting.

RONALD. Yes, and when I see on TV such real and painfully distressing scenes, injustice and poverty, my heart is torn. It weighs me down and I feel guilt for not doing more to help.

Or at least, I feel human responsibility that I ought to do something. It overwhelms me with its indescribable weight.

RM. Look, Ronald, I explained at the beginning of the retreat the sense in which the retreat is the best school for serving others. You decided to make this retreat. At this moment, feelings, pain, sense of responsibility, compassion, or guilt feelings are only distractions. On the last day we can talk about your responsibilities because they're real and important. We humans are responsible for one another, but now your responsibility is to be 100% present here. Everything else is trying to distract you. It's preventing you from coming to the center.

RONALD. That's hard.

RM. Yes, it seems hard, but this is the only way to advance on the way to truth, to reality, and to redeeming love.

RONALD. You ask me to look at everything else as distraction.

RM. Yes, for the duration of the retreat, or during meditation, regard everything that is happening outside as distraction. You're attending the best school for dealing with people; you are learning to listen and to be there for others. Union with God is an important condition for true love of others.

4.13 DICK

DICK. I can only give my time to God in a limited way. I can say that I give it to him, but I feel dishonest, because I also meditate for myself, in order to get ahead. I've often considered not renewing my intention, because it isn't quite true.

RM. You feel dishonest in doing so.

DICK. Certainly, it's best to give the time wholly to God. But I can't suppress my desire to get something out of it for myself.

RM. You don't need to suppress your desires. I asked you only to renew your intention of giving the time to God. Besides the intention, all our emotions and our unconscious are also present. These we cannot easily direct, but that shouldn't disturb us. To renew the intention is an attempt to orient oneself to God and let him give us everything else. It matters at least to try to give God the first place on the level of intention and place our interests in his hands—as if we were to say, "Lord, I will care for you, and you care for my rebellious feelings."

It's enough to renew the intention, even though you know that you don't quite live up to it yet.

4.14 CHRISTOPHER

CHRISTOPHER. I sit as though I'm in front of a closed gate, hoping that it will open. It remains closed, and I try to open it—savagely, as if with a crowbar. Then I become aware that I can't open it by my own strength. Only the Lord can do so, when it suits him. This insight doesn't help me much, for the gate continues to remain sealed.

RM. You are impatient.

CHRISTOPHER. Yes, and the tension in me increases. How long is this to continue?

RM. You are waiting for the gate to open.

Christopher Yes . . . and nothing happens.

RM. Can you turn your attention to your impatience?

CHRISTOPHER. To my impatience?

RM. Yes, to your impatience. Instead of trying to manipulate the locked gate, direct your attention more to yourself and the impatience you feel. Instead of concentrating on how to break the gate open with the crowbar, pay attention to what's happening inside you: How and where in my body do I feel the impatience? How do I feel this pressure to achieve something?

Renounce the desire for the gate to open. Nothing has to open. Everything is already there. In the present, everything is already given. And then remember that you have come to serve God, quite independent of whether the gate opens or not. It's not God who has to serve you by opening the gate, it's you who want to serve God, at least by intention, without having to reach or aim at anything predetermined. Try to give your time to God completely without expecting anything at all.

4.15 STELLA

STELLA. I'm still besieged with worries. My mother is ill; she wants me to be with her all the time. She's reproached me and that's still gnawing at me. I've also had conflicts in my job which occupy me. We want to buy a house, and I keep thinking about that. I often think of my children, whether they're being well looked after. And right before my eyes I often see the many wars and miseries in the world.

RM. All this keeps coming up.

STELLA. Yes, and as soon as I return to my hands, the worries appear again. Most of them are impressions from the last days and weeks before the retreat.

RM. Stella, when we begin a retreat, we take a complete turn, turning from the outer to the inner world—from your world to God's world. We let go of all worries, desires, interest, and expectations, and turn to the presence of God. Our only concern should be to care about him. The only desire that remains is to serve him. Our only interest is worshipping him.

The only expectation is God himself. It really isn't sufficient to keep returning to him as long as you haven't let go of your worries and interests in your heart. If your heart remains attached to the other things, returning to your hands is ineffective. It's impossible to try to chase a dog away as long as you hold it fast by its leash. I invite you to change direction. Turn from yourself and the world of your problems to the present.

STELLA. How do I do that?

RM. It begins with an inner turning to the present. Come back to your hands with this attentiveness and with decision. Give yourself totally, and awareness will soon capture your interest and attention. The present absorbs your interest. The inner turning takes some time, but it's most certainly given.

4.16 SUE

SUE. I'm sitting as if in front of a wall. Behind it are my feelings, but I can't get near them.

RM. You aren't in touch with your feelings.

SUE. No, it doesn't happen. But I want to be in touch with them.

RM. If you want so much to get there, you should undergo psychotherapy.

SUE. Yes, I began such therapy, but the same thing happened. I didn't get access to my deeper emotions.

RM. You see, you want to reach something. Renounce it. Give
your time to God without looking for reward. Devote your
attention to him in such a way as to serve and worship him
without expecting anything.

SUE. That doesn't change anything.

RM. Possibly it doesn't. In spite of that, come back to your hands
and through them into the present. See what comes from God,
from the present. We already know what comes from you:
blockage, pressure to achieve, the urge to make something
happen. Listen into your hands and pay attention to what
comes from them and from the present. No pressure to
achieve comes from there. Listen into them.

SUE *[next day]*. I'm not getting on too well. I'm already more in
the present, but it could be better.

RM. You're still not satisfied.

SUE. Yes, I'm satisfied, but. . . .

RM. . . . not entirely.

SUE *[smiling]*. Yes, not entirely. I had a dream. I wanted to travel
somewhere. There was a queue in front of the bus. I couldn't
get on it for ages. But when I finally got on and the bus began
to move, it did so very slowly. That got on my nerves because
I should have arrived long before. Suddenly I noticed that the
bus was going in the wrong direction. I was seized with terrible rage. But the bus didn't stop. I couldn't leave it. I woke up
with this enormous rage.

RM. So, you were glad.

SUE. Glad? On the contrary, I was in a fury.

RM. Just so; your dream had led you to your feelings. That's what
you wanted all along.

SUE. I would have liked different feelings.

RM. This experience should be a great help to you. You can see
how you yourself block yourself. You want to determine your
feelings yourself, and in that way you lock yourself away
from them. You don't want to admit your feelings, but dictate
what feelings you should have. This closes you up against reality, against what is really happening, and blocks you. Let
your feelings come without evaluating them as good or bad.
Allow what is there to exist. Then your blockages and your

self-made "wall" will dissolve. You can exert influence on your actions. But give free access to your feelings.

4.17 RITA

RITA. During the last meditations I felt great reverence and devotion. A psalm phrase was present in me, constantly repeating itself: "Praise the Lord, my soul, and never forget all his blessings." This thought appealed to me very much. A few days ago I read in the Gospel the passage of the blind man of Jericho, and his petition remained in me for days: "Lord, that I may see!" This petition accompanied me for a long time. *[Rita is recalling Ps 103:2 and Lk 18:41.]* When, after awhile, the word that spoke to me so forcefully fades away and no longer awakens intense devotion in me, I seek another sentence expressing my present situation. So I'm at ease in prayer.

RM. This is your way of praying.

RITA. Yes, some words from the Gospel and Psalms are already so familiar to me that they return periodically. I remain with each as long as I'm touched by it. Then I move on to another sentence or word of Scripture.

RM. An excellent way of praying! If only many people would discover it. *[Pause.]* But I'd like to lead you a step further.

RITA. Isn't it right to do it this way?

RM. Yes, it is right. It's the deepest form of prayer before contemplation. I'm leading you for ten days, and if after this time you wish to return to your way of praying, there's nothing against it. For now, try to follow what I say. Otherwise, you won't find out whether your present form of Scriptural prayer or contemplation is more suitable for you.

RITA. But shall I leave aside Scripture altogether? I grew up with Scripture and live by it. It's the Word of God. God speaks to me through Scripture. How shall I exclude the Word of God?

RM. Look, Rita, Scripture is like a letter. When you get a letter from your friend, you rejoice, sit down quietly, and read it. The letter unites you to your friend. Her handwriting, her thoughts, and her message touch you and you feel that she's near.

Then imagine that the doorbell rings while you're reading. You open the door and are astonished to see that it's your friend. You wouldn't say, "Dear Rosemary, or dear Margaret, wait here a moment; I'm just reading your letter. Don't disturb me, because I want to be in touch with you."

It's the same with God. God has given us his message in Sacred Scripture. We contact him when we read the Bible. But God is also present. He's in you, in your presence, in the reality that surrounds you. In him we live, we move, and have our being. He speaks to us from within. The kingdom of God is within us. He doesn't only speak in human words; he also speaks in the silence, through being, which can't be put into words. His living word is reality itself—existence—so you are God's word.

When we look into our own reality we meet him in a much more immediate way than through a text of Scripture. The written word is already in the heart of anyone who can be introduced in this way to contemplation. Contemplation isn't a rival of the Word, but a continuation, an experience of the content of Scripture. How could anyone orient herself to the risen and now present Jesus Christ if she hadn't assimilated the good news of the Gospel beforehand?

RITA. Yes, but this attention to my hands doesn't lead me to devotion in the same way as the Psalms do.

RM. I'm glad. In prayer we seek consolation, devotion, sublime feelings, and many more things that lead us to God. But religious feelings are by their nature changeable. They come and go. They are religious, but only feelings. Contemplation wants to lead us to the level of being. This lies deeper. In order to reach this deeper dimension we must detach ourselves from our religious feelings. The way to contemplation leads through the desert. We must become empty and let go of our religious feelings. They are not God. In order to come to God we go by the road that leads into depth.

RITA. But that is a very hard way.

RM. There is no other way to Jesus Christ than to let go of everything else: To orient ourselves to him until we no longer have, and can no longer do or be, anything. We experience more and more our complete helplessness. But everything is given us as a gift. We care wholly about God and trust that he will care for us and our feelings.

RITA. Thank you. And what must I do?

RM. Let go of Scripture texts for the moment and try to feel your hands.

4.18 JUDITH

JUDITH. I'm very distracted in meditation. I hardly ever get into my hands. A long time passes before I notice that I'm elsewhere. It's as if I have no strength to get back into my hands. Even when I notice it, it takes a long time before I return. It's as if I had no interest in the meditation. But I *am* interested; it's my will that's so ineffective. Perhaps I should put more will-power into it.

RM. You feel weak-willed and undecided.

JUDITH. I don't know.

RM. You don't know *[pause].*

JUDITH. I want to be present, but in vain.

RM. You want it with your head, but your heart is elsewhere.

JUDITH. Yes, that's more like it.

RM. Where is your heart?

JUDITH. Where is my heart? . . . *[more than five minutes' pause]* . . . Yes, my heart is elsewhere. I can see that now. *[She speaks a long time about the problem which occupies her heart, and then remains a long time again in silence.]*

RM. Meditation can only deepen if, at least for the moment, God takes first place. Everything else has to be dropped. Meditation depends on letting go. Whether a bird is tied by a chain or only a thin thread, it can't fly away. So also in contemplation. As long as your heart is held by something inessential, the all-embracing thing (the one thing necessary) cannot capture your attention because it's already caught by something else. Drop it. You won't be sorry.

4.19 CHARLOTTE

CHARLOTTE. I meditate much better outside. When I meditate in my room, in the meditation room, or in the chapel, it's tough

and laborious. I feel no recollection. I move about as if in a
morass. Every minute is strenuous, hard work. If I meditate
outside amidst nature, it becomes effortless, I relax at once,
and I'm much more present. Lately I've spent my time of
meditation nearly always outside.

RM. You find more recollection when you are outside.

CHARLOTTE. Yes, but I have certain doubts. If I meditate in the
house it's laborious. If I go outside afterwards, I'm more relaxed and alert. But meditating in nature for a long time at a
stretch doesn't lead me to recollection so well. My meditation
is very distracted, especially during daily life, but I feel better
outside.

RM. Without doubt, nature is a great teacher of contemplation. I
believe, however, that you're overlooking something. If
meditation is tough and tense, you probably want to reach
something. Perhaps you get thoughts like, "I'm meditating, I
must proceed, I want to get deeper into recollection." You
want to achieve something, and that brings tension. Then you
go into nature and feel free from this pressure of having to
reach something. That's why you think it's better to meditate
outside.

CHARLOTTE. Now I realize, in fact, that in sitting, I'm under pressure to get somewhere, and in the open I'm not. That is true.

RM. But in nature there are many distractions. Beautiful nature
isn't a true desert, where nothing distracts you. On your seat
in the meditation room or in your corner you're more in the
desert. It is a more direct way to recollection. You should
learn to let go of your urge to achieve. You can recall for a
moment where in nature you were free from pressure. When
your intense urge to achieve is resolved, remain in meditation.

4.20 CONRAD

CONRAD. The last meditations seemed to me endlessly long. I had
the impression they would never end. I often looked at the
clock. Time dragged on monotonously. I felt the half-hour
would never end.

RM. You were bored.

CONRAD. Yes, I was really bored, became sleepy and began to yawn. I find meditation very tiring.

RM. Well, Conrad, boredom in meditation is a sign that one is not in awareness. As soon as awareness begins, the present becomes interesting. It becomes alive and fascinating. Time flies. Awareness makes meditation so absorbing that one doesn't want to stop.

But when we don't attend to the present, but to what will come next, if we become preoccupied with something in our thoughts, or if we strive for something—then we want to get away from meditation, and the time seems to last longer. At such moments, I'd recommend that you prolong the meditation.

IV. REVIEW & TRANSITION TO THE FIFTH DAY

We are at the end of the Fourth Day.

Dear Reader! You aren't in retreat and don't need to keep to the times of meditation. May I nonetheless ask you a question?

Do you read this book like a novel, or do you pause from time to time? Do you take a moment of stillness when something has touched you? It's advisable to pause repeatedly, in order not to read this book in a merely intellectual and impersonal way.

Dear Retreatant! Perhaps you have already reached a state of calm, so that you no longer ask about the meaning of the retreat or the meaning of the meditations. I hope you already feel joy in remaining in the awareness of your palms. It's quite possible that you already feel the palms continuously during meditation, even though many thoughts still pass through your mind. The sensation of the palms leads us directly into the present, and so into the way to the presence of God. Should someone meditate in this way even for thirty years, it would not be a waste of time. You may with a good conscience continue to remain in the awareness of your palms.

When has the time come to move ahead to the Fifth Day? It's good to remain in the simple awareness of your hands until you are constantly aware of them, even if thoughts still move around in the background. Another experience that indicates that we should move on is that the hands constantly call us back from our distractions. In the midst of distraction we suddenly feel our hands and are instantly present again. Now I'm afraid you'll say, "Yes,

during retreat we don't need to reach anything, but there are standards to measure up to, so results are introduced again in a roundabout way." Don't allow yourself to be pressured. It all depends on
your inner rhythm and not on the speed with which you get to the
end of this book.

The Introduction to the Fifth Day describes the internal procedure
of contemplative prayer, so that we're prepared for the time of crisis. During the stillness, the things we have not worked through in
ourselves come to our consciousness, and this leads to a crisis. You
must know about this in order to react in the right way. During the
meditations we supplement our attention to the palms with a word.

Much joy to you in the days to come!

FIFTH DAY

I. INTRODUCTORY TALK: REDEMPTION

1. Abduction

During a long abduction I underwent an important inner development, which may help us understand how redemption takes place
during retreat. It was the time of the civil war between the extreme
right-wing and left-wing groups in Argentine society. The university students were very agitated by the events of this time. The
pressure to join the guerillas was great. I was living at the time
with a fellow Jesuit at the edge of the slums of Bajo Flores in
Buenos Aires. We were theology professors at two different uni-
versities. We wanted to bear witness to the fact that, while
wretched life conditions existed, it was possible to take the part of
the poor by peaceful means. We had received an express mission
from the official Church and from our superiors to live among the
poor. In spite of this, our presence in the slums was a thorn in the
flesh to many people whose political stance was the extreme right.
These people interpreted our presence there as support for the
guerrillas, and planned to denounce us as terrorists. We knew
which way the wind was blowing, as well as who was responsible
for the malicious talk, so I went to this particular person to tell him
that he was playing with our lives. The man promised me he would

communicate to the military that we were not terrorists. According to later statements by an officer, and the testimony of thirty documents that eventually came into my hands, it became irrefutably clear that he had not kept his promise but, on the contrary, had given false information about us to the military. This account should be sufficient background for the story that follows.

On 23 May 1976, a Sunday morning, 300 heavily armed soldiers with police vans surrounded our shack on the edge of the slum. After cutting off all access from outside, they invaded our house, brutally tied our hands behind our backs, pulled narrow hoods over our heads (which made us choke), and abducted us. For five days, almost without food, I lay on the stone floor with the hood over my face and hands tied behind my back. My fellow Jesuit fared much worse. He was given drugs in order to extract from him information he otherwise would never have given. As we later learned, he had—against all expectations—talked about God and Jesus Christ. The military were deeply impressed. Until then they had been convinced that we were terrorists.

On the fifth day they brought us to a private house. They replaced the hoods with eye bandages which gave us relief from the choking fits. They fastened the handcuffs in front, which was a relief when we were lying down. On this fifth day an officer came and told us we were innocent, and that he would ensure that we could return to the slum as soon as possible. These were the last words we heard regarding our abduction for five months, during which we remained handcuffed. We each were chained by one leg to a heavy canon ball. Our eyes were blindfolded until our liberation.

We had both long before begun to meditate with the simple repetition of the name of Jesus. Day after day, from morning to evening, we kept to this simple prayer.

After the officer had told us on the fifth day that we would be freed, he evidently said the same thing to the eight subordinate officers who guarded us. One of them said to us the same evening that prisoner releases always took place on Saturdays. I rejoiced since it was Friday. But Saturday came and went, and we were not released. I became extremely enraged. The injustice of being kept under arrest in spite of our proven innocence evoked helpless rage and great anger in me. My rage was more and more directed against the man who had given false witness against us. After a day of helpless rage, I was overcome by great fear of what would happen, including the thought of execution. The fear, together with an inner shaking, lasted a day and a half. After that I got very depressed: all was lost. (My fears don't seem exaggerated to me even today. After several years, when a court case was prosecuted against the commanders involved, there were no surviving witnesses from the 6000 people whom this particular group had abducted. Only we two survived. All the others had been killed.)

On the fourth day after that I sank into indescribable sadness. Another day had to pass before I could weep for hours. Only then could I feel relieved and become calmer. I waited for the next Saturday full of hope. It wasn't far off, for my inner process took several days. When again we weren't released, the whole process began again: Rage, fear, depression, sadness, and then weeping. I passed through all these emotions over three or four days, until hope again flared up at the approach of the next Saturday. This inner process repeated itself in the same form week after week, for three and a half months. All the time, I continued to meditate on the name of Jesus. In spite of inner rebellion and violent feelings, I constantly tried to forgive. I also constantly prayed for our persecutors and the people who caused our abduction. After three and a half months, the cycles of the process became shorter, but repeated themselves every day until the day of our release: rage, fear, depression, sadness, weeping. Occasionally there were more quiet days.

After our release, my friends urgently counseled me to stay for a while outside the country, and so I spent more than a year in the United States, hoping to return soon to Argentina. When, after a year, my return was still thought to be inadvisable, I came to Germany. I began to give retreats, and I also noticed that a great change had taken place in me. A kind of depression, which had always been in me under the surface, and a certain aggressiveness were completely gone and never returned. The months of abduction, imprisonment, and closeness to death, along with the constant repetition of the name of Jesus, had brought about in me a profound purification.

I have kept the description of the events very brief, in spite of the months of imprisonment and so many impressions and profound experiences. It's sufficient to describe how I was incredibly transformed in the silence of meditation. Stillness can set a great deal in motion in the human person. Attention to Jesus Christ connects us to his healing power, and I'd like to describe in more detail this purifying process that takes place in an extensive stillness—and so also in retreat.

2. Confronted by the power of darkness in the desert

The only thing the Synoptic Gospels tell us about Jesus' stay in the desert is the temptations by the devil (Lk 4:1-13). I see in this description Jesus' "retreat diary." It's remarkable that we don't hear about meaningful spiritual experiences or consoling encounters with his Father, but solely of three moments of crisis, followed by a short remark that angels came to minister to him (Mt 4:11).

In the fourth and fifth centuries, the Egyptian desert was the home of more than 10,000 hermits and monks are called Desert Fathers. They went into solitude with the desire of imitating the life of Jesus in the desert. They also reported conflicts with the devil.

When confronting a desert experience, the seeker meets the darkness and a battle ensues with the powers of darkness. What happens during this confrontation in the desert? Why is it precisely in the desert that people are confronted with evil? We want to look at this more closely.

Every human bears good and evil in himself, light and shadow. We don't like to know about the darkness within us. We suppress into the unconscious our shadow side or dark corners and create a self-image composed of our positive qualities only. Slowly but surely we convince ourselves that we really are what we would like to be.

But we carry ourselves around with us everywhere we go. And so we also continue to carry inner darkness all the time. It's active in all we do and often, against our will, determines our actions. For example, we want to love all other people. In fact, our encounters look very different. We're often impatient, rejecting, or aggressive in spite of our firm intention to be well disposed toward others. We are surprised by our reactions because we don't want to accept the source of our behavior. Frequently, therefore, we don't see in ourselves what is obvious to others by our behavior, the fact that we are marked by our darkness.

This suppressed darkness is part of us and wants to return to our consciousness. But because it's unpleasant, we push it down again energetically. We do this in different ways. We distract ourselves, so that it can't disturb us. When the darkness returns and tries more powerfully to enter our consciousness, we defend ourselves more forcefully. Much unsolved conflict, and thus much darkness, lies buried in a human being, and when the darkness tries to erupt into consciousness, ever more violent means have to be used to make it disappear. Some people spend three or four hours in front of the TV every day in order not to feel their loneliness and despair. Others try smoking or alcohol. When the pressure of the shadow becomes unbearable, some use drugs or narcotics. If the pressure shows itself more mildly, good Catholics particularly find help in the defense mechanisms of holy activity. Some overburden themselves with apostolic activity to such a degree that they no longer feel their shadow at all.

What is this darkness? We experience it in habitually negative feelings: discontent, insecurity, fear, hopelessness, rage, anger, abandonment, depression, sadness, disappointment, stress, feelings of inferiority or guilt, indifference, jealousy, self-pity, and much else. Most people relate such feelings to external events and don't realize that they arise from our own darkness. Instead, external events trigger the feelings but are not their cause.

3. Sin

This darkness is sin in its essence. Many Christians think that sin is only something that we do wrong. That is the so-called personal sin, which makes up only a small part of real sin and which one could call the less harmful failings. We can repent our freely chosen actions and be converted. In confession we are freed from the sin and can trust in God's mercy and forget our wrongdoing.

It's different with our habitual negative tendencies. They are located at such a depth that they easily escape our consciousness, and so we feel rather helpless about them. Frequently, we don't feel them as sin, because we don't freely commit or consent to them. Sin, however, isn't only what we consciously commit, but rather everything on a deeper level that separates us from God and other human beings. Deeply rooted negative feelings do this. The Church calls these sinful roots in us "original sin." We have such limited access to them that we can only be redeemed from them. In real life, original sin and voluntary personal sins are inseparable. Original sin makes us act sinfully. And these acts in their turn make apparent the deep-down darkness.

4. The good core, the dark layer, and the outer rind

In the creation story, we read how God created human beings and saw they were good (Gn 1:31). Man and woman lived in harmony with God and the whole creation. After a time Adam and Eve sinned. They were driven out of the Garden of Eden (Gn 3:1-24). This story shouldn't be taken literally, in the sense that a long time ago two people were driven away from a place. It is a description of the actual human situation. The creation account describes our present reality in the form of a story. It tells us that each of us has a good core where we are whole, and where we become conscious that God loves us and holds us; we experience there who we are in God. This original state was symbolized by Paradise and the Garden of Eden (Gn 2:4b-25).

The Fall that followed expresses the fact that around this good core of every human a dark layer formed (Gn 3:1-24). It isn't what is deepest in us. It is a secondary reality added to the first. It only covers the good core; it doesn't belong to human essence. This is expressed in the story by the implication that the Garden of Eden was not destroyed, but that the first human beings were driven out of it. An angel with flaming sword guards the entrance and prevents our returning there.

The new place for human beings is described as a place of thorns, of toil, of pain and death. Human beings had to work hard for themselves in sweaty, daily toil, meaning an unbearable existence full of suffering. This place, like Paradise, is a human reality. It's the dark layer that formed around the good core and which we can experience daily. In order to live with less pain, human beings overlaid that painful state with a protecting skin. This skin represents our resistance to the suffering of darkness. It's our defense mechanism *per se.* It lies like a cement slab on top of all our feelings. We can't penetrate to our feelings, and so to our good core, without lifting this slab. So we live on the surface of our being, without access to our good core, to the Garden of Eden which is still present in us.

This is our present situation: we have an inner good core through which we could experience who we ourselves are in God, how we are loved and carried by him—that we are children of God, temples of the Holy Spirit and members of Christ—how the Holy Trinity dwells in us. Around this healthy core lies the dark and painful layer of sin which keeps us at a distance from the good core. In fleeing from our dark layer, we set up a barricade which I call here an outer rind. It's intended to protect us from our shadow and enable us to live with less pain. The price of our protection is that we are also separated from our true inner being, our deepest identity in God.

5. Pre-contemplative and contemplative behavior

In the Introduction to this book we saw the qualities of pre-contemplative and contemplative prayer and their differences. Because they play an essential role in the process of purification described earlier, we have to look at them again more closely.

The spiritual life is divided into two periods. The first we call pre-contemplative. Spiritual progress is achieved through our own effort. We need to reflect, evaluate, examine our conscience. We consider, decide, and make resolutions. These resolutions are renewed and put into practice, until the desired change in ourselves has taken place. Love and faith have to grow in us. It goes without saying that all these endeavors are impossible without the accompanying grace of God. All the same, it is we ourselves who make the effort to progress spiritually; it is we who work for the kingdom of God 'in the sweat of our brows.'

After a certain time, we are led into the contemplative phase. Our procedure changes. Instead of exerting ourselves to make progress, we now need to learn to look at God alone and let go of everything else. We trust that, if we orient ourselves solely to God, everything else will be added to us. The difference is very important. In the contemplative phase our sole endeavor is directed to our relationship with God. Everything else happens by itself, occurs, is given. We no longer worry about the course of things on earth. This doesn't mean inactivity, but our activity has lost all anxiety. We are gradually becoming independent of results. The pressure for achievement disappears. During the pre-contemplative phase our effort was directly turned to changing ourselves and the world. We need to get results, and that causes pressure, worry, and stress.

These two forms of the spiritual life stand in a peculiar relationship to the inner reality of the human being—to the outer rind, the dark layer, and the good core. The outside of the rind represents the sphere of pre-contemplative prayer. Within the rind lies the sphere of contemplation. This means, in concrete terms, that the laws for changing the world are valid outside the rind: we have to *think actively* and *reach goals.* Our reactions in daily life are like this. If something disturbs us, we immediately ask ourselves about the cause and try to change it. Within the rind, in the dark layer, and in the good core, we can neither think nor act. The moment we begin to think or to act, we are already outside the rind.

How are we to behave in the contemplative sphere? First of all, *look, gaze.* This is a purely spiritual activity with which we don't aspire to reach anything. To *look* always implies letting go, being directed toward something. Second, we can *trust.* Third, we can *love,* but this isn't love as we usually understand it. It's the pure love that no longer expects anything from the other. It's like the sun which always shines and does not cease to shine even when its rays are not received or reflected. This love comes from looking and can't be made. If we remain in looking, in contemplating, it grows in a natural way. Fourth, we can *suffer:* Sin that is suffered in contemplating and loving is redeemed and never returns.

In meditation we gradually grow calm. This leads us to the rind we mentioned, our resistance to our sin. If we continue to devote our attention to awareness, the rind breaks open, and we enter the zone we called the layer of darkness. We experience our negative feelings, which separate us from God and from others. Our spontaneous reaction is to think and do. We ask ourselves from whence this darkness comes, why it is here, and how we can remove it. Thus we become active and have fallen back into our old habits of thought and action. Since, however, we neither think nor act on the contemplative level, we realize that we've left the contemplative sphere through our reaction, and find ourselves again outside the rind, in the pre-contemplative sphere.

If we want to stay in contemplation, we must keep looking. In our case, looking means to direct our attention to the sensation of our hands, and through this to the awareness of the present. It's looking in the direction of the good core, the presence of God. We enter more deeply into the dark layer, which causes pain. To remain in contemplation we must admit the pain and bear it. But whatever is suffered through in this way, while we are looking toward God, is redeemed. It does not return. So much light and strength comes to meet us from the good core, that we find the courage to continue.

Redemption in the Gospel sense means the same thing: Jesus Christ has passed through and suffered the great dark zone of all mankind. He invites us to go with him. He carries us through our darkness. All we need is to be ready to shoulder our cross and bear this suffering. Paul says that he is prepared to bear Christ's suffering and death in his body, so that Christ's resurrection may also be manifest in his body (2 Cor 4:10).

6. In the following of Christ

We are on earth in order to be redeemed. Sin, the darkness in us, separates us from God and from others. We are wholly received into the eternal love of God only when all the darkness in us is dissolved. We see God only after the dark zone in us has been redeemed through suffering. That is the goal of our earthly existence.

A person who has suffered his original sin to the end, in love, and has followed Christ in this sense, has not lived on earth in vain. But a person who has evaded this redemptive love during life has to continue the way of redemption after death. That is the Church's teaching on purgatory.

We are on earth in order to allow our own and others' darkness to be redeemed. Love alone dissolves the darkness. When a human being is loved, he or she is more and more enabled to accept the darkness, to suffer it and allow it to be redeemed. We don't go this way for ourselves alone, but also for others. If someone wants to help others in this process, he or she has to radiate much love. Should you believe that you can work for the redemption of your fellow human beings without allowing yourself to be intensely involved in the redeeming process, you deceive yourself. We radiate only what we are. The radiation touches the human being from within, on the level of contemplation, there where redemption takes place. Every work with others, be it pastoral care or charitable or social work, depends for effectiveness more on your own transformation than on what you do.

7. Concrete description of the redeeming process in meditation

Against this background, dear Retreatant, I would like to describe how redemption takes place in meditation, so that you can see clearly what is happening in meditation. The description is meant to help you handle the difficult times during meditation and to react in the right way.

When we begin a retreat, all worries and thoughts of our daily life at first attack us. After about two days of intense stillness, this first restlessness subsides. We experience a deeper recollection than usual. We come to ourselves and so approach our shadow. On the one hand, we want to find ourselves; on the other, we don't want to come so near that our darkness arises. Consequently we remain in meditation, but escape unconsciously into small distractions.

The process goes this way: After a few half-hours of meditation, during which we were already quite well in awareness, a host of thoughts suddenly arises. This puzzles us: Why are we troubled with thoughts again? Now and then we recognize persistent themes that conceal worries. Most often, however, there's simply a constant flood of unimportant thoughts. Through the silence, through the absence of distractions, flight mechanisms, and repression of thought, something has begun to move in our unconscious and wants to come to the surface to be redeemed. We're frightened by this flood of thoughts and ask ourselves what we did wrong. With this, we are back in thoughts and have left the way. We have moved from the contemplative sphere back to the level of the outer rind. If we don't make this mistake, but courageously remain in awareness—that is, the awareness of our hands and of the present—then the process of redemption begins.

In the course of this process, thoughts can continue to increase, or they can be replaced by a reaction of the body. The pressure of the unconscious can, for example, express itself in pain in the knees or the back. The shoulders also can hurt, or some other place in the body may respond with unpleasant feelings.

If we don't analyze why these somatic expressions come and where they come from, but simply remain in awareness, the pressure can become stronger. It expresses itself often in the form of tensions in the body: Breathing becomes flat and no longer descends into the abdomen. We feel oppressed, as if a big stone were lying on our chest. The abdomen gets cramped, the throat tight. We may feel unwell, may break into sweat or find that swallowing irritates us. Sobbing or coughing, itching, yawning, weeping or dozing can appear. These phenomena frequently cease at the end of meditation, but as soon as we begin again, they reappear.

What's happened? The pressure of the unconscious has spread to the functions proper to the body. Since it meets blockage in the body, various tensions and pains occur. Again we shouldn't look for the causes or reject the unpleasant phenomena. Everything that is there is allowed to be there. The darkness makes itself felt in order to be redeemed.

The process can continue by a strong feeling arising—for example, rage against our parents or someone else with whom we normally live in tension. A deep sadness could also overwhelm us. Another time it may be the feeling of meaninglessness or loneliness (or any other feeling). The pressure from the unconscious takes the form of a negative feeling. After a wave of darkness, comes a calmer and more recollected time.

Whatever has been suffered through during contemplation is redeemed. It never again returns. There may be further waves of the same or similar feelings, for these unconscious feelings are not usually cleared in one meditation. But with time, everything unredeemed in us is removed, layer by layer, as when a mountain is strip-mined. Thus redemption takes place.

The pressure that comes from original sin shows itself most often in these successive steps: Thoughts increase; physical pains occur in the body; tensions and cramps are felt in one or several parts of the body. Then frequently, but not necessarily, comes a feeling. Just one of the physical reactions may then be resolved. Or there can be several resolutions, in different order. The reactions have in common that they show themselves more strongly during meditation than outside of it. Often they've disappeared by the end of meditation. There is a firm rule with regard to bodily pains: if they continue for a long time after meditation, one should make sure that they aren't organic. Pains in the knees, for example, are often caused by inner processes. But if they persist after meditation, they could be caused by a physical knee injury.

Dear Retreatant, it's important for you to be able to interpret these states and not let yourself be tempted into thinking and doing. Everything that is there in meditation is allowed to be there, but we don't occupy ourselves with the pains, tensions, or thoughts that may occur. We try to remain in awareness, willing to suffer all that may come. It's like straddling a ridge: On the one hand don't repress anything, and on the other, don't become occupied with the pain.

If pains arise, we treat them as we would a wound. The wound is cleaned and bandaged, and then we return to work. It will continue to hurt for a while, but we don't need to be preoccupied with it. It heals by itself. To be more exact, the wound heals through the life-energy which has been given to us. So also with the shadows in us which reveal themselves in pain. Looking at them is bandaging the wound. When we allow what shows itself to be there, we don't need to keep on tending to it any longer. We can return to work, which in our case is the renewed awareness of our hands. Our pain is going to be healed. The power of the Spirit will dissolve the darkness if we remain faithfully in the present.

I hope that through this Introductory Talk we can understand why Jesus Christ has drawn our attention to the meeting with darkness through his stay in the desert, and that we can interpret our unpleasant times during meditation as necessary for our redemption.

II. INSTRUCTIONS FOR MEDITATION

As I said at the end of the previous day, the experience of the center of our palms is a prerequisite for proceeding to meditation on the Fifth Day. If you're making a Closed Retreat, meditate daily for four units of two half-hours, as on the previous day. Be sure to keep to fixed times. Gradually add two or three more half-hours to the daily program, perhaps in the time before breakfast and then after supper. Divide this time according to your own rhythms. By the end of the retreat you may easily reach six units of two half-hours each. If you attend daily Eucharist, you will then be spending about seven hours in prayer, and that corresponds to an Ignatian retreat day.

In the case of a Retreat in Daily Life, divide the times for meditation as before. I ask you again to begin each meditation by renewing your intention of surrendering to God or worshiping or praising him. Then briefly become consciously aware of your body, and finally feel into your hands, as you have done so far.

As soon as you are fully present, say with every breathing out a prolonged *Yes* into your hands. It should be a word inside you; don't move your lips. Say it with an inner sound and listen to the sound. Listen at the same time into your palms, to see whether your *Yes* arrives there, and how. You don't have to reach this goal, but simply pay attention whether and how a gentle streaming becomes perceptible in the center of the palms as you're saying, *Yes.* After some attempts, say this *Yes* every time you breathe out. Listen to the inner sound, and what this sound, *Yes,* brings about in your hands. Don't enter into a philosophy of the *Yes.* Don't reflect whether your life is a *Yes* or a *No.* Take the word simply as a sounding word. Remain with it the whole of the Fifth Day.

There are movements of energy in the body. Most people aren't conscious of them. With a little exercise and patient listening we gradually become aware of them. But it takes time. And it isn't the same for every person. Some feel the movements spontaneously and at once; others take longer. To become aware of these energy movements, it's very helpful to direct attention to the outgoing breath. The center of the palms is also a privileged place where they can be especially felt. As soon as you sense an indication of awareness, add *Yes* to intensify the transmission of power.

III. DIALOGUES

5.1 OLGA

OLGA. I don't have success with the *Yes.* I try, and really remain with it, but get very tired. I'm exhausted after each meditation.

RM. This *Yes* exhausts you.

OLGA. Yes, it really does. Every *Yes* brings something of my life before my eyes. I said *Yes* to my job, to my husband, to my children, my mother, my father, to my difficulties, and so on.

RM. You had to force yourself to do that.

OLGA. Yes, I had to force myself.

RM. You didn't really feel like saying *Yes* to everything.

OLGA. Yes, I wanted to. I want to say *Yes* to my life.

RM. Something fights in you against the *Yes*, otherwise you won't have become tired.

OLGA. It was as if I were standing in water up to my neck, when all the time I wanted to run.

RM. Something acted like a brake on you.

OLGA. Yes . . . *[long pause]* . . . yes. . .

RM. Perhaps there is a *No* hiding in a little comer of your heart?

OLGA. But I don't want it, I want to say *Yes.*

RM. The *Yes* and *No* clash against each other, fight each other, and the exhaustion is complete.

OLGA. How?

RM. Your unconscious half says *No* and your active consciousness, *Yes.* Your energies cancel each other out and you have no more strength.

OLGA. That's right, I feel this loss of strength.

RM. When a full tram stops in front of you, you politely allow people to get out so that you can get in more easily. Be courteous to your *No.* Let it come out. It wants to get out.

OLGA. How does one do that?

RM. Feel into your hands and find out whether a *Yes* or a *No* is coming. If it is a *No*, let it come and repeat it, until it ceases. Let come whatever is coming.

OLGA. Am I to say *No* all the time?

RM. Why not?

OLGA. I interpret the *No* as a *No* to my life, but I want to say *Yes* to it.

RM. I see that. You can't get into the tram with your *Yes*, because your *No* is still sitting inside. Be courteous and let it come out. Say *No* until it stops by itself.

OLGA. Will it stop?

RM. You need not work yourself up into a *No*. Just stay attentively there, whatever is coming. When your passenger has left the tram, a *Yes* will come. But don't say *Yes* or *No* to individual things. Pay attention to the word and its sound.

OLGA. I'll try to do that.

5.2 DANIELLE

DANIELLE. For some days I have been in the center of the palms with all my attention. I felt so intensely held in the present that I found it difficult to decide on the *Yes*. I finally did it two days ago. It was difficult at first. It seemed too much to me to bring the hands and the *Yes* together. But I kept at it and noticed that I was blowing a tensed *Yes* into my hands. I was actively doing it, so it couldn't be right. Then I tried to let the *Yes* flow into my breath very gently, and it happened almost imperceptibly. I tried to listen to the sound. I was fascinated by it. Only first, I couldn't understand how a word that moved neither lips nor throat could produce a sound. After awhile I noticed how I could really pay attention to the reverberation of the *Yes*. This was a turning point. My breathing became slower and deeper. I was perceptibly more in the present and fully awake, so that the times for meditation became much too short. Through the *Yes*, I felt circulation through my whole body, and to me this little word is a great help.

RM. You feel happy with it.

DANIELLE. Yes, I like staying with it. It leads me more intensely into the present. I feel more at one with myself.

RM. I'm glad.

5.3 MARGARET

MARGARET. The last few days were very difficult. So much from my past and my inner attachments came up that I felt quite exhausted. These aren't present shadows. It's my own inner structure which is all wrong and sinful. I've never had such deep insight into myself.

RM. You were shaken.

MARGARET. Yes, and it led ever further. I ended up in real despair. At first a sense of helplessness about my faults arose. I looked deep into the abyss of myself. Then rage and impatience followed, working me up into real despair. The inability to get out of my entanglements changed into hopelessness and pushed me still deeper into despair. I believed I couldn't endure it any longer.

RM. That was a terrifying state.

MARGARET. It's still the same. I find no way out of it and I'm afraid there isn't any.

RM. There is a way out. It's the radical turning from an attitude of self-centeredness to trust in God. It's even a grace to pass through this hopelessness. Only then we grasp that we can't do anything ourselves except turn humbly to God and beg, "Lord, I am helpless and desperate. But you are my Lord and my God. You can lead me out of this despair. You can change me and heal all my wounds." This turning is necessary. Despair leads to the firm conviction of one's own powerlessness and to the realization that the way can only exist in radical trust in God. . . . May I ask you something?

MARGARET. Certainly.

RM. Do you stay with the *Yes* during meditation?

MARGARET. In my despair I abandoned the *Yes*.

RM. Did you at least try again and again to return to the awareness of your hands?

MARGARET. I didn't get that far.

RM. The very road to trust is a determined return to the *Yes*. If you follow the steps I show you, I will lead you out of the entanglements in yourself.

5.4 GABRIEL

GABRIEL. During recent meditations something important dawned on me. I was sitting on my stool when I suddenly became aware how I was mentally waiting for the end of meditation. I returned to my hands and to my *Yes*. Soon I found myself thinking about what to do after meditation. So I said to myself, "You are here now. Stay in the present," and returned to the *Yes*. But the distraction didn't leave me alone—I'm still in meditation and already thinking of what I will do the next hour. And when I went for a walk, scenes came to mind in quick succession in which I could discover a similar process. During a mountain tour two weeks ago, I kept thinking, "If I were at the back of this mountain," or, "If I were already at the top. . . . " And so I really experienced very little joy in the climb or in nature, because I was never present where I was. I was always one or two hours ahead.

It was similar with my studies; in my head I was already in the next term. On weekends I think about what I'm going to do the next weekend. I'm thinking about what my friends and I will talk about a day before we even meet! And when I am with them at last, I'm occupied with my next date. After breakfast I'm already at lunch, and while I'm eating I see the afternoon's agenda before my eyes. I live nearly exclusively in the future. And in meditation it's almost worse. Perhaps I only notice it more then. When I'm sitting in meditation, I am already on my walk outside, and the other way round.

RM. You live in the future.

GABRIEL. Yes, that's it. *[Pause.]* I've often asked myself whether my flight into the future is caused by fear of encountering the present reality.

RM. That is why we learn in meditation to live in the present. By living in the future we don't really live; the future isn't yet here. We miss out on living our life and are always elsewhere than where we are. By remaining where we really are, we stand on firm ground.

It isn't sufficient to keep returning to the present. Place your heart into this one present moment. Enter right into the present. Where your heart is, there is your attention. If you return to the present a thousand times, but don't have the desire to remain there, your endeavor will be in vain. Your attention will turn where your inner focus is.

God's presence is hidden in the present itself. It will reveal itself from there. The present moment is the field in which the treasure lies hidden (Mt 13:44). Buy this field and you won't be disappointed. Experience this present now in your hands and in the *Yes* you say today, and remain there with all your senses.

5.5 VICTOR

VICTOR. I have difficulties concentrating. I do keep returning to the hands and the *Yes*, but immediately it's gone again. So I'm very distracted. My weak willpower is the trouble. I can't force myself to concentrate.

RM. You suffer from weak concentration.

VICTOR. Yes, it's plagued me since childhood.

RM. Look, Victor, let's try without willpower or concentration. It could be that you keep returning to awareness, but that as soon as you feel you've arrived in your hands, you are satisfied with that, and so your attention fades.

VICTOR. Yes, that's how it is.

RM. When listening into your hands in this way, try to remain listening. Tell yourself, "Now it's beginning!" and listen with interest, even when you are aware that it's always the same. Open yourself, as if you want to experience something very quiet and delicate. As if you were stopping to become aware of the slow movement of the hand of a clock, or to behold how a flower opens after the dew is gone. Awareness of one's hands can also take our breath away if we're present with our whole heart and interest. Willpower and concentration destroy this gentle and sensitive attentiveness, because they only look in order to reach something.

5.6 ARNOLD

ARNOLD. I like meditating, and I come to a certain state of recollection especially in retreat. When this state deepens, a lot of fear arises, and I close up. I block it. Nothing continues after that.

RM. The fear threatens you.

ARNOLD. Exactly. The thought comes immediately: What will happen if the fear increases? I feel a deep foreboding.

RM. You fear your fear.

ARNOLD. Yes, the fear that something very dark might come suddenly, and I won't be able to cope.

RM. You don't trust yourself to let the threatening things come.

ARNOLD. No, I don't dare. There's no reason for the fear; it's just there: no concrete cause for my anxiety.

RM. Could this fear also come outside of meditation—for example, while you're walking through the woods when it's getting dark?

ARNOLD. No, I won't even dare go into the woods.

RM. These fears have been with you for some time.

ARNOLD. Yes, years ago these states of panic were much stronger. I noticed it in my dreams. Murder and killing followed me, monsters with claws came to meet me, the abyss was bottomless. I often fell into it, and it took ages to hit the ground. Scenes like that were usual with me. I used to wake up bathed in sweat in the morning.

RM. Now they have become less threatening, but in meditation they continue to terrorize you.

ARNOLD. Yes, that's right. It's only during meditation that I lose the firm ground of my security.

RM. Can you look at these fears and let them be?

ARNOLD. Let them be? . . .

RM. I'll explain it to you. First of all, come back from the *object* of fear to the *feeling* of fear. Don't think about what could happen, but say to yourself, "I'm terrified." Then you are no longer lost in your fear, but more with yourself, in reality, in awareness, and can more expressly perceive your feeling. When you can look into the face of your fear like this, come back to your hands and your *Yes*. The fear may still go with you. But you are no longer with the fear. That's the central difference. You are in the present, looking at what comes from there. No fear comes from the present.

ARNOLD. But at these moments I can't look at my fear.

RM. Then look at your inability to do so. You don't need to be able to do it. Tell yourself, "I'm now in a state in which I can't yet look at my fear." Then you are already looking, and the fear of your fear has become relative. Calmness, safety, and assurance can seep through you a bit. You'll find that with this quiet, reassuring sense of safe keeping, you'll gradually be able to look at your fear.

ARNOLD. Sounds hopeful. . . .

RM. Stay with all your senses with the *Yes*.

5.7 MANUELA

MANUELA. I have a hard time with the *Yes*. The awareness of my hands also came slowly for me. I was with my hands in recent days, and now you ask me to do something different again!

RM. Hm.

MANUELA. I tried, but I didn't succeed too well.

RM. It's rather a burden for you.

MANUELA. Yes. I feel it as a burden. On the other hand, I know it's an introduction. I feel it's necessary to experience thirst for a time in order to appreciate the quenching glass of water.

RM. You are prepared to accept that.

MANUELA. I get annoyed now and then, but I'm prepared all the same, and even enticed by what remains to be discovered. So far my efforts haven't really been in vain.

RM. Yes, stay with it.

MANUELA. What should I pay attention to?

RM. Accompany your breathing with a very quiet and listening *Yes*. Pay attention to whether and how it arrives in your palms. Say the *Yes* during the whole length of your outgoing breath. The more gentle it becomes, the more the *Yes* will flow into your hands. Say it with an inner sound and listen to this sound. When you're alone, you can even sing it out loud! It will slowly become a more quiet and internal sound. Remain with it the whole time and during all your meditations.

5.8 BEN

BEN. I don't know what's happening with me. I began the retreat quite well. I was present full of joy and expectation. But for the last two days I seem to have lost orientation. The question constantly arises, what is this stupid sitting good for? Then follow doubts and annoyance because of the loss of time, and all this hanging around doing nothing.

RM. You feel like you're lost.

BEN. Yes.

RM. I hope you don't try to answer your questions by looking for meaning.

BEN. I didn't for the first two days. Now I surprise myself by constantly discussing the meaning of the meditations.

RM. And when you notice it, do you return at once to your hands and to the *Yes?*

BEN. Not always.

RM. Questions of meaning occur in the head, on the mental level. That isn't our business at the moment. Don't enter consciously into them at all.

BEN. Yes, but I don't know why I should meditate. I'm not motivated.

RM. You don't need to know "why" now. It's natural for questions of meaning to come. For this reason I asked you at the beginning of the retreat whether you want to be introduced to contemplative prayer and whether you are prepared to let yourself be guided. You wanted to make this experiment, and so I asked you to renounce the questions of meaning until the end of the retreat. I know from experience that these questions will necessarily return, and that they must be dropped for our purposes. You aren't able to answer them now. All I can do is keep inviting you to walk the way along with me.

Before you've finished this ten-day journey, you can't make the judgment as to whether meditation is the way for you or not. After that, I'll even ask you to make a discernment regarding your experience and to decide whether this retreat has given you something for your own path. If not, you may forget it then. But at this stage you can't make this evaluation because you haven't yet had the experience. Meditation leads of necessity through times of crisis, where meaning becomes obscured. The retreat has a lot to do with trust. You entrust yourself to a guide who, you believe, can lead you a step further. This trust is limited to the duration of the retreat. During this time you don't need to have a certainty of your own. Your certainty lies in trust. Your motivation lies in your following someone to whom you have given your trust, even at times when it becomes more difficult.

BEN. Yes, but I don't feel oriented.

RM. You may feel like that. Look at this feeling of helplessness, and then return to the awareness of your hands and to the *Yes*. See what comes from there. The lack of orientation comes from your feelings, but listen to what comes from reality. Your loss of orientation doesn't come to you from there. Discover what comes from the present.

5.9 TANYA

TANYA. I was very restless during meditation. I made myself calm by telling myself, "Stay calm," and, "I am calm." And I really did calm down and could feel into my hands. I do something similar with distractions; I tell myself, "I remain in the present." Or when I begin to doze, "I'm awake."

RM. You have practiced "autogenous training" (a method of auto-suggestion).

TANYA. Yes, and it helped me.

RM. Autogenous training has a good method. We give commands to our unconscious, and the unconscious accepts them. In this way we can, for example, become quiet and even reach other states. Autogenous training is a kind of self-hypnosis. It has a concrete and intended effect.

TANYA. What we're doing is nearly the same.

RM. Contemplative prayer is different. Though both methods seem to be similar because they lead to quiet, they actually represent opposite attitudes. In contemplation we are convinced that true life lies slumbering deep within the soul. It's there and needs only to reveal itself. Our task is merely to allow whatever happens to happen, and to listen to whatever comes from our real nature. From there come charity, unity, strength, and love. From there comes the experience of God's presence. Because one is convinced of this, one renounces every "doing" and "reaching out." We surrender to what gives itself, what takes place, whatever shows and reveals itself. In autogenous training, on the other hand, we send out orders. We want to effect something. We want to urge ourselves on to what is good. That means that we want to bring something about. In contemplation, we take care not to interfere from the outside and to allow our deepest being to show itself, allow the Trinity to reveal itself to us. Contemplation is a process of becoming conscious.

TANYA. I see that, but shouldn't I calm myself down (at least at the beginning of meditation) by means of autogenous training?

RM. Autogenous training isn't bad. You're well used to this method. It isn't impossible to bring yourself to quiet before meditation by means of self-hypnosis. But when, with time, you come to feel the power of awareness, you'll notice how quickly and deeply listening will lead you to reality and peace. It's much better if you direct yourself from the beginning of meditation to contemplative listening and to the self-revelation of the indwelling Holy Spirit.

5.10 HERBERT

HERBERT. I experience deep calm in meditation, even though a lot is moving inside me. But during the night I dream very intensely and sleep restlessly, much more so than outside of retreat. Last night I dreamt, for example, that I was in a large castle. On the top floor the boss was sitting in a very high-class office in front of an enormous desk with many telephones. I was in the cellar in a dark musty room. I wanted to go to the boss to tell him that I wanted to buy a ship and start a business. But I didn't reach the top floor and couldn't get to the boss. I tried several times, and never succeeded. One time, a dog barred the way, another time I got lost. New hindrances constantly appeared. Finally I stood at his door, knocked, and entered. Then I woke up.

RM. How do you interpret this dream?

HERBERT. I see behind it a problem with my father. He was very strict with me, and today I'm still afraid of him. In comparison with him, I'm still in the cellar. I want to be his equal and don't manage it.

RM. You know how to interpret your dreams.

HERBERT. Yes, I always analyze them.

RM. It's very helpful to become conscious of the message of one's dreams. They reflect exactly what is taking place in our own emotions.

But it's important not to confuse the interpretation of dreams with prayer or contemplation. During meditation and during the whole retreat, one shouldn't ascribe special meaning to dreams and shouldn't analyze them. When you feel your way into the meaning of your dreams the next morning, in the shower or while brushing your teeth, that's all right. But don't do more than glance at your dreams during the retreat and don't lose time interpreting them. Dreams aren't God. That's why one should leave them aside during retreat and return immediately to God.

HERBERT. Yes ... *[reflecting]* ... dreams are not God, that's true.

RM. You can continue ahead on your way without having understood a dream. If an important feeling arises in a dream and clearly stands out, you can look at it as you look at other feelings during meditation. If the dream isn't clear enough at first glance, don't actively look for an interpretation, but leave it alone. Either the feeling evaporates, or it will reveal itself more clearly later. Your general readiness to suffer, and your contact with the present are sufficient. In retreat and meditation it's better to renounce interpreting dreams; otherwise they distract us from the essential.

HERBERT. I understand.

RM. I hope you are fully with your hands and your *Yes*.

HERBERT. Of course. The *Yes* helps me to deep recollection. I've discovered the power of the inner sound. When I say *Yes* with that inner sound, I'm more alert and the stream of energy in my body is stronger.

RM. Keep going this way.

5.11 BASIL

BASIL. During meditation I feel a kind of rebellion against authority. Aggressions arise against dignitaries and all those "higher-up" people. Then I sense a bad conscience and get the impression that I don't achieve enough. Yes, I feel I'm a failure. It's as if I had no right to live unless I have a lot to show for it. So I'm dependent on the opinions of others.

RM. You don't feel your own ground under your feet that enables you to be independent from others.

BASIL. Right. I face authorities enraged and helpless. I'm left hopelessly in rebellion.

RM. Don't stay with these thoughts. Listen into your hands, into the present. Hear what comes from there. You already know what comes from your world of thoughts. It's this conflict with authority figures. Whatever comes from comparing yourself with others doesn't help you either. Listen into your hands, into the present and into your deepest being. See what comes from there. No such feelings do. There, you experience that you are. You experience your true self. This gives you a sense of your own worth that other people, with their opinions of you, can't take away. It's untouchable. It's also independent of authorities. In this awareness of your own being, you will find your own identity.

BASIL. And what shall I do about my problem?

RM. You can wallow in inferiority feelings forever . They'll always pull you down. But come, look in the direction of God, of what comes from him and from your true center. Then you'll feel the ground under your feet. Only then you'll experience the unshakable ground within yourself. Everything else becomes relative. Then you won't have to keep your self-worth alive by your own merits. It does not come from achievements, but from your being. Discover this inner existence that carries you and gives serenity and independence. When you rest in yourself and stand by yourself, you'll also be able to handle authorities.

BASIL. I don't find this ground.

RM. Yes, it's clear that you have not yet found it.

BASIL. Why "not yet"?

RM. Because we are traversing a path, and I'm leading you step by step into this experience.

BASIL. What are these steps?

RM. The next one we are just taking is the *Yes* which I gave you today. Say this quiet, flowing *Yes* every time you breathe out, with an inner sound into your hands.

BASIL. I've tried that already, but I'm not getting it.

RM. Yes, that's quite possible.

BASIL. I don't understand that either.

RM. You can't say *Yes* because there is still too much *No* in you.

BASIL. And what must I do?

RM. Say *No*.

BASIL. But I want to say *Yes*.

RM. To the authorities?

BASIL. No, not to the authorities.

RM. You see, Basil, there's still a *No* in you that has to come out first.

BASIL. Should I defy the authorities in my meditation then?

RM. No, Basil, not like that. Simply come to your hands, and when you are already in awareness of them, look into yourself to see whether a *No* or a *Yes* comes from your depth. Don't think about your problem with authorities, but simply look what comes from within, without premeditation, and let it flow. After the first wave of *No* has died away, test out whether now a *Yes* will come naturally. But you can return to the *No* whenever you're urged to it from within.

BASIL. I'll try.

5.12 NORBERT

NORBERT. I am getting along just fine. The meditation also goes well. Now and then, I'm afraid that I meditate too little.

RM. Too little.

NORBERT. Yes, I won't like to meditate if I feel driven. Normally, I'd put myself under pressure, but I became conscious recently how unnecessary that is, and have tried to free myself from it. I've already examined this pressure from all sides, and find it comes from my mother. She always demanded so much from me. I had to fulfil all her wishes, at once and exactly as she wanted. When I resisted, she reproached me that I didn't love her, and so on. But she would do anything for me. She was constantly blackmailing me with her demands and complaints. I can feel the pressure sitting on my neck. I'm busy dissolving it.

RM. You're already dealing with it.

NORBERT. Outside of retreat I work at it. Though I'm conscious of it during meditation, I feel this isn't the time to be occupied with it. I work hard at it outside of retreat.

RM. Now we're doing something different.

NORBERT. Yes, I'd like to have a definite answer: Should I meditate more with the risk of getting under similar pressure, or should I meditate less in order to do it without pressure?

RM. You're uncertain what to do.

NORBERT. Yes, I'm uncertain.

RM. How long did you meditate yesterday?

NORBERT. This is my first contemplative retreat. Yesterday was the fourth day, and I meditated for three hours. Is that right?

RM. You can decide for yourself. Objectively, one might on the fifth day of the first retreat meditate four to six hours, if nothing intervenes. It's not helpful to meditate under pressure. If we're susceptible to such pressure, it would be better to meditate a little less for awhile.

It seems important, however, not to keep *reacting against* pressure, for that, too, is still depending on pressure to get where you want to be. The true solution is a change in motivation. It's one thing to want to free oneself from pressure, another to listen into yourself for a longing for God, for the essential, for the true home. When you go to meditation with this longing, you won't get tensed up. You won't get tired, and the hours will pass by without your noticing it.

People who are interested in the contemplative way carry, in different ways, a longing for God in themselves. This longing is the power that leads to contemplation and stillness. If you find this longing and listen to it, you can meditate from it. The pressure to achieve lessens, and we no longer meditate because we must or ought to, but with a lively interest.

NORBERT. How can I know whether I'm meditating from the pressure to achieve or from my longing for God?

RM. You don't need to know. Feel into yourself, find your longing for God—for the heights, for union with your origin—and try to meditate from there. If pressure to achieve becomes mixed with it, it doesn't matter. But you learn to listen to the longing inside, and the feelings of pressure can retire into the background.

5.13 ANGELA

ANGELA. I felt a very great longing for God during meditation. I was wholly enraptured, so I tried to feel God's presence.

RM. And you felt it.

ANGELA. For a short time it went very well, then something disturbed me, and nothing happened after that.

RM. The way is to open yourself completely; to feel into yourself whether and how the presence of God becomes noticeable. To be wholly ear. Nothing but listening. That's where the way continues.

ANGELA. What was it that disturbed me and made everything vanish?

RM. Very often at a moment when you experience something new, you get a half-conscious desire to hold onto it. As if you were to tell yourself, "I've grasped this at last! Now I know—once and for all—how to get there." At the same moment, everything that's really spirit vanishes, because we can't possess anything spiritual. Truth gives itself to us. If we hold onto it, it withdraws. If you remain in pure wonder and surrender yourself to it, you'll be led more and more into it. Then it gives itself even more intensely. That's why it's good advice to make oneself, on principle, independent of any current experience. Meditation is as it is. It comes as it comes; it's good in whatever form it passes. Renounce the effort to buy God's grace with your fidelity and hard work.

When you feel longing for God, it's sufficient to look into the longing. The presence of God is already in your longing. It has been awakened by God to help you find the way to him.

5.14 ALPHONSE

ALPHONSE. Yesterday you asked my neighbor where her heart was. That has struck me deeply. During my walk outside, this question went with me. I found many things I'm attached to, and saw that I have to let go of a lot of them if I want to find the essential. When my enslavement to the things I cling to became clear to me, I realized that these are the very things that turn up during meditation as major preoccupations. There are times when many scattered thoughts fly around in my head. But more persistent distractions are always concerned with these attachments.

I tried to let go of them. It took a long time before I had the impression that I could give up everything. In between, fear arose—fear of losing something I am attached to. When I could let go of these in my thoughts also, I felt relieved. Meditation went much better after that. All the physical pain was gone. My back was free, and my breath could freely flow into my belly. I would never have believed that these two experiences hang together so much.

RM. You were surprised.

ALPHONSE. Yes, and the first question, "What's my heart clinging to?" was the beginning of something else. I asked myself (this was also during my walk) whether God loves me. Of course he does, I told myself. I felt how theoretical it was even while formulating the question. Then I asked myself again whether God really loves me. Spontaneously, an unbelievable longing for the love of God came over me. That was something indescribably new for me. I was moved to tears . . . *[pause]*. . . . I still feel this consternation . . . *[pause]*.

RM. This longing for God is the love of God for you. God himself awakens this longing, in order to show you that he is there and in you. The longing *is* his love for you.

5.15 MICHELLE

MICHELLE. It's slow, tough going. There are moments when meditation seems to be going very well. Then I'm somewhere else again. When it doesn't go well for a moment, I ask myself spontaneously whether I am doing it right and how it is when I am present. I observe when and why I become distracted. It's the same with the *Yes*. I make the effort and want to do it right. But somehow I'm not able to stay there for long.

RM. You're afraid of doing something wrong.

MICHELLE. Yes, I am afraid because I want to do it well.

RM. It's good that you are committed and take the trouble to enter into meditation—or better, to enter into the presence of God. But you take too much trouble if you want to know whether every step is exactly right. You'd like to control yourself and your meditation, in order to be certain that you don't do the wrong thing. With this, you fall back to the mental level.

The question whether your meditation practice is right or wrong distracts you from awareness. Meditation is much simpler. Let go of your control. You don't need to know at all whether you're meditating correctly. Simply stay with it. Then it's right. If perhaps something or other still needs to be corrected, you'll notice it a bit later, without policing yourself constantly. The need for control isn't directed to the present, but to your actions. Orient yourself toward God and forget how you're doing.

5.16 JUAN

JUAN. This afternoon during my first meditation, I got furious, even desperate. But it was different from other times when I've had these feelings. At first I didn't know what made the difference. Gradually I realized that, before, I always felt ashamed of these feelings and wished them away. That feeling of shame was gone. I could allow the rage to be there. Shortly after that, I noticed how tensions in my spine disappeared. I believe that because I accepted these feelings and didn't fight against them, they disappeared. Gradually peace came.

A little later, during the same meditation, I became conscious that I wanted to hold on to this peace and to all the beautiful things I experienced. I got sad when I realized that it's exactly this that keeps me from staying in the present. With that insight, tensions disappeared in my shoulders. I was then—perhaps for the first time—relaxed for a while. I was drawn still more intensely into the experience of the present by awareness of my hands and saying *Yes*.

RM. That's a very helpful experience. We fight something or we cling to something. Either involvement excludes remaining in the present.

5.17 HAROLD

HAROLD. I've been meditating for years and have found that this is my way. I can't and don't want to live without quiet times. I feel I'm more myself through contemplation and know this is the right way for me. But lately I've felt a bit depressed. Meditation pulls me down. During meditation, I have the impression that there's a big stone sitting inside me that I want to break up but can't. I know that the problem lies in me. It's original sin, it's the shadows I have to dismantle. These are feelings of heaviness and depression. I'm ready to suffer them through until they are dissolved. But they oppress me, and often there remains a fear that I will sink into them.

RM. The meditation depresses you.

HAROLD. Yes, it does.

RM. You tell me you have to "dismantle" your shadows. In this way you dig yourself into your depressive feelings. The depressed state increases until you are more occupied with your shadows than with God. Look at him. He will dissolve original sin in you. Remain in awareness, with your hands, with your *Yes*. Look what comes from that. To be aware of feelings means to look at them only for so long, until we can accept them. Once we've reached this state, they no longer interest us, even though they may still disturb us. Move on at once to awareness. Direct yourself wholly to God. Leave your sins to him. You care for him, and he cares for you.

5.18 NICKY

NICKY. I often get discouraged in meditation. I don't make any progress. I can't stay with it and want to give up. I don't find the way into my hands. If I feel anything, it's only for seconds. I'm immediately elsewhere. I'm also annoyed that I don't notice when I get distracted. I circle in thoughts and don't get away from myself. This situation is from way back! I ask myself seriously what I'm doing wrong and what I can do differently. My restlessness gets on my nerves. Nothing gets any better.

RM. It annoys you.

NICKY. Yes, I don't get further, and don't know why.

RM. The problem lies right there: You want to get further. With that, you place yourself under pressure. The further you want to get, the more the pressure mounts. You want to reach something at any cost. This excludes contemplation.

NICKY. I want to be free from my inner burdens, to come to Jesus Christ, to love him and serve him. It's the longing for God that urges me on. Should I prefer not to have the longing?

RM. Something isn't quite right in your fundamental attitude. You want to reach something, even though it's a holy thing. Jesus Christ is there. He's with you. You don't need to force him to come to you or urge him to change you. He is with you and will give you what you need. Let go of your anxious desire to come to God. You don't need to see either progress or no progress. Try with determination to stay at your task, or come back to it. Something will grow in you without your noticing it. It's not important whether you succeed in feeling your hands. It's sufficient to try, with determination, to remain present.

NICKY. But three days ago, I was already much more recollected.

RM. Yes, because that was true, something could get moving in you in order to be redeemed. This puts pressure on your thoughts and your mood. As long as the process is taking place, you feel tension and restlessness. Bear patiently with this state.

NICKY. And what is it that wants to come out to be redeemed?

RM. You don't need to know that. If you're alert to the movements in yourself, you can read from your present state what wants to be resolved: Impatience, the need to achieve, self-will. These will disappear by themselves if you're ready to continue remaining in the present and suffer whatever comes.

5.19 MAX

MAX. When I discovered meditation, I was still very much in my head. I wanted to understand and explain everything. Before I really started anything, I looked for detailed explanations. That's the way one goes about it at school and in university. I found the same thing in daily life. My head had to catch on first; nothing could get started until that happened. So it was very difficult for me to follow the instructions for the meditations. After I had begun to meditate, I had to fight long and hard against my thoughts, and I got annoyed at them. I wanted to eliminate them, convinced that meditation isn't very good if thoughts still present themselves. Now that I hardly notice them, it's almost the same to me whether or not thoughts buzz about in my head, or how many there are. I've noticed how much I fought against and rejected them before. The center of my meditation is shifting. . . .

RM. . . . to something else.

MAX. Yes. . . . How shall I describe it? I exist, and this existence has drawn all my attention to itself, so that the thoughts are on a sideline. It's as if it were not I doing the thinking, or as if the thoughts had nothing to do with me. They've become uninteresting. There are still times, at the beginning of meditation or otherwise, when I'm not yet recollected—then thoughts still disturb me. At other times I'm more intensely in the present, so that the train of thoughts doesn't even come to my attention.

RM. You're more independent of your thoughts.

MAX. Yes, I no longer get annoyed and don't pay attention to them.

5.20 LAURA

LAURA. I notice that I'm very determined and ready to enter into this stage of meditation. But during meditation itself, a great deal rises up from my childhood.

RM. Lots of memories.

LAURA. Lots. Especially memories relating to my relationship with my father. I have a very weak father. It always was as if he weren't there. I missed having a father. I still notice that I'm often looking for a father in men. I feel the lack of support and security that a father gives. I'm also expecting support and security from God. I remember very clearly how my parents once sent me to a family in the country for a long time. The family was very hard on me. My father never visited me even once in six months—the whole time I was there. I thought I couldn't stick it out. I only survived by going out a lot into nature. In my despair, I felt I was part of nature. I could remain in that feeling for some time. Somehow I felt

my own self and came to myself. I could endure my abandonment this way .

RM. That was a great grace because you were shown the right way
through this experience. You see, parents give their children
their first security. But later, the young person or young adult
has to discover security in himself or herself. This happens
quite naturally when the parents have given security. You
didn't receive much security from your father, but you were
shown how to find your own inner stability.

LAURA. Yes, that's true.

RM. Try this now also. Feel into yourself; feel, as you did at that
time, that you are there. Be wholly alert and listen into yourself, whether or not the essential security comes from existence itself. That's the genuine security. You can always return to it, as you already managed to do in a way in your
childhood. I'm not saying that your father's absence didn't
leave a wound in you. But in spite of this, the road to essential security lies open to you. This security dispels all other
insecurities. It's always there when you enter into yourself.
No one from outside can rob you of it. Awareness of your
hands and the *Yes* lead you there.

5.21 CORNELIA

CORNELIA. I've been very distracted for several days. I have a
great many thoughts and look on helplessly at everything
that's going around in my head.

RM. You find it difficult to recollect yourself.

CORNELIA. May I tell you what happens to me in meditation? If I
can just once get it all out, perhaps I will then be able to find
myself again.

RM. With pleasure.

CORNELIA. First there came an active phase, and I planned and
planned. Hundreds of ideas came to me about how I could re-
organize my work and my apartment. Then came a time of
dreaming that all my wishes are going to be fulfilled: prosperity, success in my work, and meeting the ideal person for
me. There was a restless time when I couldn't break free from
confrontation. I argued repeatedly with friends, colleagues,
and my parents. Later I was bored. Questions of meaning

arose. I discussed with myself whether meditation is meaningful or not. I felt great anger at this "mindless sitting."

In another meditation I was beleaguered by insistent sexual fantasies, and I couldn't get rid of them. During the next unit I became sleepy, yawned, and dozed off. I tried hard to stay awake, but my will was powerless. I continued to fall asleep. Another time it was a tune that constantly returned; I couldn't shut it off. Often it can be nice memories from my youth. They attract me, and I try to disengage myself from them, but they constantly return. Another recurring theme is the fantasy about how I shall teach others meditation, or—when I'm scheduled to see you—I'm occupied for a long time beforehand with what I shall say about my meditation, and I watch myself and comment on what I do in meditation and how I behave. During the last minutes of meditation I think of the clock and wait for the signal to end.

RM. A vast range of distractions.

CORNELIA. I'm glad that I could express them.

IV. REVIEW & TRANSITION TO THE SIXTH DAY

We're at the end of the Fifth Day. I hope that you found your way with *Yes*. It's possible that thoughts haven't yet disappeared, but that the *Yes* has strengthened your recollection at times. Perhaps you've been more attentive to your hands. However, you don't need to believe that you are now recollected. One can meditate for years with this *Yes*. If you are happy to continue meditating with this *Yes*, you're ready to proceed to the Sixth Day. If you feel the urge to move ahead, look into yourselves to see whether impatience, or the need for activity or results, is the cause.

We saw on the Fifth Day how redemption takes place in contemplative prayer. The readiness to suffer plays a role here. In the Introductory Talk of the Sixth Day, we'll return to the need for willingness to suffer. It's very important. In meditation, we pass on to the name—the name of the Mother of God.

SIXTH DAY

I. INTRODUCTORY TALK: WILLINGNESS TO SUFFER

1. Condition for following Christ

Whether or not redemption takes place in meditation depends on our remaining in contemplation and being ready to suffer. I spoke of this in the previous chapter. The right attitude in meditation is very simple, even though not always easy. To meditate well we need to pay attention to only two things: orientation to God and willingness to suffer. Let us look more closely at the latter.

Jesus redeemed the world through his suffering. He came into the world, was a child, worked, preached, healed, taught the apostles, and did much else. But he redeemed the world by his suffering and death. He calls us to walk this way of redemption in joy and suffering with him. Anyone who wants to be a follower of mine, he says, must carry his cross and follow me (Mt 16:24). Readiness is the only condition for following Christ. If we read the Gospel with the question in mind, "What is the most important condition for Jesus to accept someone as a disciple," we might think the answer would be love for the Father or for one's neighbor. It's astonishing that these are not the conditions for following Jesus. Jesus himself wants to lead his disciples to love for the Father and the neighbor. But beforehand, he only asks for their willingness to suffer. Jesus has traversed the great dark sphere of humankind in his suffering. Whoever wants to come with him has to go through the darkness of his own sin. He carries us. Our task is to accompany him and to suffer our part.

2. Two memories

At the age of five I was confronted with Christ's death on the cross in a seemingly unimportant incident. I had at that time no consciousness of any "readiness to suffer," so the experience provoked in me more incomprehension than insight for a long time to come.

It was shortly before my First Holy Communion. I was engrossed in table games with my brothers and sisters, mother, grandmother, and aunt. I objected to a small mistake that had been made. We briefly discussed my objection, and the decision went against me. I believed I had been treated unjustly, became furious, threw everything down, and ran away. As I said, I was five years old. At the time, my mother was preparing me for my First Communion. On one of the following days we spoke about Christ's death on the cross. She said that Jesus was unjustly executed. I accepted this information as I did all the other truths of the catechism I was learning. My mother went on to say how Christ suffered his death with great willingness, and contrasted this to my own behavior in becoming so enraged over that small matter a few days earlier. I countered that these two events could not be compared, for it seemed to me that an unheard-of injustice had been done to me. She replied that Christ also suffered unjust treatment. I cut her short, again protesting that a real injustice had been done to me. The example of Jesus Christ must have challenged me deeply, for the conversation has remained so clear in my memory that to this day I remember where we were standing at the time.

Years later I was again confronted with this theme in an experience which became important for me. It was at Mons, a town in South Belgium, where I spent two years during the 1950s in practical training at the college run by the Belgian Jesuits. It was a very difficult time for me. As a foreigner (I had studied philosophy for three years at Eegenhoven-Louvain in Belgium before that), I hardly knew the local language in the beginning. I found the dialect and rather common French of the pupils particularly difficult to understand. This led to unpleasant situations and numerous misunderstandings. Many pupils had great problems at home and caused disciplinary problems. The school had a kind of built-in punitive system by which the pupils were kept under control. These disciplinary measures were, on the one hand, distasteful to me personally, but as a foreigner, I wasn't entitled to mete out punishment. My pupils liked to take advantage of this. To make things worse, on Saturday afternoons I had to supervise the pupils who were being punished. They were mostly given writing tasks—for example, to write 300 times that teachers had to be treated with respect. The situation was not easy. I struggled to cope, but had, on the whole, a difficult time. My working hours were also burdensome; they began at 6 a.m. and lasted until 10 p.m.; free time was very scarce and mostly confined to Sunday afternoons.

My recreation consisted in going after dinner every Sunday to the chapel to pray the Stations of the Cross. In contemplating Christ's Way of Sorrow, I was able to offer up my hardship, weep freely, and unload my burden. After that, I went to walk in nature for an hour or an hour and a half. My suffering intensified during the week, when I was constantly on call and there was no time to seek relief from the pressures of the job. But on Sundays, before Christ's cross, free from external duties, I could admit all the pain and let go of it. No one had taught me this. From within, I was spontaneously given a way to suffer what life had laid on me.

3. What do we have to suffer?

What do we have to suffer? It's sin which requires redemption. More especially, original sin in us needs to be redeemed through suffering. When we come close to our center, we reach the dark zone of original sin which separates us from the Garden of Eden and obscures our original consciousness of God's presence. In other words, when we go into silence we come face to face with ourselves. In solitude everything unredeemed comes to the surface and forces its way into our consciousness. This can be very painful. The sin we speak of includes personal sin as well as original sin. Personal sins are less traumatic than the pain caused by the darkness that lies deeper. While the original sin of our fellow human beings causes us enough suffering, we are almost completely spared this during meditation, because we are confronted almost exclusively with our own original sin. That is what must be suffered through. Only in this way can we be accepted into the love of God.

These are not exotic or masochistic torments that come to us. We don't need to look for pain. We are asked to suffer what life itself lays upon us and what is necessary for the redemption of sin. As long as the world is not totally redeemed, suffering necessarily belongs to the way.

Not everything that has been suffered is redeemed, a fact that is not as self-evident as it may seem. Each of us is acquainted with people who at some time in life have suffered a deep hurt and could not forgive. They keep recounting the hurt with all its complicated details. They tell it a hundred times and more, and their wound doesn't heal because they keep it open with rage, hate, anger, feelings of revenge and self-pity. Had Jesus Christ suffered his death on the cross with rage, hatred, and annoyance, we would find it difficult to believe in the redeeming power of his suffering and death. Only what is suffered with love—in touch with our center, with God—is redeemed.

Often, suffering itself is not the deepest pain. It's essentially more painful not to be able to love people who make us suffer.

4. Keeping the willingness to suffer alive

We have to make ourselves ready to suffer. We fear suffering and flee from it. The unconscious has been loaded, so to say, with rejection of suffering. The outer rind, which separates the dark layer from the sphere of thought and action, resists suffering. We flee by any means from suffering and personal distress. We are convinced that only the guilty should suffer. So we're always in search of a scapegoat on whom we can unload painful punishment. We justify ourselves and accuse others in order to escape suffering. Behind all human harshness lies the fear of having to suffer. With every hurt received comes the desire to retaliate. The alternative to an aggressive reaction is swallowing everything—by which, however, nothing has been suffered through. It has only been repressed and is stored in the subconscious like everything else that is already waiting there for redemption. How many distractions we invent during meditation! They only serve to prevent the confrontation with our darkness, because it is painful.

Redemption takes place only through suffering. But since our nature resists suffering, we always need to strengthen our inner readiness to suffer what life imposes on us. Our readiness to suffer can be compared to a swinging door. If someone wants to go through it to another room, it quickly opens wide. Yet it begins to close as soon as the person passes, and is shut in a flash. And so with our readiness to suffer: In a moment of good will, we're only too ready to take up our cross and follow Christ. But in another moment, our readiness disappears quietly, unnoticed, until we once again reject everything except the more pleasing moments of following him. Active readiness is very important. In the silence of meditation we come to face ourselves, and so our unsolved conflicts begin to stir up our unconscious and force themselves into consciousness to be accepted—that is, redeemed. But if, at that moment, active readiness to suffer is lacking, we do not even become aware of the fact that we have again suppressed the unredeemed shadow into the unconscious.

With active readiness to suffer, our times of meditation become more painful, but also more redemptive. What is suffered in love is healed. We learn to welcome suffering. We become aware that something is hurting and accept it: It is all right to feel pain. The process of redemption can begin. As with a wound or scar, it hurts. We notice the pain and accept it, bind it up, and return to work. The wound still hurts, but we are no longer actively occupied with it. We are conscious of the pain and know that it will of necessity continue to plague us, but we're already back at our task. The wound slowly heals and leaves a scar. That visible sign perhaps remains for a long time, but without hurting. It is the same with redemption. When something rises up from our unconscious we let it come. We suffer from it. When we're able to look at it, we return into the present, and though the wound still burns, we are no longer occupied with it.

The powers of our nature heal it. Slowly everything is being suffered through. The wound becomes a scar. It is still there, but without hurting.

5. To suffer or retaliate?

In a retreat, whenever I speak about suffering, many questions come from the participants. Why do we Christians have to suffer injustices without defending ourselves? Why do we have to circumvent problems by passively suffering everything? Do we not become unfit for life if we look on without doing anything? Do we not become incapable of sustaining conflicts if we don't confront them and stand up to other people? Why should we tolerate everything without setting limits? Isn't it criminal to look on passively while injustices are taking place? Why should we not fight actively against the oppression of the poor?

It's very important to me to reply in detail to these fully justified questions. What I say must always be seen from the viewpoint of contemplation. We know that there is a sphere of daily, "other-directed" or societal, life where we're active in thinking and doing. There we have to achieve results. There we can do, produce something, influence others, fight, and confront. In this sphere we can keep the Commandments, acquire virtues, look for psychological and character change. There we can organize political and social activities.

But there is also an inner sphere, contemplation, where we can only see, love, trust, and suffer. Thinking and doing—showing results and reaching goals—are no longer possible here. Both spheres exist simultaneously in us. Take an example: Someone hurts me in a conversation. How do I react? I can hit back with a similar retort, or suppress everything by telling myself that there is no offence. In neither case will any healing take place. Hitting back is an outward reaction. It brings no redemption. (On the contrary, my opponent will probably retaliate even more vigorously.) But if I swallow the hurt, it remains like a lump in my throat. Nothing is redeemed because suppression and retaliation are evasion of pain and remain in the sphere of doing.

How does healing take place? I accept the hurt and feel, "This is a hurt; it does hurt. It is all right that it hurts." With this, suffering the hurt begins. It is neither doing, nor achieving, nor thinking. It is pure suffering. Healing has begun. If I don't need to answer immediately, I don't react to the one who hurt me. I need time to let the wound become a scar. According to how deep the hurt went, I sleep on it—once, twice, or seven times. When it has ceased to hurt, it has become a scar. It is still there, but in being a scar it has lost its threatening aspect. I can return to the other and speak to him or her about the hurt. I can do so energetically, but without hatred. The pain is gone; I can react more lovingly.

As this example shows, external and internal reactions can be different. Let's imagine I was hurt and can't sleep on it seven times because external circumstances demand an immediate reaction. Even in this case I first accept the pain. I feel again, "This is a hurt, and it does hurt; it's okay that it hurts." At this moment, redemption begins. Since the circumstances demand prompt reaction, I have no time to let everything heal. My reaction will be marked by a certain amount of animosity underneath, since not everything has been redeemed. It will not, however, be full of hatred, since the healing process has begun. When external circumstances give us more time, more redemption takes place. The circumstances generally determine the timing of our reaction.

We can summarize the answer to the challenges mentioned above: when advocating suffering, accepting, admitting, not placing limits, not defending ourselves, we always means the inner, not the outer reactions. During our contemplative retreat I address only the inner dimension. It is there that we learn a new kind of behavior. External behavior, on the other hand, depends largely on external circumstances. Our outer reactions can be determined by outer necessities. It's better to react when the wound has healed and we can do it in love, but the circumstances may justify a quick reaction, even when some feeling of animosity is still present.

Many psychologists hold the opinion that one has to learn to defend oneself. That is right, but it concerns our outer reactions. If someone disturbs me and behaves in an unsuitable way, makes unjust demands on me, or is aggressive, I can determine the outer limits of passivity. But I should not put up inner walls to limit my love for that person.

In Latin America I saw many outrageous injustices and knew many people who work for justice. Some of them couldn't bear to see these evils and fought against them with hatred. Others were able to fight these atrocities and those responsible for them with love, because they had accepted their inner rebellion and no longer felt hatred against these perpetrators of injustice. They had the insight that the unjust by their actions also destroy themselves, and wanted them also to be redeemed. Those who were filled with hatred did not appear to me more effective than the others who acted from love.

6. Becoming more and more Christ on earth

Through our willingness to suffer whatever life demands of us, we become disciples of Christ. We often feel that we have much to suffer. St. Paul, however, is convinced that the sufferings of this present time cannot be compared with the glory to be revealed for us (Rom 8:18). That is why he preached Christ crucified (1 Cor 1:23). He wanted to fill up what is lacking in the afflictions of Christ (Col 1:24). He carried about in [his] body the dying of Jesus so that the life of Jesus may also be manifested in [his] body (2 Cor 4:10).

This union with Christ is deeper than we think. Jesus Christ came into this world to redeem us. He laid the foundation for this in his life and suffering. The redemption is not completed. Christ wants to continue his work of redemption through human beings. He wants to become human again in us, until we have become *alter Christus,* that is, a new Christ on earth.

This can be realized only in human beings who open themselves to Christ to such a degree that his grace can flow through them to others. It can happen only to the degree that we let go of ourselves in order to become wholly permeable. That is a first condition.

Another is to become defenseless to such a degree that sin can flow through us and can be accepted by Christ. When willingness to be open to unredeemed darkness without defending ourselves grows in us, then Christ can receive it and redeem it. Perhaps these few sentences make clear what a deep union with Christ can be created through suffering what is unredeemed.

Jesus Christ redeemed us by his suffering. He continues to suffer in us, until we are totally redeemed. His deepest pain is not caused by our sin, but by our inner resistance to this process of redemption. We want to give him our best, we want to become wholly good people for him, but we forget to give him our worst also. He asks us to suffer our sins through him and with him. Anyone who wishes to go this way should always strive to keep the willingness to suffer alive.

II. INSTRUCTIONS FOR MEDITATION

You have said *Yes* into your hands. Now I ask you to say, instead of *Yes,* the name of the Mother of God. You may say, "Mary," or "Mother of God."

We have come thus far in order to come at last to the name. We consciously walked a part of the way with *Yes* so that the name doesn't become a means to greater recollection or more intense meditation. The name and person of the Mother of God must not become an instrument to achieve a goal. That would not be compatible with the dignity of her person. So we began with the *Yes.* God is Father for us. He is equally Mother. But he is not human and can't be father or mother like our earthly parents, only in a divine manner. So we have to say that in a certain sense God is neither father nor mother. The first access to God lies in his motherhood, just as in human life the first relationship is built up in the mother's womb. The child finds security and belonging there. With birth, entry into life, the child leaves this security and opens itself to the world, and so also to the father. The immediate relationship between mother and child, which grew up in the nine months of pregnancy, changes at birth, but the mother instinctively remains the first personal relationship for the child. In every mother and every woman, God's motherhood reveals itself. In the Mother of God it does so in a privileged way.

I ask you during the Sixth Day to make the transition from *Yes* to the name of Mary. Continue to renew your intention to be there for God; to give him this time as surrender, service, or praise. Be aware of your body until you come into your hands. Listen into your hands. After you have felt them, say *Yes* a few times and pass on to the name of Mary. Say her name, if possible, with great reverence. Reverence can't be produced on demand. If you feel no reverence, say it simply as you are able. Say it, like the *Yes,* with an inner sound. But try to listen to it rather than say it. You don't need to say it aloud. Do not connect a picture or representation with the name, but listen to the sound. Say it with every outgoing breath and listen attentively as it arrives in your hands. It should not be an invocation or cry for help, but a simple addressing of Mary, with a quiet inner attentiveness to her person. What is important is simply this attention and presence, not any images, stories, devotional feelings, or spiritual meditations.

If you feel resistance to saying the name of the Mother of God (for example, if you are a Protestant), say the name of your own mother; address her as you usually do. It is possible that you also feel resistance here. Try all the same to remain with it.

It could be that you have the initial impression that you have to pay attention to too many things—the sitting, the hands, the breath, the sound, the presence. One can expect difficulties at the outset comparable to those in driving lessons. There also we feel overwhelmed to have to pay attention to so many things all at once: accelerator, brake, clutch, steering wheel, gear shift, indicators, windshield wipers, lights, and the road as well! To the beginner, this seems impossible. To an experienced driver it becomes quite natural.

It is the same with meditation. You will quickly find the harmonious interaction of breath, hands, name, and presence. These belong together and lead to a great and intense union.

Do I still have to remind you of the renewal of your intention? I don't think so. I'm sure it has become habitual. If you are making a Closed Retreat, you will have meditated more than eight half-hours daily. Take, if you like, an extra half hour here and there in addition. During a Retreat in Daily Life, stay at least two weeks with the name of the Mother of God.

III. DIALOGUES

6.1 URSULA

URSULA. I'm not getting on with the name of Mary. It is too much for me. The name doesn't say a lot to me. I repeated it a few times and when it wouldn't go I stopped it.

RM. You found no access to it.

URSULA. The name of the Mother of God doesn't mean much to me.

RM. That's why you stopped saying it.

URSULA. Yes, I stopped saying it because it only disturbed me.

RM. Do you feel the center of your palms in meditation?

URSULA. Yes, I can feel it well.

RM. What did you experience with the *Yes?*

URSULA. The *Yes* didn't mean much to me either.

RM. Then I ask you to return to the *Yes*. With every breath say a gentle, ringing *Yes* into the center of your palms and remain with it during the coming days.

URSULA. And if I feel nothing?

RM. You will not lose time if you listen for years to this *Yes*. It will lead you into the presence.

6.2 ADAM

ADAM. A few days ago something important happened to me. I became aware that I meditate under pressure according to a fixed timetable. Perhaps unconsciously, I then expected that God must do as much for me as I invest in him. Without realizing it, I wanted to force him, "You must repay me my hours of meditation." If it was four hours, I wanted to be paid for four hours. And if as much as six hours, I expected a remuneration for six hours. In hindsight it seems to me I wanted to put a pistol to God's head. Consequently, my meditations were tense. Yesterday it was more relaxed. I no longer make rigid plans about how many hours and with how much energy I want to meditate. There's less pressure and I feel more free. My motivation seems to have changed. Instead of meditating under the pressure to achieve, I feel something like a conviction arising in me that this is my way and that I want to take it. Slowly I feel a conviction rather than a striving to get somewhere.

RM. The pressure is gone and you meditate more from your center.

ADAM. I'm more myself.

RM. More at one with yourself.

ADAM. Yes, freer, much more sure. At the moment I can accept myself as I am, and God as he is.

RM. This gives serenity.

ADAM. I saw something else in this change. I discovered that I was looking for suffering. When my legs were aching in sitting, I felt joy and told myself that this makes me more like Jesus Christ, and that in this way my darkness would be redeemed more quickly. Such was my obsession, and I endured my pain at whatever cost. In order not to lose the chance of a quick redemption, I meditated even harder at those times. That has disappeared. I believe I treat myself a little more gently. It's unbelievable how much pressure I had always involuntarily imposed on myself.

RM. These are important insights.

ADAM. Something more. Before, when I meditated under pressure, I returned from distractions more tense than ever. When anger rose up repeatedly during meditation, I noticed I came back like a windstorm. My conscience immediately dictated the command to bring myself back promptly and with force. I realize now I was too hard on myself and that I repressed my anger too forcefully. I didn't handle it gently enough. It becomes more and more clear to me now that this prompt return was an escape from my anger. I'm now able to welcome this rebellion. I experience my rage and let it be. The anger doesn't appear so terrible to me, and I notice that my negative attitude towards it is slowly disappearing.

RM. Adam, I don't need to tell you how important this insight into your inner compulsion was. But it goes so deep that you can't make it disappear once and for all. You will be surprised again and again by the return of the pressure. But gradually it will become weaker until it disappears completely. Attention to the gentle light of the presence of which you become aware through your hands and the name will dissolve the harshness in you.

6.3 TERRIE

TERRIE. It's wonderful to meditate with the name of the Mother of God. Before this I had no relationship with her. The ugly and sentimental pictures of her put me off. But then, when I was there with fullest attention and repeated her name with reverence, great joy arose in me. A door has opened. For the first time I experienced a positive relationship with her. This union with her lasted for half an hour. It was important to me. I wanted this experience again during the following meditations, but it didn't happen.

RM. You longed to have that experience again.

TERRIE. For a time I did. But then I remembered that I don't need to attain anything, so I dropped it. Since then it has no longer been important whether I feel it or not. I repeat the name with reverence and listen attentively to the sound. I haven't felt consolation, but feel instead that it's right this way. The repetition slowed down and the sensation of the present became stronger.

RM. You sense its rightness.

6.4 MIRIAM

MIRIAM. I'm not wholly satisfied. I'm quite all right and can sit for longer stretches; I am present, even though not always and not wholly, but I have the impression that I stand as if before a wall. There should come a breakthrough, and it doesn't. Something is closed.

RM. You feel blocked.

MIRIAM. Yes, it's gradually becoming clearer. I am, as it were, sitting impatiently before the wall. Yes . . . you spoke of being willing to suffer. Well, I'm ready now, and because of this I expect that whatever lies behind the wall in my unconscious should break through.

RM. You don't need to direct your willingness to suffer to something that hasn't yet happened. You can suffer whatever comes along. The wall is there now. This wall has been given to you to endure. This wall that blocks you and prevents you from going further is your cross which has been laid on you at this moment—not whatever you imagine may be behind the wall. Whatever is there is all right being there. All that comes to you has been given to you to lead you on the most direct way to God. At this moment it is the wall. Renounce your desire to go further. Let go of what lies behind the wall and simply remain there as you are with everything that blocks you.

MIRIAM. Hmm . . . I see that.

RM. Miriam, may I ask you something?

MIRIAM. Yes, please.

RM. How far are you with the name of Mary?

MIRIAM. I'm not there yet.

RM. Begin now.

6.5 ROMAN

ROMAN. I feel a strong resistance to saying the name of the Mother of God. I struggle with it because you asked for it, but it's very troublesome; it's like sand in well-oiled machine.

RM. You feel resistance.

ROMAN. Yes, it's very difficult to repeat the name.

RM. Did you try to use the name of your own mother?

ROMAN. I call her "Mummy," but that would be worse than using the name of Mary. I feel no relationship to Mary, and I feel at a distance from my mother.

RM. So the difference is not very great.

ROMAN. I have also noticed that.

RM. Roman, you see, there is still an obstacle in the way of either of them. If you had already been meditating for a year and knew habitually how to handle your thoughts and feelings, I would say you should stick to it, so that these obstacles are removed. It would take some time. But you are taking the first steps in contemplative prayer. It's sufficient that you are conscious there is still a way ahead of you. Return to the *Yes* and remain with it.

ROMAN. OK, I agree.

6.6 CAITLIN

CAITLIN. The meditations are difficult for me. I often ask myself why it's all so tiresome. I circle round myself and don't get out of my own orbit.

RM. You have many thoughts.

CAITLIN. Yes, memories of my mother often come. She was a very determined person. I believe I'm still suffering from it. When I come back to the present, the class I teach comes to mind. The pupils are so troublesome this year. Every day I go home exhausted and ask myself why I have to put up with all this. Sometimes I'm worried because I have so few friends, and why the few I have leave me so alone. I also remember my university exams when I received unfair marks. Then again,

I'm disquieted because I've been looking for an apartment for so long without finding one.

RM. You suffer a lot.

CAITLIN. Yes, I suffer a lot. It makes life so difficult, and in meditation it all comes up. *[She weeps.]*

RM *[Only listens.]*

CAITLIN *[Weeps for a while and then slowly becomes calm.]* I often ask myself why all this is happening to me.

RM. Do you know the name of the feeling you have experienced these last few minutes?

CAITLIN. Pain . . . ?

RM. Isn't it rather self-pity?

CAITLIN. Self-pity? . . . *[pause]* . . . I've never looked at it like that.

RM. Your problem is not that you suffer, but that you complain about your sufferings. You say, "My mother was like this and that, and I'm still burdened with the consequences." You pity yourself because of the pupils in your class, and because of your exam marks. You complain about your friends and lament about your fruitless searching for an apartment. Look, that's self-pity. You spend your time of meditation complaining.

The important thing isn't that you change the external circumstances of your life, but that you change your attitude toward them. What would happen if you were to suffer willingly what you cannot avoid? What if you were even to thank God for your difficulties? Every unpleasant circumstance is given us for our purification and transformation. Renew your readiness to suffer and you will become a follower of Christ. You will share in the work of your own redemption and that of others.

As your complaining destroys your meditation, so it destroys your relationship with those around you. Someone who forever grumbles about their wounds becomes a burden to others. And more, most people experience the laments of others as a reproach to themselves for not helping. Stop lamenting, and people will like you and help you.

CAITLIN. Shall I stop meditation also?

RM. You can stop meditating any time you want. But that's not what I wanted to say.

CAITLIN. What did you want to say?

RM. Meditate properly!

CAITLIN. How?

RM. Look, Caitlin, you say you can't get out of circling around yourself. But your attention always turns to people and situations about which you lament inside. In fact, you're in an orbit very far from yourself. You aren't even aware that you aren't attending to your feelings. Constantly recurring thoughts always hide feelings we're not yet conscious of.

CAITLIN. I see that.

RM. Learn to listen to your feelings. Learn to look at your self-pity until you can say, "Yes, that's me. I indulge in self-pity because I don't want to suffer. I blame God and the world for my fate. It's okay if I continue to have these feelings." Once you recognize your state and can accept it, then comes the positive phase: Try to prepare yourself to suffer. Tell Jesus Christ you want to be his disciple and are willing to carry the cross with him. When you've reached that point, meditation can begin. Come to the awareness of your hands and to the name, and remain present with your whole attention.

CAITLIN. I'll try.

6.7 HENRY

HENRY. I had a fantastic experience. It was a real breakthrough. I sat for a long time, maybe two and a half hours. I was led ever deeper into recollection. I felt totally uplifted. I was fully present, and repeated the name of the Mother of God. I could have stayed there for ever. I had no bodily pains and hardly felt my body at all. Everything was rooted very much in the ground. I was fully awake, intensely in the present, and with the name. Suddenly I realized I had no fear and wished others well and felt great love for all, without having resolved on this or tried to produce it.

The astonishing thing is that in daily life I work well and get on well, but at heart I'm a scared rabbit! I'm afraid of everybody. I worked on this myself and also through therapy. This fear comes from my father who constantly intimidated and swore at me. I can cope with it, but I'm never free from fear. And now, suddenly, I had no fear. I felt love and wished everyone well. This feeling lasted for a long time.

Then suddenly, a fear arose that this new state could evaporate. *[He laughs.]* ... Yes, you'll say, the fear had come back. Yes, it had come back in another form, but at least I was allowed to experience for a time what it's like to have no fear at all. I had already learned in therapy to accept it. It had diminished, but I was—as far as I know for the first time—without any fear at all.

RM. You were afraid to fall back into fear?

HENRY. I told myself, "Whether it comes back or not, for now I will stay with it and look into this feeling of fearlessness and love." I tried to remain there with full attention.

RM. You see, Henry, that was a grace. That state was given you as something passing, so that you could discover that it's possible to live without fear. This experience is meant to stimulate your hope and courage to keep going forward. Just now this state is not yet your own nor your natural fundamental disposition. But it's a promise that it can become so in time. It's there God wants to lead you.

6.8 GERALD

GERALD. I've been meditating regularly for fifteen years. Every day I rise early and consistently devote my best time to contemplative prayer. I feel that this is my way, and I keep to it and enjoy it. I make a yearly retreat. I remain single-mindedly with the name in meditation. I'm content, and yet not entirely. It seems to me I'm meditating with my hand ready on the brake.

RM. You don't know what interferes with your being fully content.

GERALD. No, I don't know. In some way there's sand in the machine.

RM. Do you feel the same during your ordinary life? I mean in your activities and private relationships.

GERALD. Not really. In my work I'm clear and resolved. I can hold my own and can cope with tensions. I believe I'm reliable and effective.

RM. You are capable.

GERALD. Yes, one could say that.

RM. Don't you harden yourself a little when it's a question of asserting yourself?

GERALD. That could be. Without the ability to resist and show firmness, I couldn't prove myself in the battle of life.

RM. You feel that you harden yourself in order to assert yourself.

GERALD. Yes, I see a certain steadfastness as necessary—and vigorous reactions.

RM. True, steadfastness . . . but don't you have the impression that your face and your movements show a certain harshness?

GERALD. I've never noticed that. It could be, however.

RM. Do you feel body tension?

GERALD. Yes, I often feel tense, especially in my neck and shoulders.

RM. How do you react to the fear of being hurt?

GERALD. How do I react? . . . Hmm . . . I close up inside and show a cold shoulder.

RM. You close up.

GERALD. Yes.

RM. The counterattack soon follows.

GERALD. When I feel attacked I react harshly.

RM. Hmm . . . *[pause]*.

GERALD. Why these questions?

RM. One of the greatest enemies of contemplation is inner harshness. It's like a hidden virus—not easily discovered, but it blocks meditation.

GERALD. Am I as hard as that?

RM. You don't feel that you're hard.

GERALD. In trying to reach goals, and when I'm under attack, I actually do react harshly.

RM. You could become more conscious of this harshness. For example, when you react this way, ask yourself how long the harshness remains, what influence it has on the whole of your life, and how you feel when it's absent. Keep in touch with the tensions in your body all the while. They could serve as a barometer for your inner hardness.

GERALD. Am I also too hard in meditation?

RM. Gerald, the way of contemplation is a special way. It's an inner and gentle way. It's like listening to birdsong. It's like the gentleness with which one holds an opening flower bud. If you try to open it with force and roughness, it's destroyed. It needs gentle handling. It's the same with this way. It requires the strength of a person who doesn't close up in hostile surroundings, because he or she believes in love and doesn't fear necessary pain. You are effective, capable, and also ready to fight. If something acts like a brake on you, it could be hidden hardness.

GERALD. I'll try to pay more attention to the times when I harden myself. But how do I dissolve it?

RM. Fear can make us hard. The urge to achieve always does so. Love, meekness, and mercy dissolve the hardness. In meditation, listening dissolves it. One who listens and is wholly open to receive what comes from reality—from what is encountered—becomes relaxed, gentle, and at ease. That's why I keep saying, "Don't concentrate, but listen and receive." You must not strive to "get into your hands," but let your hands draw you so as to discover what comes to you from them. Unwillingness to suffer can also make one hard. The fear of being hurt turns us to stone. The fear that something could come up in meditation that one doesn't want to suffer, is most often countered with hardness. Anyone who stands simply in his poverty before God and carries the cross of Christ with inner willingness, becomes gentle.

6.9 DANIEL

DANIEL. I'm uncertain how to handle my feelings. On the one hand I'm supposed to accept them, and on the other not to occupy myself with them. A few days ago I tried to look carefully at the feelings that suddenly came up from my childhood. You tell me not to remain occupied with them, but return to awareness of my hands, to the present, and with the name. I hear you also say continually that we're not to suppress our feelings. Must I suppress them and not suppress them at the same time?

RM. You ask for a clear explanation.

DANIEL. Yes, please.

RM. It's actually like walking on a knife edge. From awareness of the present and from the name come salvation. If we are there, everything happens by itself. That's the highest criterion, one side of the coin.

On the other hand, we unconsciously place a cover over our unpleasant feelings. We're afraid of them. In addition, we have deep-seated emotions and unsolved conflicts of which we're unaware. We carry them within us, unknown to our self. They block the healing power which flows from the deep ground of our soul. They aren't easy to reach. These conflicts are very painful. We refuse instinctively to feel them. We protect them against every touch.

DANIEL. Yes, I know something about being afraid of pain.

RM. Therefore we go into stillness, which leads us deeper into ourselves and brings these feelings to the surface. Whatever is suffered through is dissolved. The knife edge consists in our readiness to suffer our feelings without occupying ourselves with them. Salvation doesn't come from them, but from quietly remaining in the present.

DANIEL. Then I need only sit still and remain present.

RM. Exactly. Our feelings aren't really our concern. But we have to count on a great resistance to suffering. This resistance causes us to repress our feelings unconsciously, so that they don't make us suffer. That's why we should look for a moment at our unpleasant feelings, but only until we can say, "Well, there they are, and it's okay for them to be there." To give a feeling permission to exist is an express sign of acceptance in love, or at least in submission.

DANIEL. Feelings are to be accepted.

RM. Yes. But this is not an act of my will. I can't make it happen by suggesting to myself, "I accept them."

DANIEL. But?

RM. By my looking at them with tolerance and resignation.

DANIEL. That makes sense.

RM. We disengage ourselves from them in a way that isn't rejection. We don't allow a breath of denial with regard to them. We turn away from them by turning to the present, the hands, and the name. Along with this, the feelings may still remain. Dealing with our emotions rests on two poles.

DANIEL. I see. One is the readiness to suffer whatever life imposes—that is only a precondition. The other and more important pole is attention to the present. From these comes healing.

RM. If we hold fast to these two poles, the knife-edge is safe. Hidden conflicts in us, which form obstacles on the way to God, dissolve, and our real nature—love and peace—becomes apparent.

6.10 EMILY

EMILY. I have the feeling of not meditating well. I make every effort, but afterwards it seems to me that I should have done better. I can't put my finger on it; it's a general feeling. Or better—I can define it—I'm distracted. I also flee from meditation.

RM. You are afraid of meditation.

EMILY. I have the impression I also flee from God. . . . Recently I lived in a relationship that was not good. It was clear to me that I had to break it off. I was doing harm because it nearly destroyed a whole family. Of course I had guilt feelings. I stopped praying, going to church, and meditating. I've only now begun again.

RM. You feel guilty.

EMILY. Yes, I did not know what to do. Now the relationship is broken off. How I can repair the harm I did is a mystery to me.

RM. The problem itself is gone. Guilt feelings, and the desire to repair the harmful results, remain.

EMILY. Yes, my self-accusation has remained. I fear I have to make atonement; otherwise the affair will cling to me for ever.

RM. You are easily a prey to guilt feelings.

EMILY. Very easily. I had therapy. It lasted two years and cleared up a lot. My mother was constantly nagging at me, though in my opinion, I was not a particularly naughty child. She often reproached me for being ungrateful, not loving her enough, though she loved me (and so on). Well, such situations, and the feelings connected with them, became clear to me during therapy. That helped enormously. But the tendency to feel guilty has remained. I easily begin to brood and get caught up in self-accusation.

RM. Come back to the essential, to the present, the presence of God. Come where there is neither guilt nor guilt feelings—to true being. If we have harmed another person, we should repair the harm as far as possible. But this won't take away your guilt feelings. They lie deeper than the present guilt. Your torments of conscience will only be healed if you stay where there are no guilt feelings. Turn to him who changes all guilt feelings into his love. In true being, that is your inner center, only love radiates. Come to Jesus Christ who has taken all guilt on himself. You don't need to work to remove your guilt feelings, only take refuge in the light. No guilt feelings exist there.

6.11 CECILIA

CECILIA. Three times yesterday during meditation I got very worked up. A colleague who constantly hurts and upsets me kept coming to mind. Then every injustice I've ever suffered came up. Rage, or better, anger, arose. Shortly after that, I got worked up for the third time because I was interrupted during meditation. When I grew angry then I realized something isn't right with me. Why am I so easily upset?

Looking into myself with that question, I saw that I get so excited because I'm afraid of letting hurts come near me. Suddenly, at a glance, all my resistance to any kind of suffering became clear to me ... *[pause]* ... I never saw it so clearly before. *[Pause]* ... Fear of pain is very deep-seated in me. That's an important factor in my thinking and acting.

RM. You were impressed.

CECILIA. It was a shock.

RM. It was a great grace to see something like that.

CECILIA. A painful and sobering grace ... *[pause]* ... But I'm glad to be confronted with it so starkly. I saw very deep down into myself. By myself, I could never have done so.

6.12 JAVIER

JAVIER. When you spoke of surrender, I felt resistance. I had the impression of being ridden over roughshod. The suspicion that God wants something of me that I don't want to give became louder and louder.

RM. This filled you with panic?

JAVIER. Yes, the word "surrender" all by itself makes me allergic! Some years ago a priest told me that I was called to the priesthood. I was very young and entered the minor seminary. I wasn't conscious of having acted from an inner urge. Years passed by before I became aware that I did not want that at all.

RM. That God did not want it either.

JAVIER. Yes, it took a long time before I had the courage to leave, and that's the reason why your demand for surrender is so threatening to me.

RM. You fear that once again something is going to be asked of you in God's name.

JAVIER. Yes, I'm learning to listen more and more to myself—to pay attention to what I want. Recently I read in the Gospel that Jesus asked blind Bartimaeus what he wanted. He wanted to see. I'm feeling a God awakening in myself who doesn't only make demands, but also asks what I desire.

RM. You are discovering your freedom.

JAVIER. Yes, this gives me freedom and self-assurance.

RM. And when you become more free, you can also look at your wounds. You can see that you were unjustly treated and that the wound has not yet quite healed.

JAVIER. True. The wound hasn't yet healed. If what you say is right, I can perhaps look at my hurt and let it be. Then, possibly, I'll react with less resistance.

RM. Look, Javier, God does not take your freedom from you. When God wants something from you, he doesn't tell your neighbor that he demands it of you. He places a longing for it deep within you. This—your deepest desire—reveals God's will to you. You only need to listen to, and trust in, your deepest longing. We act against God's will only if we don't listen to our deepest being, but go after superficial and self-destructive wishes. Surrender is a need of love. Have you ever loved anyone?

JAVIER. Yes, I believe so.

RM. Didn't you have the desire to gift this person and share something with him or her?

JAVIER. Yes.

RM. That is your desire for surrender. That's also what happens in meditation. You meditate out of longing for God. If you are sensitive to the inner longing, you will find genuine surrender and gladly give your time to God. It's not a command from outside that could be in conflict with your inner desire. Your wound from earlier in life is still there, and that's all right. It's all right for it to hurt.

JAVIER. Yes, but you also demanded something of me. It was also a command from outside in this sense and provoked in me the same allergic reactions as before.

RM. I demand of you only what you have empowered me to demand. Our agreement at the beginning of the retreat was very important for this reason.

JAVIER. What agreement?

RM. Before the retreat I always ask about desires and expectations. You asked me for an introduction to contemplation. I answered I would gladly comply with your request on condition that you follow my instructions during the retreat. That's the agreement we made. By virtue of it I have asked something of you, but only for the time of this retreat. In this sense it is your own, not my demand.

JAVIER. And if this surrender overwhelms me?

RM. Then I will show you steps that will not overwhelm you. Look at your wounds in the light of this surrender.

JAVIER. Thank you. I'll try.

6.13 FELICITY

FELICITY. During my meditation I saw an African woman before my eyes. She was dressed in European clothes and led a small child by the hand. I was walking the same road and was going somewhere. She came to me and gave me a message (I don't know exactly what). I asked about her child and she told me that it was an orphan. She had adopted it and loved it very much. Then suddenly we were in a tunnel. A car came and stopped. The driver invited us to ride with him to the next town. He looked very kind. I felt confidence in him and we got in. During the journey he told us of his family. But the child began to cry and the African woman wanted to get out.

RM. And all this happened during meditation.

FELICITY. Yes, during meditation.

RM. Felicity, listen . . . dreams, during sleep or when awake, can reveal much from our unconscious. Psychotherapy and dream-work are appropriate and helpful ways to deal with this. Our way is somewhat different. We go to God by a direct route. Dreams take place on the mental or psychic level. We leave these levels behind and seek the level of being. There, no stories or events occur, and nothing changes. God is eternal peace, resting in his own being. He doesn't think or act. Thinking and acting can't touch him. He is eternal love, timeless and changeless Being. In him there is stillness, as on the ocean floor. He causes everything to move out of itself, without being changed or touched by it himself. Let go of these fantasies and daydreams and come into the immediate present.

FELICITY. Yes, but the dreams come to me spontaneously while meditating.

RM. They come because you encourage them, attribute importance to them, and devote your attention to them. Don't pay attention to them and don't think that they're important.

FELICITY. They're no good in that case.

RM. They are good. But we're going a different way.

FELICITY. Should I suppress them?

RM. No, you don't need to suppress them. Whatever comes, independent of your will, is all right. But don't occupy yourself with them for even a moment. Return with determination to the concrete awareness of your hands and to the name of Mary. Meditation is rooted in the earth and related to reality. The daydreams will continue to come for a time, because you are so used to them. Later they will decrease, little by little. There's something of greater importance: Let go of them inside yourself. Don't cling to these dreams; don't attribute importance to them. Let go of your interest in them, and be interested in what is true, essential, ever present, in the formless present. Look toward what is there where nothing stirs. Contemplation is living consciousness and an eventless flowing of the love of Jesus Christ, who receives us into himself.

6.14 NORA

NORA. During meditation I get pain behind my eyes, at the back of my head, and in my neck. I also have pain in my back and my legs, but these are bearable. Those in my head are almost unendurable.

RM. Meditation is a torment for you.

NORA. Yes, I came in the hope that it would stop.

RM. Do you feel inner tensions?

NORA. I'm not conscious of them.

RM. Do you make great efforts in meditation?

NORA. Yes, I'm completely exhausted by the evening.

RM. During your next meditations, sit quietly and don't try to meditate, but simply sit. You can place your hands together, but without concentrating on them. You can let your thoughts come, play with your fantasies, let your feelings distract you. I would like to make only one stipulation: Don't do it intentionally. Let everything happen as it comes. Spend all your meditations until our next dialogue in this way.

NORA. You want me to sit there, not meditating or doing anything.

RM. Yes, do that.

NORA *[Next day]*. I tried to do as you said. I tried to sit there, come what may. After a very short time I felt my hands more strongly than ever before. Suddenly a huge fear of life came over me. It had unexpected force. I found myself beginning to meditate in a tense way . . . *[pause]*. Then I told myself, "No, do not meditate! Endure it!" Well, I couldn't endure the panic for very long. I let it come up repeatedly, but couldn't let it be for long.

RM. We've taken a big step forward. Meditation served you as a way to suppress your fear.

NORA. I wasn't conscious of that. *[Long pause.]* I'm well aware I have many such fears and that they could rise to the surface. I shrank from these fears, but was not aware that I suppressed them with meditation.

RM. We've discovered one of these repressive mechanisms. You have experienced how earnest meditating can suppress a vast number of feelings.

NORA. What am I to do in future? How do I continue?

RM. Try just to sit for a period of time without meditating. When the fear arises get accustomed to it and let it come. Then feel gently into your hands, but without seeking any results, without striving or willing, only listening, hearing, and receiving whatever comes. In this way you will slowly learn to meditate in a relaxed way.

6.15 THOMAS

THOMAS. I feel a lot of joy in meditation. I was rather exhausted and strained when I came here. Now, after the first five days, I have become calmer and can remain in peace. I experience how contemplative prayer can be recuperative.

RM. You are content.

THOMAS. Yes, I'm content. I received a few good ideas for my work today. I see much more clearly.

RM. I hope you didn't occupy yourself with these ideas.

THOMAS. They were in fact important insights. I have consciously admitted them because they will help me greatly in my work.

RM. Are you occupied with your insights during meditation?

THOMAS. Yes, I gave myself the time of meditation. They were important ideas.

RM. Were they more important to you at that moment than orientation to the presence of God?

THOMAS. Can one make such a comparison?

RM. When we become quiet in meditation, we put a distance between ourselves and all other things which are normally important to us. Quiet also gives clear thoughts, because many things in us can settle down and be set right. I have nothing against your writing down briefly one or another good idea, as long as it doesn't occupy you further. The fundamental question is whether you seek God himself, or quiet and clear thoughts for the improvement of your work situation. You have intentionally given the time of retreat to God, or at least, the half-hours of meditation. During this time nothing is more important than God himself. Give exclusive attention to him. In this way you signify that he is more important to you than your work.

You said just now you are content because you have become quiet and have recuperated. This could be very egotistical, if you're only seeking your well-being. My suspicion is reaffirmed when you now use the time you wanted to give to God for planning your work.

THOMAS. Do I not work for God?

RM. Your final goal is God, I don't doubt that. But contemplative prayer consists in devoting ourselves to God and forgetting one's self, one's worries, one's wishes, one's tasks, one's past and future. God alone suffices. This devotion is put into practice through wholehearted attention to him. If you continue as you are doing, your daily meditation will soon become a preparation for your sermons or work conferences. You'll think about your pastoral concerns with individuals. It's more difficult in normal life than in retreat to resist these distractions. Your time of prayer is contemplative only when you forget your cares and tasks and devote yourself wholly to the presence of Jesus Christ.

THOMAS. I understand.

6.16 TILLIE

TILLIE. In meditation I'm confronted with my inner inconsistency. On the one hand, I feel that God is the ultimate meaning of my life; on the other, I feel resistance to him.

RM. That must produce tension.

TILLIE. Yes, it tears me to pieces.

RM. You cannot admit your resistance to God.

TILLIE. I don't want to resist him.

RM. Of course you don't, but there is something unwanted in you against God which tries to tell you something.

TILLIE. What shall I do with it?

RM. Admit it and look at your resistance.

TILLIE. I'm afraid the resistance could increase, so that in the end I will resist him.

RM. Look at this fear; it will then fade a little. You'll grow in confidence that your innermost self is good. Whatever arises against God is only disordered and wants to be released. After looking at your resistance, return to your hands and to the name, and see what comes from there. Look at what comes from reality. God lives in the deepest center of your soul. Anything that fights against him in yourself is only something in between. He himself will dissolve this resistance to himself. You can also pray, "Lord, I am powerless against my resistance. But you can take it away. With or without resistance, there is no other way but to turn to you. You will redeem me."

6.17 PHILIP

PHILIP. My meditation varies. Often I give my attention to the name and the hands, but then I'm off. When I return to the name it doesn't take long before I'm gone again. My attention is very weak. I'm distracted and have a feeling of indifference or a lack of interest. My meditation just plods along.

RM. Something isn't right.

PHILIP. Yes, but I can't do anything about it.

RM. Are you committed to your times of meditation and your retreat?

PHILIP. I don't feel much resolve. I tell myself at such moments, "You must now return to your hands," but it's not very effective.

RM. It's weak.

PHILIP. Yes, and that's why I'm often absent.

RM. It could be lack of determination. You cannot fully give your-self to the way and force yourself to feel your hands. In con-templation nothing works with a "must." Lively interest opens the way: What am I discovering? What comes to me from there?

PHILIP. How can I become more resolved?

RM. It depends on what your orientation is. Do you know what you want from the retreat? Do you know what you want to do with your life?

PHILIP. I don't know whether I know.

RM. Then you don't know. Be aware of your lack of purpose. It wouldn't be a bad thing to work at that and to become clear why you came to make this retreat. Resolution is a precondi-tion for meditation. It grows when we know what we want.

The real motive for meditation is longing for God. That's the compass of our life. It leads us into retreat and lies behind the desire for meditation. We can't always feel it, but it's always present. Every human being carries at least a breath of it in-side. Search into this longing, be aware of it, discover it—with that it will grow. In order to come to God by way of contemplation, it would be sufficient to look constantly at this longing. It awakens desire, a passion to seek God and surren-der to him, to serve him and praise him. Only then are we wide awake and resolved in prayer.

6.18 MAUREEN

MAUREEN. I was for a long time recollected and very peaceful in meditation. Then thoughts came, and the quiet was suddenly gone. I didn't feel very good and also noticed back pain. My thoughts were quite confused at first. Then they centered more and more on my future. I'm a pastoral assistant and am changing my parish. My thoughts circle around my future work.

RM. The change is hard on you.

MAUREEN. I was thinking whether I won't be overtaxed by the work in the new parish. It's a large parish, and the parish priest seems to be rather stiff and hard.

RM. You're afraid of him.

MAUREEN. Yes, my thoughts are also circling around my fear. I have had various practical work experiences. I have always been lucky, so I don't have any reason to be afraid. My brother came to my mind. He is also a pastoral worker. He is doing very well. He is older, more gifted, and is always successful. I had secretly determined, this time, to do better than he.

RM. You compare yourself to him.

MAUREEN. Yes, I always compare myself to him. For once, I'd so like to do better than he, but I can't. So I often feel incapable. I try, but in vain. In the end, feelings of inferiority arise which I can't get rid of.

RM. This comparing is an inner need for you, an inner compulsion.

MAUREEN. It's my problem. Whether I want it or not, it's always there.

RM. Well. I will show you a way. Turn to the present, listen into your hands until you become aware of yourself and sense your own being. Then you will be more one with yourself, and the comparisons will fall away. It's the same when you come to the name of Mary. Security and a sense of belonging will arise and you will be wholly with her, with her name. Everything else will disappear; the comparisons will become superfluous. It won't matter any more if someone is greater or smaller. The experience "I exist" is sufficient and depends on no exterior event. All comparisons are superfluous. To be one with the inner ground of being gives true security and a sense of belonging.

MAUREEN. That means I must discover more of myself and God.

RM. Yes, and when you are one with yourself, and your security comes from within, love will well up in you. Love will cause you to see your brother from a different viewpoint. You'll rejoice in his wellbeing. His success won't threaten you anymore. You will experience his success as your own, because you will feel more and more one with him.

6.19 ERNEST

ERNEST. For days I felt great tension in my chest area. It only dissolved when I had the shattering insight that I have always suffered from massive guilt feelings. I hadn't realized that before. At the same time, I became conscious that, until then, I hadn't meditated in the right way. I only sought quiet, release from my guilt feelings. I heard from you a thousand times that we should give the time to God. I wanted to do that and renewed the intention to serve God in meditation. But on a deeper level I always meditated for myself. I'm shocked at myself and my self-centeredness *[long pause]*.

RM. *[Looks into Ernest's eyes and is silent.]*

ERNEST *[After a longer pause]*. It hurts to see that. But it's also healing, because now I'm a little more with myself and my reality. But how do I get away from my guilt feelings and self-centeredness?

RM. *[Again says nothing.]*

ERNEST *[After another pause]*. I feel more calm.

RM. You have taken the first step. It's an insight, it's a grace. Without God's light we can't discover these feelings. It's also a promise that the next grace that dissolves these feelings will be given.

ERNEST. How will it be given?

RM. Grace comes when it's given. We cannot force it. We can go the way I have often shown you.

ERNEST. Which way?

RM. The rays of divine grace dissolve your guilt feelings if you don't suppress them and remain tuned to the essential. Not to suppress means to be ready to suffer everything imposed on us by life. It means to admit the guilt feelings and suffer them until they have been taken away. To be tuned to the essential means to remain in awareness, to listen into the hands, to attend to the present, and to keep repeating the name. These feelings will then rise like smoke through a chimney, dissolve, and leave you free.

ERNEST. Shouldn't I instead go into this guilt in order to discover where it comes from?

RM. When we're with God, we have no guilt feelings. Focus on the essential, on him. This is the simplest and shortest way. It will transform you. When you're in union with Him, the guilt feelings will evaporate.

6.20 ALFRED

ALFRED. I discovered what it means to give one's time to God. Until now, I had always said this intention, but it didn't alter my meditation. Yesterday I remembered how my wife from time to time asks me to occupy myself with my children. When I can do it, I go to the children's room for awhile. Most often, I experience the children then quite differently than at other times. I become aware of them with their needs, wishes, and worries. I can put aside my own cares and simply be with them. All the day's pressure falls away. There's nothing to achieve, and there's no hurry. I'm simply with them and am much more accepting of them as they are. I'm interested in them and can listen to them. I'm there for them.

When I remembered this I saw a parallel to meditation. I told myself, "You have nothing to aim at. You can simply be there with God and for God. You can give your attention to him." It was liberating, and I was much more present. Now I begin to understand that we're not aware of God because we don't turn ourselves fully to him and don't let go of everything else. We can't take him as he is, but only as we want him to be for us.

RM. You can be there for God and for your children without any other agenda.

ALFRED. Yes, I get an inkling of how great a joy it can be to be there only for God.

IV. REVIEW & TRANSITION TO THE SEVENTH DAY

Dear Retreatant, we are now finishing the Sixth Day. I hope you have no more difficulties with the daily procedure of the retreat. Please don't talk or telephone and don't take up other activities like playing music, knitting, crafts, and the like. I'm even hoping that you are not reading, and that you don't miss it.

It's also part of the process that you read only a little of this book at a time. Did you have the courage to omit some dialogues and not read them at all?

How did you get on with the name of the Mother of God? Did you try to say it? Did you remain consistently with it? If not, I'd recommend that you remain with this Sixth Day and begin with the name. If this is the case, do not move on. You wouldn't get far if you were to go to the next day. Just the opposite. Everything needs its time.

On the Seventh Day, the Introductory Talk will treat the second precondition for meditation: attention to God, the central goal of the retreat. In meditation, we come to the name of Jesus Christ and remain with it for the rest of the retreat.

SEVENTH DAY

I. INTRODUCTORY TALK: ORIENTATION TO GOD

1. Eye contact and distraction

From our innermost being we are oriented to God. It is written into the ground of our being that we come from him and can find our ultimate home only in him. The longing for God is our inner compass which turns us toward him that we may learn to listen to him, to look at him, and to trust him. It should be our constant endeavor to direct our attention to him. Through orientation of our attention to him we become more and more like his Son.

In the story of Jesus' walking on the water we have an outstanding example of the power of being turned to God, and of the danger we're in of losing this most essential contact.

Matthew tells us that after the feeding of the five thousand, Jesus sent the apostles to the other side of the lake (Mt 14:22-33). He himself went up a mountain and remained in prayer until dawn. The apostles had a head wind the whole night, and the boat was tossed to and fro by the waves. Suddenly they saw a figure coming toward them over the water. They were panicked, for they believed they were seeing a ghost. They began to call out in fear. Jesus calmed them by making himself known to them.

Peter was the first to react and went from one extreme to the other. He forgot his fear, the boat, the wind, and his companions in his desire to get to Jesus. He begged for the wonderful power to walk on the water and go toward him. Jesus agreed, "Come, Peter!" Peter was enthralled by Jesus. He relied wholly on the call of Jesus, and I can't imagine it otherwise than that he looked into Jesus' eyes and left the boat without paying attention to the water. He saw only the eyes of Jesus. Through this eye contact, strength flowed into him to enable him to walk on the water as if it were the marketplace of Capernaum. He was wholly turned toward Jesus, and through eye contact was as if one with him.

Suddenly a gust of wind touched his face. Fear rose in him. He will have asked himself, "How strong is the wind?" "Will the waves rise higher when the wind grows stronger?" He had begun to doubt, "Will I be able to continue to walk on the water? Will I not sink and drown?" Occupied with his fears and questions, he forgot the eye contact with Jesus. Probably he even wanted to look back to know what he should do in the situation, whose help he might call on in case of emergency. Immediately he was up to his neck in the water. Perhaps he had already swallowed some water before he could get out his cry for help with his remaining strength. Jesus at once grasped his hand and drew him out.

Our situation is similar. We go to meditation with the best of intentions to turn to God, to Jesus Christ. Through awareness of the hands and the name we keep eye contact with him. He carries us across the water. It is his strength which directs our attention to him. Yet when the first pain arises, when the first negative feeling expresses itself, when something moves in the unconscious, the first disturbing noise from outside becomes noticeable, fear grips us and we lose contact with him. We turn to the newly arisen problem. It often seems to me that we are extremely adept at handling problems. I suppose that we're only waiting for an excuse to interrupt our essential contact with God in order to return to our ego. We withdraw from the presence of God in order to brood over our problems. We succumb to the illusion that we want to attend to the problems only in order to return as quickly as possible to the present.

2. The vine branches and the pressure to achieve

Often it's the urge to achieve that keeps us from being turned toward God. In the Gospel, Jesus describes his relationship with the apostles using the image of the vine (see Jn 15:1-8). He himself is the vine, the apostles are the branches. The branches that bear fruit are being pruned by the gardener—that is, the Father. The branches that do not bear fruit are all cut off. The actual heart of the image shows the necessity of being turned to Jesus.

What is the task of the branches? They have to produce grapes. They direct their whole strength to producing grapes. They dread not bearing enough fruit at the right time. They worry about their survival. In this fear, they throw themselves into the production of grapes, which brings with it a tremendous pressure to achieve. Under this pressure they are occupied night and day with their fruits. Even during winter, when the issue is dormant, they plan their grapes. They tell themselves hundreds of times what the grapes must be like, how they could grow better and more quickly, and produce sweeter juice. And when the first fruits are forming, they try to infuse more sap into them. They compare their fruits with those of other branches and convince themselves that the bunches on the other branches are bigger. They complain that there hasn't been rain for long enough and that that's the reason why their grapes did not get enough sap. Then they measure theirs against the neighboring grapes and protest that the sun seemingly only shines on the others. The more they concern themselves with their fruit, the more they circle around their problems. The more they endeavor to press more sap into the fruit, the less vitality flows into the grapes.

Jesus also wants the grapes to grow. Jesus sees how the branches, laden with anxious care, pressure themselves and wear themselves out in misguided attention. The meaning of the parable is to say to the branches, "Stop! This is not the way! Make a 180° turn!" Instead of concentrating on the grapes, unite yourselves with the vine. Then the strength of the vine will flow through you and you will bear rich fruit. At the same time, you'll be freed from your pressure, your compulsion to compare yourselves with others, and your tensions. You are occupied only with yourselves, with your cares, your success. Turn back, unite yourself to the vine. Remain with it with all your senses and your strength. The vine takes care of the rich fruit. You are so occupied with yourselves that you don't notice that your connection with the vine has already been broken and that no vitality is flowing into you. Turn back to your source, and everything will be given. Sun and rain, vitality, and rich harvest—everything will be given you without cost. You deceive yourselves when you believe that you are producing grapes by your own strength. It is the power of the vine that works through you. Close union with the vine is the one thing necessary. Direct your attention from the grapes to the vine."

We are the branches. Behind our urge to achieve, our worries and fears, our circling around ourselves, and our inner pressure to succeed, lies a deep-seated misunderstanding: We think we have to do everything ourselves. But it is God who does everything through us. The lilies have no cares. God clothes them splendidly. Our only care should be to be always with him. Instead of worrying about ourselves, our achievements, and our survival, we should pray, "Lord, I care about you. You care for me. I leave myself wholly to you. Your strength will work in me." Thus we can carry out our usual activities either with worry or without worry. The decisive issue is, to whom is our eye directed—to ourselves or to God?

We do not need to make ourselves perfect, but to unite ourselves to God, who is perfect. Through this contact, God can work in us. Through our constant attention to him, he changes us.

3. Sadness over our sins

I'd like to give an example to show that even preoccupation with our sins and the wish to be perfect distract us from the essential. The Franciscan Eligius Leclerc describes in his book about the life of St. Francis how the saint was on the road with Brother Leo, and that in crossing a brook and admiring the purity of the water, they thought of purity of heart. Francis noted that Brother Leo had become sad.

> He said to him, "You seem to be brooding."
>
> "Yes, if we had a little of this purity we would also have the bubbling, overflowing joy of our sister spring and the irresistible strength of her water." A bottomless homesickness vibrated through Leo's words. With an air of melancholy he stared at the brook, the image of a purity which forever escapes human beings.
>
> "Come," said Francis, pulling him along.
>
> The two continued on their journey. They were silent for awhile. Then Francis asked, "Do you know, Brother, what a pure heart is?"
>
> "When one has nothing with which to reproach oneself," answered Leo, without much thought.

"Then I understand that you are sad, for we always have something with which to reproach ourselves."

"Exactly, and that is why I have given up the hope of a pure heart."

"Ah, Brother Leo, do not be too concerned about purity of heart. Look at God! Admire him! Rejoice that he is the altogether Holy One! Thank him for his own self. It is this, my little brother, that makes a pure heart. And when you have thus turned to God do not, ever, turn back to your own self! Don't ask yourself where you are standing with God. Sadness at not being perfect and at discovering the sinner in oneself is a human, an all too human feeling. Lift your eyes higher, much higher. God exists, his infinity and his changeless glory exist. A heart is pure when it doesn't cease to adore the living and true Lord. It shares deeply in God's life and is so strong that even in all its misery it can be touched by the eternal innocence and joy of God. Such a heart is at one and the same time empty and full to overflowing—that God *is* God is all-sufficient for it. From this certainty, it derives its peace and all its joy. And holiness of heart—that too then, is nothing else than God."

"But God demands that we make efforts and remain faithful to him," Brother Leo objected.

"Certainly, but holiness doesn't consist in self-realization nor in the fulfillment which one achieves oneself. Holiness is first of all the emptiness which one finds in oneself, which one accepts, and which God fills in an equal measure to which one opens oneself to his fullness."

(E. Leclerc, OFM, *Weisheit eines Armen, Franziskus gründet seinen Orden*, Dietrich Coelde Verlag, 1981, 2nd Edition, p. 74 ff. Trans. Sr. Lucia Wiedenhöver, OCD.)

We often make the same mistake as Brother Leo. We want to make ourselves perfect and are too preoccupied with our imperfections and problems, with our sins, our guilt feelings, and self-reproaches. Instead, we should orient ourselves constantly to God. He will transform us. If only we had an inkling of the tremendous transforming power of the presence of God! Constant attention to his presence and giving ourselves up to him in trust—these uplift and purify as nothing in the world does. Without doubt, psychotherapy can be useful and at times necessary. Various forms of therapy can help us become more aware of many things, but real healing comes from the presence of God. It flows through the contact with our center, with the divine spark within us. Constant and fully surrendered contact with God heals our misery.

We deal with our imperfections, failings, sins, and guilt feelings like one who is standing in a dark room and beats about with a stick in order to destroy the darkness instead of lighting a light! We do not have to destroy the darkness. We need only go to the switch and turn on the light. Then every darkness disappears. It is the same with our sins. We need only enter into contact with Christ. In him there is neither sin nor guilt.

4. Orientation of the human being to God in Sacred Scripture

The essential message of the Old and the New Testaments is orientation to God. One cannot plumb its depths because nearly everything in Scripture speaks of it. It is the constant theme of the Old Testament. Whether with gentle and quiet wooing or with severe reproaches, the message is always putting God first in our feelings, our thoughts, our actions. Scripture demands that we have no other gods and proclaims that we cannot find happiness except in the one God. Only consistent fidelity and orientation to him can bring us permanent peace. The first of all commandments is the orientation to God. Original sin is the embodiment of all sins. Adam and Eve are the first who allowed themselves to be distracted from God and who through their egocentricity placed themselves at the center.

St. John's Gospel tells us in detail of the moving example of Jesus. As he is one with the Father, so we should always look to him. He lives wholly in the Father. The Father is always before his eyes. He is within wholly turned to the Father. He speaks only of what he hears from the Father; he does only what pleases the Father. He lives this contact with the Father before our eyes; he has no other center than the Father. With his inner eyes, he looks always at the Father and so teaches us how we can live as he does.

In the Synoptics, this orientation is most often portrayed as faith:

- St. Joseph, who allows himself in simplicity to be led by God.

- The Mother of God, who feels herself to be the handmaid of the Lord and says "yes" to the Incarnation.

- Mary sitting at the Master's feet, lost in him.

- The sinner in the house of Simon the Pharisee who surrenders herself totally.

- Zacchaeus, who expresses his faith in generosity.

- The blind man of Jericho, who keeps pleading in his faith.

- The Centurion of Capernaum, who in his trust asks for no proofs.

- Matthew, who promptly rises from his money table.

- One of the criminals who was crucified with Jesus.

All these and many others are presented to us as examples of resolute orientation to God. Besides these examples, at the Transfiguration of Jesus, we hear the Father's voice asking us repeatedly to turn toward his Son.

As to St. Paul, we find insight into his personal orientation not only through his theology, but even more strongly in the ethical recommendations to his communities. Everything without exception is founded on God. When he writes that the members of the community should not quarrel, he gives as reason that they are members of Christ. When demanding that the Sixth Commandment be kept, he argues that the body is the temple of the Holy Spirit. When he speaks of the order in the family, he justifies everything by reference to Christ. Paul lived entirely with his inner eye on Christ.

5. The example of the saints

I have also learned this attitude of orientation to God from the saints. All of them have it in common. I have to mention St. Ignatius in particular, for the retreat is nothing but a school of orientation to God. The ideal of St. Benedict was "to walk in the presence of God." St. Alphonsus Rodriguez, a Jesuit Brother who for years was doorkeeper at the College of Palma de Mallorca discovered Jesus Christ in everyone who visited the College. Day and night he lived with his gaze on Jesus Christ.

6. The most frequent mistake in meditation

If we want to know whether we meditate correctly or incorrectly, the discernment is simple and can be found in the answers to two questions. The first is, "Am I with God, or with myself?" I'm with myself if I'm occupied with my problems, worries, wishes, thoughts, feelings, or anything else that pertains to myself. The second is, "Am I ready to suffer?" If I'm with God and ready to suffer I'm on the right path. All discernment of spirit in contemplation has taken place with these two questions.

For years I have been showing the way of contemplation to countless people, work which includes the task of correcting mistakes. Outwardly, faults can rarely be seen, so I have to ask each person how he or she goes about it. Since, however, these mistakes made in meditation are not conscious ones, they can't be communicated directly. The Retreat Master has to look behind the scenes. The conviction has grown in me, through long experience, that the most frequent mistake that constantly haunts retreatants is the occupation with oneself. I can't repeat it often enough, and remind you again, that our attention should not be directed to our problems, cares, wishes, thoughts, pains, feelings, bodily attitudes, past, future, or whatever else relates to our Self, but solely and uniquely to God himself.

7. The desire for immediacy

To focus on God means, for many people, to have the intention of giving God first place in their lives. He is the final end. However, the first thing in our intention is the last in execution. When I want to reach a town, I first have to use all different modes of travel to reach my destination. The town comes first in my consideration but is the last attained. Many people therefore believe that God exists for them only in incalculable distance, in eternal life. So we're always in danger of directing our attention only to the means and not to God himself.

This is a disturbing problem in the Church. What is published as spiritual literature or presented as spirituality often seems to direct attention not to God himself, but to a means that will lead us to God. God or Jesus Christ are the end, but only indirectly. Our attention is most directly focused on changing ourselves and the world. We give our attention to a text that speaks of God, look at a picture that reminds us of God, devote ourselves to a problem that we want to solve with the help of God, or plan actions we want to carry out according to the mind of God.

Images, texts, and symbols are in fact means to come into his presence. As means they help us on the way to him, until the moment comes when we shall no longer need them. Then they become an obstacle. But it is hazardous to aim for immediate relationship with God. That's why the world often remains in the spotlight of our attention, with God behind the scenery.

The desire for contemplation lies in discovering the immediacy of attention to God. It is the desire to seek no longer God's gifts, but God himself. No longer to use the means that lead to him, but to dare direct contact with him. That is the reason why, in this book, I stress the development of awareness and attentiveness. We began with awareness of nature. Then we learned to remain with breathing and the hands. Attention is directed to God even more explicitly when we attend to the present. Still more so through the simple and single repetition of the name of Jesus Christ.

II. INSTRUCTIONS FOR MEDITATION

Before I ask you to pass on to the name of Jesus Christ, I remind you of the exterior framework of your retreat day. A fresh recalling of instructions given earlier won't do any harm.

I presume that you have become accustomed to silence by now. I take it that you are refraining from speaking; that, except for keeping a diary, you do not engage in any writing, not even letters; that you don't use the telephone or watch TV, you don't listen to music and do not pursue any occupation. Apart from some fitness exercises like jogging, you spend all the time between meditations in nature. Relaxation is linked spontaneously with the time spent in nature.

To the four hours of meditation which we have been making since the Third Day, you have already added the one or two half-hours. Continue to meditate each day between five and six units of two half-hours each. Always renew your intention to give this time to God, and at the beginning of each meditation, briefly direct your attention to the different parts of your body so as to be more fully present. If you are devoting yourself to a Retreat in Daily Life, remain for two weeks at least with the Seventh Day.

In the same way in which you have spoken the name of Mary, move on now to the name of Jesus Christ. We shall remain with it to the end of the retreat. If you want to practice this kind of meditation after the retreat, I would recommend that you meditate always with the name of Jesus Christ. You have come to awareness

through following the steps recommended for meditation. With
every exhalation now say the name of "Jesus" into your hands with
an inner sound, and with every inhalation, "Christ." At the beginning you might want to say the name with every second breath, or
you might simply want to say "Jesus." Little by little, however,
come to saying the name of "Jesus" with every outward breath and
"Christ" with every inward. When our attention is still held by the
movement of the air it seems to us more natural to say "Jesus"
when breathing in. But when the consciousness of streaming air
deepens, we experience the breathing out as coming first. Accustom yourself from the beginning to say the name while breathing
out. Listen how the name arrives in the palms of your hands and
say it with an inner ring as you did before with the name of
"Mary." Do not embellish the name with representations, images,
or memories, but stay with the simple repetition.

With this name, turn to Jesus Christ himself. You will experience
that his name and his person become one. The name should be
neither a cry for help nor a petition, but a loving attentive contact
with him. With reverence, turn to the present Christ. Everything is
created in him, everything exists in him. You yourself, too, exist in
him. He is present in you. He is present in the innermost center of
your being, in your consciousness. He lives in your alert attentiveness. That is why the name of Jesus Christ can fill you with a certain devotion which will have to be purified later through a period
of dryness. During those "darker times," you'll feel that nothing of
your contact with him has remained. But as long as you give your
attention to the present moment, the contact exists even though you
may not feel it. However, if you are aware of feelings of superficiality or routine, you have ceased to be in awareness. Instead of
giving up the repetition of the name return to the present through a
more intense awareness of your hands. The ever-present Son of
God will take you into his love.

III. DIALOGUES

7.1 BETTY

BETTY. I feel resistance to the name. The meditation goes much
    better when I do not say it. I find it too much. I have said it
    now and then, but gradually dropped it.

RM. You feel resistance to the name.

BETTY. Yes. I do not feel resistance towards Jesus Christ himself, but toward the repetition of his name.

RM. Only against the repetition of the name, but not against himself.

BETTY. It is somehow strange to me to say the name of Jesus Christ without connecting it with a petition, a theme, or an image from the Gospel. I miss the corresponding correlative: a person.

RM. A matching partner.

BETTY. One says a name to someone, and not just into emptiness. When I have a word from the Gospel or a scene from his life before me he is much closer to me.

RM. If it is a question of nearness, the name is more helpful than your previous way of praying.

BETTY. How?

RM. When you take an episode from the Gospel you think of the earthly Jesus of Nazareth. He has died, is risen, and as Christ is present everywhere. In him everything was created. He penetrates everything and is present in everything—also in you, in your consciousness, your hands, your breath, but very specially in your expressing his name. The kingdom of God is within us. When we look into ourselves he reveals himself to us and shows us how we are his mystical body, how we are children of God. This takes place not so much in images and thoughts, but in your own being, in the place where *your being* and *the Being* touch each other. In the experience of your present moment, the all-pervading presence of the Son of God touches you. You need no image, no thought, no memory, no feeling, no other support but the name alone. This is not the only way, but this is the way I'm showing you. His name is given to us from heaven, in him is our salvation.

In this way say the name of the risen and all-present Son of God, the name of the Logos, the Wisdom of God, as he is present in your being, and as he is *the reality* itself in *your reality.* Say to him who is everything in you, "Lord, I am nothing, you are everything." Then Jesus Christ is nearer to you than anything else, nearer than you are to yourself.

7.2 FRED

FRED. I am more recollected in meditation than I usually can manage. I'm always present in my hands. Thoughts do come as well, but not too many, and I am with the name. I listen with interest and I wait for what comes. I'm present with lively curiosity. Now and then I'm disappointed that nothing comes.

RM. You are waiting for something new.

FRED. I don't know. I'm looking for what comes from reality. Mostly nothing comes, and then I feel frustration moving in.

RM. What are you expecting?

FRED. Somehow I'm looking for new experiences.

RM. For something exciting.

FRED. At least for some progress.

RM. Nothing new needs to come. We're so used to measuring and judging progress in relation to the *thing*. We watch a TV program, then a second and a third. . . . When building a house, we lay brick upon brick. We read a novel and constantly expect something new to happen. The TV programs, the bricks, the pages of a novel are all external objects which replace each other. We do the same in prayer. We talk to God about our life, formulate petitions, make reflections, and see to it that we always have something new to bring up. In our religious feelings the same happens. When one feeling dies down, we already wait for another uplifting sensation. In contemplative prayer, however, these changes are unimportant.

FRED. Is there nothing new?

RM. Nothing new has to occur in contemplation. The new, the fascinating—which could surprise us—is always already there. It is covered up by much that is superfluous. When the superfluous falls away the new and exciting shows itself.

So you are always there, but you are not consciously aware of yourself. God is there and you are not aware of him either. The light of your consciousness is there and you rarely or never turn your attention to it. The present as such is there, but you don't pay attention to it. Being is there, yet you don't take notice of it.

When you quietly remain with your hands and with the name, gradually everything that covers up true being will fall away: thoughts, feelings, imaginations, dreams, expectations, wishes, worries, interests, and whatever else is unimportant. The more everything episodic fades into the background, the stronger and clearer all-penetrating reality which can never be absent comes to the fore.

FRED. That is new to me. It makes me even more curious.

RM. Curiosity is not the right attitude. Curiosity is a greed, a self-centered expectation. The right attitude is one of surrender, of willingness to serve, of adoration. These are reality-related. The more everything that normally occupies and absorbs us disappears, the more the present can move into the center. With this, the presence of the risen Christ who penetrates everything with his goodness can move into the center, and you become more and more one with this presence of the risen Lord. This happens not as a result of awareness but *in* it. However, nothing new is happening in this process. You only become conscious of what was there already. You also become conscious that everything has always been there. That is why you don't have to expect something new, but have only to look into yourself. When you are with the risen Christ peace is revealed to you that is eternally resting within itself, and love that is eternally self-emptying, overflowing.

7.3 JOSÉ

JOSÉ. I have tried to say "Jesus" in breathing out, and "Christ" while breathing in. I don't get on with it and feel strained saying the name with every breath. My breathing gets all confused. Sometimes it gets quicker; then again I feel I want to control it. Also, the name is too long, my breath is rather short. I get hectic inside. That really isn't for me. I stopped it.

RM. You stopped it.

JOSÉ. Yes, I stopped because it makes me restless.

RM. Does it have to go well from the start? Can we not have a learning process?

JOSÉ. I tried it repeatedly, but I only get restless.

RM. We're learning something new which you don't yet know and of which you have as yet no experience. One has to keep on patiently.

JOSÉ. Can I not say another name?

RM. *[Says nothing.]*

JOSÉ. Well then, I will go on trying.

RM. Begin again. Say only "Jesus" when breathing out. Say it with an inner sound and into your hands. Say it ever more gently until you hear the name rather than say it. You need not move your lips, it is mental speaking. While you are repeating the name, listen with attention into the center of your hands and feel whether the name arrives with the movement of your breath. Do not try to change the rhythm of your breathing, but adapt the rhythm of the name to your breathing. It takes time to sort itself out. Later on, it becomes natural and harmonious. Wait until you have become familiar with this before you say "Christ" when breathing in. Repeat the name with every breath out and in. Only when you are very distracted return to the awareness of your hands.

JOSÉ. Is this step necessary for the way?

RM. It's necessary for this way.

7.4 CLARE

CLARE. I don't know whether I should use the name. I used to meditate with it. With time it became rather empty. In hindsight, it seems to me that I used the name only to quiet down. I don't want to continue doing this. That's the reason why I dropped it. Now I don't know whether I should return to the name or not.

RM. You feel a resistance to saying the name.

CLARE. Yes, it's as if there were a wall. I sit in front of it and nothing moves on. I feel emptiness within myself.

RM. Yes, the emptiness must come. We must pass through that; otherwise we don't move from the level of religious feeling to the depth of contemplation. We like to cling to religious feelings. They are pleasant and help us along in everyday life. But they are only feelings and by their nature changeable. There is no sure foundation in them. Return to the name.

CLARE. Yes, but I don't want to use the name as a means.

RM. If you notice that you use the name in this way, return to awareness and pay attention to the hands. When you are thus in contemplation, so much assurance and security will come from the hands that you will no longer use the name as a means.

CLARE. I still have the impression that I'm using the name as a means.

RM. Then pray like this, "Lord, I want to say your name with reverence and not misuse it, but I can't yet say it unambiguously. You, however, can do everything; you can give me your grace so that I no longer use your name as a means. Help my weakness and powerlessness. Accept my miserable and self-centered meditation as a praise of your name." Remain with the name. It leads you forward on the way. It is a contact with Jesus Christ himself. Through his name he works in you and purifies you.

7.5. SIMON

SIMON. The meditation is going quite well, but I'm not satisfied with my progress all the same. I should have got further by now. I still have thoughts and other distractions. It still takes too long before I find my way back. I work at it, but don't really advance.

RM. You feel pressure to make more progress.

SIMON. Yes, I feel pressure. The others who are on retreat with me have already advanced further. They meditate much more than I do.

RM. That the others, in your opinion, have advanced much further puts you under pressure.

SIMON. Yes. The same happens to me in everyday life. I'm youth chaplain and have group meetings often until late in the evening. Then in the morning I feel under pressure to be in the parish office at 8 a.m. because the secretary is already there.

RM. The secretary finished her work at 6 p.m. and you worked until 11 p.m. You could get to the office later with a good conscience, or you could have a longer break in the afternoon.

SIMON. But she doesn't know how long I go on working in the evening.

RM. You could explain that to her.

SIMON. Hmm, . . . true . . . I must admit that the pressure comes also from me. I pressure myself.

RM. The pressure lies within you.

SIMON *[after a longer pause]*. That could have something to do with my father.

RM. With your father.

SIMON. Yes, with my father. He always demanded much of me. I did not want to and couldn't possibly disappoint him. I always had to bring home good marks and come up to his expectations.

RM. You wanted to satisfy him.

SIMON. Until now I haven't been conscious of it. I had to buy his love with my achievements.

RM. And so you developed the need to achieve. With this pressure to achieve you react to all the demands of life. You don't even want to disappoint your secretary.

SIMON. Yes, but life does demand a lot of me.

RM. There is pressure from outside and pressure from within. We all have to live with controls and demands from the outside. Daily life demands results, demands our commitment to others; it wants to challenge our creativity.

Usually, we can cope with such demands. They frequently help us discover and develop dormant abilities. However, what is not healthy and what can make a person ill in both body and soul is when we add inner pressures to the outer ones.

SIMON. Yes, I experience this inner pressure a lot.

RM. That is why I'm showing you a way to free yourself from inner pressure.

SIMON. How?

RM. By taking away the outward pressure for the time of meditation. We have agreed that you don't have to achieve anything during your retreat. You don't even have to achieve a proper meditation. It suffices that you enter into the individual steps.

If you don't succeed, you begin again and try anew. Only enter wholeheartedly into the exercises. Then it doesn't matter whether or not you reach the goal you've set for yourself.

SIMON. But the inner pressure remains. Isn't that much worse?

RM. Yes, it is. It is harder for you to bear the inner pressure because you can no longer say that you are overworked by your father, your secretary, or your boss. You find out that the pressure comes from yourself.

I will show you how the way continues. Through awareness of your hands and the continuous repetition of the name of Jesus Christ, you will find peace and quiet. If you are aware of the quiet and the ever-present moment, you'll be able to be there without the need to achieve. As long as you are with yourself, with your true being, you'll be free from the pressure to achieve.

SIMON. And what if I feel the pressure all the same?

RM. Then look at it and allow yourself to feel like that. Welcome it. Tell yourself, "I'm feeling this pressure and it's okay." Then turn your attention again to the present moment. When you stand in the present moment with all your senses, you will no longer feel an urge to achieve.

SIMON. At the most only for a few moments.

RM. Right, only for the duration of the *now*. But precisely then a slow but sure process begins. Through it, the inner urge to achieve gradually fades. This doesn't happen in a day, but if you regularly arrive at this momentary independence, the gradual decline of your urge to achieve is unstoppable.

7.6 DENNIS

DENNIS. I often have sexual desires. Many women attract me. I fall in love easily. I feel the lust to enter into sexual relations with them. Then I control myself, but feel very frustrated. Often such thoughts linger for a long time and even follow me into my meditation. I don't know how to deal with them because there is always a feeling of frustration and a kind of disappointment. Yet I love my wife and don't want to be unfaithful to her; this feeling of being unsatisfied leaves me bitter.

RM. You are looking for a way out of this situation.

DENNIS. Yes.

RM. You say you are reserved towards other women.

DENNIS. Yes, for fear of the consequences.

RM. You see, Dennis, that's a negative motivation. You act out of fear. You are not the only one who has such thoughts and desires. Learn renunciation from a sense of devotion. Tell yourself, for example, that you want to be faithful to your wife, that your marriage is the real meaning of your life, and that you accept this renunciation consciously and voluntarily for the sake of your marriage and your family. There are many men who live with many women, but have no home and family. They don't know real love. You have a harmonious family. Your wife and your children love you. That's a positive motivation to enable you to accept the renunciation. You will, of course, feel the loss, but without frustration.

DENNIS. And does that have something to do with meditation?

RM. Meditation lifts you to a higher plain. It lifts you from the level of lust and desire to the level of being. When you come to the awareness of the present, lust and sexual desire decline. When you utter the name of Jesus Christ with due reverence, these other feelings quickly quiet down. You'll be led quite naturally from the level of your senses to higher ones, and will experience them as more appropriate. You'll feel more at one with yourself and be more aware of the presence of God.

DENNIS. Doesn't that mean that I'm suppressing my drives and feelings?

RM. It should not be suppression. That's why it's important that you accept your sexual desires as natural and as belonging to you, not as something repulsive. It's important that you don't reject them, but pass on to higher things. In this way they disappear quite naturally.

When, on your walk, you come to a crossroads where three paths beckon, and you choose the one that is right for you, no one can blame you for having bypassed the other two. You simply leave them aside because they are not your paths. In the same way, it isn't suppression when you don't follow your passions, but follow the direction that is more fitting for you.

7.7 MAURICE

MAURICE. Concentrating on the hands is hard work for me. I became very tired and was drenched with perspiration by the end of the meditation. I was incredibly strained.

RM. You feel exhausted and tense.

MAURICE. That may well be, but simply from exhaustion—I don't feel the tension.

RM. Look, Maurice, you make every effort and concentrate on the task with full engagement. We connect concentration with an attitude that's too hard for meditation. It's strenuous and tires one out. I asked you to listen rather than concentrate. Listening relaxes and does not tire. In listening we put out our antennae. We're ready to receive everything that is there, that comes from the present. We need only hear, without effort, without strain. Pure awareness is relaxation which doesn't burden us. We become tired only when we make strenuous, superfluous efforts—for example, if we unconsciously want to attain something. It isn't listening or looking itself that exhausts us, but the effort of the will.

MAURICE. I've concentrated too much.

RM. Yes, pass on to listening. Contemplation does not tire. It is pure awareness. Just as contemplation re-creates us, in the same way every genuine recreation leads to contemplation. Try to discover relaxed attentiveness, and meditation won't exhaust you.

7.8 SONIA

SONIA. I had many thoughts during meditation, and suddenly I became conscious of many things. I'm always criticizing everyone and everything. I constantly find fault with myself and others. Many specific scenes suddenly came to mind in which I reprimand and correct others. I felt sick of myself because I recognized my discontent. I've always projected everything on others, put them in a negative light, instead of recognizing my discontent. Suddenly a sense of hopelessness came over me, and I felt I was blocking the feelings that wanted to come. I felt discouraged and was furious with myself, but couldn't really let them come.

After meditation I went out of doors. I sat down in a meadow and looked at the flowers dancing in the gentle breeze. Their beauty gradually touched me. I was filled with wonder. I had let go of myself and felt in the present. At the same time, trust and hope awoke in me. They became stronger during the Eucharist. Almost without thinking, I experienced a reconciliation with myself, with God and the world.

RM. It happened by itself. You were given an insight. Then you became obsessed with negative feelings, and you were freed from them out of doors. This transition from circling round yourself to wonder at everything that is, was given you spontaneously in the meadow. You can learn from it. When you are locked into circling around yourself, turn to awareness. If awareness becomes stronger than your circling, the negativity can disappear.

7.9 JOSEPH

JOSEPH. In every meditation I sit as if before a closed door. I'm blocked, I do not get further, and the door is shut. I stagnate and remain stuck there.

RM. You want to get further.

JOSEPH. Yes, I have been trying for a long time and it went well at times, but now I'm sitting before a closed door.

RM. The door need not open. Nothing needs to happen.

JOSEPH. That's a contradiction. On the one hand you say that longing for God is necessary, and on the other that I'm to remain frustrated because the door need not open at all?

RM. You don't have to go through the door to encounter God. He is in front of the door. He is there. Don't you mistake longing for God with your wanting to succeed? You want to succeed by going through the door. Everything is in front of the door. Everything is there already.

JOSEPH. Yes, but the longing for God drives me to him.

RM. You want to *reach* God. *Longing for God* is something different. Now and then one can feel it, but it's very quiet and without tension. Most of the time we don't feel the longing for God but recognize it only in its effects. For example, if the meditation is difficult and you can stay with it in spite of that, you know that you are carried by the longing for God. Or when you can keep up the daily meditation after the retreat, it's the longing for God at work. Other people make grand resolutions without keeping them because the longing for God is still weak.

This longing isn't a feeling, and we often have to pass through stretches of time when we don't perceive it. We have to exchange a level where one is supported by feelings with the level of being. This can only happen when our feelings are withdrawn from us and we continue to act with the strength that comes from our longing. The longing doesn't seek results. Expectations, however, are always tied to results.

Once again, you need not go through the door. That's an expectation which comes from your desire to attain something. You want to get the door open. Longing for God gives you the strength to remain before the door, but doesn't urge you to go further. The longing means that God is already there. God is even in the very longing. When you look into the longing you will find everything.

7.10 JOYCE

JOYCE. I fared badly in meditation for a long time. *Badly* isn't the right word. Let's say that it was tough going. But the evening before last, I felt the presence of Jesus very strongly. This continued during the Eucharist in the chapel and when I went to bed, even during meditation in the morning. After breakfast, I suddenly had stomach cramps and the feeling of the presence was gone. But I understood for the first time in my life that God is present, whether I feel him or not. It became clear to me that I had to go through this state. Not feeling anything is part of the way. It's a purification.

RM. What did remain of this presence, in spite of everything, after it had gone?

JOYCE. What remained? I don't understand the question.

RM. You experienced his presence. After that it seemingly disappeared. But you knew with inner clarity that God is present even when you can't feel him. Look into yourself. What has remained there in spite of the absence of feeling? While experiencing the presence were you perhaps somehow so touched by him, that this touch remained, even though the feeling had already passed away?

JOYCE. I'll let this question speak to me. I can't yet answer it.

7.11 CAROLINE

CAROLINE. I'm not doing well in my meditation. I can see that others are much further along. I try hard, but don't get ahead. It's the same when I think of my husband. I have a bad conscience about him because he's so good to me. I think I ought to do much more for him. *[Pause.]* . . . I often laugh at myself and say, "You try to redeem the whole world so that God will be content with you. In the end you still have a bad conscience, because the world isn't wholly redeemed and you should have done more. If you had redeemed the whole world, God would probably still not be satisfied!"

RM. You always reproach yourself.

CAROLINE. I feel like a failure.

RM. It isn't a new feeling.

CAROLINE. No, a very old one. As a child I felt that way before my mother. I have already worked a lot at it, especially during therapy a few years ago. I'm learning to live with it. Without realizing it, my mother always gave me a bad conscience. Nothing was good enough for her. I often had to hear that I was ungrateful and not worthy of her love. I can live with it, but here in meditation it becomes acute again. . . . *[Pause.]* Now that I can say it I feel better again.

RM. Your guilt feelings could become less, and with time disappear altogether.

CAROLINE. Really?

RM. A bad conscience always exists in relation to someone. In this case it has attached itself to me. I asked you to remain with the hands and the name. You've built up a bad conscience towards me because you were afraid of not being able to satisfy my demands—even though I never demanded anything from you in that sense. Not being able to comply brought about self-reproach and guilt feelings that are connected with your mother and finally with God.

You project your guilt feelings on God too. God can't be dissatisfied or he wouldn't be God. But the bad conscience always exists in relation to someone. It always surfaces when your self-image is derived from someone else.

CAROLINE. I can't live without relationships, of course.

RM. You don't need to. But your understanding of yourself doesn't have to be dependent on others. When you direct your vision towards yourself, you can find a sense of yourself in your own inner self. Deeper still than this sense of yourself, you can perceive your existence in the center of your own being. It is there you feel that you are. You experience that it is good as it is. There are no longer any guilt feelings. So turn within, to the root of your being. There you don't depend on anybody; there you rest in yourself. When afterwards you go among people again, your self-image will be independent of them, and you can enter into healthy relationships.

God isn't a person who demands something of you from outside. God is the center of your being. He is deeper in you than anything you know of yourself. That is why Christ says the Kingdom of God is within us. Come where no guilt feelings exist, only love always overflowing, and peace eternally resting in itself.

CAROLINE. How can I do that?

RM. You can't bring it about. You can be on your way. That's all that matters. You are being led, and at the right time everything will be given to you. We can't reach this state by our own efforts; otherwise you'd get new guilt feelings because you haven't reached it. Whoever is on the way is in the right place, no matter whether someone is at the beginning, in the middle, or at the end of the way.

CAROLINE. And what is the way?

RM. The way is the same as at the beginning: listen into your hands and come to the name. Remain in the awareness of your being and you will be led to what is essential.

7.12 VERENA

VERENA. I'm getting on well. I like to meditate and am able to stay with it for long periods. I'm experiencing a lot of quiet and have the sense of being at home. I quickly get into a kind of absorption. I can't say where I am in such a state . . . *[pause]* . . . I don't know. I don't experience my body then. When I come to the end of the meditation I'm in a restful state. These times are beneficial to me.

RM. You're content.

VERENA. Yes, content.

RM. You are fully alert and in the present the whole time.

VERENA. I don't think so. . . . I don't know what happens at these times, but I don't think I'm in a wakeful state. I'm in a peaceful state, and peaceful is also the effect this time leaves behind, but I can't call it wide awake.

RM. Verena, on this way we remain clear and present to ourselves in every state. Concrete contact with reality always remains. A kind of vague state or absorption has to be avoided in every case. We remain wide awake in the present and with our feet on the ground of reality. God is reality itself, God is pure consciousness.

Don't get yourself into this unconscious state. We're going the concrete way of awareness. As long as you are in awareness, especially in the awareness of your hands, and as long as your attention is directed to your breathing and the name, you'll remain in contact with reality. It can be given to you to have no thoughts or not to feel your body, but you must always remain wide awake. Otherwise meditation easily leads to the occult and paranormal, about which I need to warn you.

VERENA. Thank you. That's an important correction.

7.13 KURT

KURT. For a long time I was impatient and discontented in meditation. I didn't know why. It was a creeping but permanent dissatisfaction. I clearly felt it and looked at it, but didn't know how to let go of it. I hadn't looked through to what lay beyond it. Yesterday I suddenly realized that I always want something from God. I want him to give me something—consolation, hope, or clarity about my faults, change of character, removal of my faults like my impatience, my anger, my sadness, or that God give me the feeling of advancing. . . . I understand that through these wishes I stand before God wholly egocentric. I have recognized that I half-consciously seek a relationship with Christ only in order to get something from him.

So it dawned on me how I fall into the same pattern in other situations in my life. The problems with my wife have a lot to do with the fact that I always want something from her. I expect attention from her. Yes, I want love and tenderness. On my side, there's sometimes little to be seen of love and surrender. In my work it's the same. Well, this attitude won't be the whole answer, but yesterday it became clear to me how I always want something from others and how selfish I am. I became conscious of all this through my egocentric attitude toward God. I'm shaken to discover how I circle around myself. Even when I give the impression of being with God and others for their sakes, too often I'm only with them for my own sake.

RM. An important insight.

KURT. Yes, I was really stunned. These weren't isolated insights; it seems to me that I've become aware of the root of all this self-centeredness. This has shaken me.

RM. Hm. *[Pause.]*

KURT. And what do I do with it now?

RM. Nothing.

KURT. How "nothing"?

RM. It's important that you learn not to do anything with it.

KURT. Things are to remain as they are?

RM. Exactly. Everything is to remain as it is. Try to live with this insight and endure it. If you've really seen the root of your actions you can't fundamentally change it. You could at most acquire some new ways of acting, but that wouldn't amount to much. The root remains. It lies much deeper. But deeper still than this root, there lies in you an unbelievably selfless love and a tremendous power. Allow this very deep ground in you to become effective. It will dissolve your egotism, as the sun dissolves the early mists.

KURT. And how do I do that?

RM. By allowing your egotism to continue to be there, enduring it, and while doing so, directing your attention to the present and your deeper center. Everything else will follow by itself.

When you remain in the present you will go still deeper into yourself, there where no egocentricity exists.

KURT. Is that the way?

RM. Yes, that's the way.

7.14 GEOFFREY

GEOFFREY. I was recollected, and suddenly a scene with my mother came to my mind. It was a quarrel with her that took place ten years ago and which I believed I had worked through long ago. I felt a great rage against her, and was so possessed by it that I couldn't get into my hands at all. These strong emotions have frightened me.

RM. You wouldn't have thought it possible.

GEOFFREY. No, I wouldn't have thought it possible of myself. I was panic-stricken at the thought of whatever else might come up and overwhelm me. I felt the rage seated deep within my very being.

RM. Panic and rage in your very being.

GEOFFREY. At first I couldn't look at my rage. After a while it was possible. I could admit to myself that I was feeling rage and panic, and allow these emotions to be there. Then I tried to get back into my hands. I asked myself what I was aware of in them, but I couldn't get into awareness.

RM. You went on trying.

GEOFFREY. I knew that the rage was still so great that it could completely keep me from being aware of my hands. I've accepted the rage and the fear with love—well, let's say, with resignation—and endeavored with patience and endurance to return to awareness in spite of lack of success.

RM. You just stuck with it

GEOFFREY. That was yesterday afternoon. I was prepared for anything in the next meditation. But this morning I experienced instead a kind of recollection I haven't known before. I was simply in the present until midday, and wide awake the whole morning. I could leave the chapel, begin anew with meditation, and the intense experience of the present was there again. I had nearly no thoughts. Or better, I believe I was for a good while without any thoughts, but I don't want to fool myself. I haven't had the chance to make sure of it. I was certainly wide awake in the present as never before. My sacrum and lumbar regions became quite hot. I could never have imagined such an intense clarity as entered my consciousness. My heart grew vast and wide, and I felt a warm, pulsating love for everybody.

RM. In this love Jesus Christ was present.

GEOFFREY. Undoubtedly.

7.15 PAUL

PAUL. It's tough. I follow the directions and try to do everything right, but it doesn't flow. I often have the impression that something drags and blocks me. Yesterday I went for a walk and sat on a tree trunk not far from the path. After a while I noticed how dry and dead it was. I became sad and said to myself, "Yes, I am as dead as that."

RM. Then you wept.

PAUL. I would have liked to weep, but I can't weep . . . *[pause]* . . . I haven't wept for years . . . *[pause]* . . . I did not even cry at my mother's funeral.

RM. You can't weep. *[Pause.]*

PAUL. When I was a child I was sometimes told, "Don't cry."

RM. You weren't allowed to express your pain.

PAUL. No, even when the lump was already in my throat I had to swallow it.

RM. *[Pause.]*

PAUL. I didn't want to burden others with my pain.

RM. Pain and sadness thus remained and were not allowed to show. *[Pause.]*

PAUL. Most likely.

RM. Now they are returning and want to show themselves. *[Pause of more than ten minutes.]*

PAUL. *[Tears are slowly falling. Then he begins to sob. After a quarter of an hour the weeping stops, still followed by a time of silence.]*

7.16 JASON

JASON. When I look back on the last retreat days, I can be content. Several feelings arose. Sadness about a friendship which broke up last year, tensions with my mother, and a certain conflict with my boss. A few things concerning my future also became clearer to me—it's constantly working in me. This also expressed itself in body pains. For a time I felt some pressure on my chest, as if a big stone was weighing on it.

RM. A lot is happening.

JASON. Yes, things are beginning to move.

RM. You're glad about it.

JASON. Yes, I'm glad about it and I wish that more will start moving so that more will be purified and redeemed.

RM. Well, Jason, I'm afraid you're too occupied with yourself and your progress. Your attention isn't centered on God but on your purification. Change your perspective. Instead of looking at what is happening in you, direct your attention to God himself. Let go of your desire for progress. This desire focuses your attention only on changes in your feelings and inner emotions.

The way to go is to attend to the essential and therefore to the present. Focus your attention solely on God. We're transformed through uninterrupted attention to the risen Christ, who penetrates everything and who holds everything within himself. Leave all your cares with him. God alone suffices.

7.17 LENA

LENA. It was strange. I was meditating and present as always. Thoughts came and went, but I could always come back. Slowly I began to notice an urge to move away. I wanted to get up and go, no matter where—just away. I wanted to creep under a blanket and pull it over my head. I felt the urge to escape from the situation, in whatever manner—only away from myself.

RM. You wanted to flee.

LENA. Yes, I felt the urge to flee. This feeling came over me with great force, and I wanted to run away in a panic. But I didn't do it. I told myself, "Now more than ever you remain here and look at what is happening." I looked at the feeling of panic. For a time it got still stronger so that I felt I couldn't endure it. I was already secretly regretting that I had resolved to remain. Suddenly I became aware of a parallel in my daily life. When something unpleasant rises up in me, I always experience this panic which pushes me to take flight. At first I was tormented by flight, from my workplace, then from my circle of friends and from groups. Afterwards elemental images from my childhood came up. I was amazed at how often I've already run away. Whenever something didn't suit me, I fled. At first it only meant a flight from the actual situation, but then also a flight into eating, sleeping, music or activity. I believe this is part of my fundamental mechanism.

RM. You were surprised at this discovery.

LENA. Yes. As the images from my past surfaced, I didn't feel the need to take flight any more. I could even sit there quietly. These insights were partly embarrassing, partly pleasant.

RM. You have looked more deeply into yourself

LENA. Yes, and it was a new experience for me that I could just let it be. I didn't have to make resolutions, I didn't feel like changing anything. The insight itself was sufficient.

RM. As we come nearer to contemplation, we begin to understand that one can just be, without having to change oneself. The effort to change still belongs to the ascetic stage.

In that pre-contemplative phase we don't yet have sufficient composure or enough trust in the power of grace. In the contemplative phase it becomes possible to entrust oneself to the center, to the presence of God, and to let everything be given to us. We simply move into the depth; from there flow the light and the strength which change us. In the Gospel, Jesus Christ says, "the Kingdom of God is within you." St. Paul says, "the Spirit of God dwells within you." If we're concerned about God, he will be concerned about us.

As we unite ourselves with our center, with the presence of God within us, we become transformed by him into his Son. We're taken into his eternal love. After that, our external activities flow without accompanying anxieties. Life becomes clearer and more simple. Our activities become more dynamic and more effective because more and more God works through us instead of our having to achieve things on our own. We become instruments in his hands. Instruments have no anxieties, no problems. Then power flows from our center. God works through us.

7.18 JOAN

JOAN. I got angry at the way you sing here during the retreat. I can't stand this slow singing and this style. I like to make music and to sing, and I believe that I have a feel for it. My sense of music is offended when I hear how you sing here.

RM. You suffer under it.

JOAN. It isn't merely suffering. I feel indignant. I can't stand it.

RM. Come back from the music to yourself and look at your indignation and annoyance. Leave the exterior, what the music is like, and look into your indignation. Look at the feeling. When you have looked at it for a while return to awareness.

JOAN. *[A day later.]* I did what you suggested.

RM. And how is it now?

JOAN. The indignation is gone. But something isn't quite right. Nothing happened. The singing continues as before. Nothing has changed.

RM. Nothing has changed in the singing. That's true. But something has happened to you.

JOAN. Yes, so it has. . . . Yes, something has happened to me. *[Pause.]* I didn't think it was important, but, . . . yes, something has happened. . . . So it is . . . I'm no longer indignant.

RM. That's very important. If we weren't on retreat you could now, after having faced your indignation, do something constructive to improve the quality of the singing. Your reaction to it would then no longer arise out of disapproval but out of love and inner calm.

We're always looking for changes from without. Through meditation something changes within us. Something in us is healed. As a consequence, we're able to respond to the exterior situation with more love.

7.19 STEPHEN

STEPHEN. I was firmly convinced that I meditate without ulterior motive, but I felt your request to give the time to God without expectations or plans to be something new and surprising. I did give the time expressly to God and continue to do so conscientiously. After each meditation I consistently check if I'm satisfied. I was shocked to discover that I don't sit there without any ulterior motive, but that I always want to reach something. I can renew my intention to give the time to God, but not yet without a motive. At the end I experience a certain amount of dissatisfaction if my meditation didn't quite go as I had anticipated it.

RM. You experience yourself as dissatisfied.

STEPHEN. Exactly. I have the desire to come closer to God. When this desire isn't fulfilled I become discontented.

RM. The longing for God makes you discontented.

STEPHEN. Somehow this is a contradiction, but it seems to be like that.

RM. The root of the desire is the longing for God. This is most precious and a precondition for the way, its inner strength, and the energy that drives you forward. It is important not to want to translate this longing into concrete ideas, but simply and exclusively to focus on the longing. When you listen to that longing and stay with it, it becomes stronger, more present, more all-embracing. It leads directly to the presence of God. You can pay attention to this without any other motive. The longing and the presence are there without concrete ideas or expectations as to how they are to be realized. How the way continues and what is going to come of it we leave to God. We rest in this contact with him and that is sufficient. That is surrender, service, adoration. It is longing and fulfillment in one.

IV. REVIEW & TRANSITION TO THE EIGHTH DAY

Dear Retreatant, we are coming to the end of the Seventh Day. We have completed the individual steps of the introduction to contemplation. From now on I'll give you no new instructions. Remain, if possible, always with the name of Jesus Christ. I hope you have already experienced a little of the power of this name. If not, be patient and continue with the meditation. It's worthwhile. He is our Savior and Redeemer. Even though you may not have much hope based on your own strength, trust in him. He himself will lead you further.

As a review you could ask yourself whether you gave the time agreed on to meditation and kept to the framework conditions of stillness, nature, and recollection.

In the Introductory Talk of the Eighth Day we shall speak of forgiveness. It's a very important topic. Open yourself to it as far as possible.

I wish you a time full of blessings.

EIGHTH DAY

I. INTRODUCTORY TALK:
FORGIVENESS

1. A memory

As I write this, the specter of Communism has disappeared from
Europe. It wasn't always so. I've already spoken of the war and the
post-war years. There is still something more from that time that I
want to share. My father owned land, and we lived in a beautiful
large home. He had been an officer for the whole of the First
World War, and in the Second World War he was again in uniform. My brother George was, like me, attending the military
academy. My mother was at home with my five sisters and two
little brothers. The Russians were approaching. My parents didn't
want my sisters to fall into the hands of Russian soldiers and decided to flee to the West. In our village, Gyal, a suburb of Budapest, there was bitter fighting and equivalent destruction. Our
house was severely damaged by weeks of artillery fire. It took a
whole year after the war had ended before we were able to return.

The first to return was my brother George. The devastation was
indescribable. Our land had been declared state property by the
Communists. Only a small section was left to us. Whatever had not
been destroyed by the war had been stolen. The farm machinery

and equipment had disappeared. No furniture, no windows, no roof tiles—only debris remained. My brother counted sixty doorframes; the doors belonging to them were gone. Later we recognized much of our property in the neighborhood. The house had lain deserted for months, and many people thought we would never return.

When we returned from the West in March, 1946, my father was arrested at the border as a former officer and landowner. He was later declared innocent by the court but not released. He was dragged to the dreaded Secret Police headquarters in Budapest at 60 Andrássy St. and poisoned. He died shortly afterwards.

After we had crossed the border I accompanied my grandmother, who had been with us in the West, to an aunt's home. I was therefore not present when my mother, together with my now eight brothers and sisters, entered the house. The basement was covered knee-deep in rubble, but it was the only part of the house in which they could settle. All the other sections were completely uninhabitable. They arrived with their miserable possessions of clothes, mattresses, and other things which they had been able to save through their year as refugees. My paternal grandmother, who, together with my brother, had been living in the basement for a number of months already, had prepared supper. The joy of reunion was great, but the sight of our home was depressing. They had a look around, ate supper, and laid out the mattresses for the night. When they were ready, my mother called them all together. The whole family knelt on the mattresses and said evening prayers. My mother had them pray for all who had suffered or who had caused damage in the house and in the surrounding neighborhood. That was her first reaction to the devastation. As she said later, she didn't want to allow hatred or resentment to take hold of my brothers' and sisters' hearts. It was also she who later taught us to forgive. I don't remember ever having been aware of feelings of hatred or revenge in our family. I myself was more susceptible to anger and resentment. God sent me this experience that I might learn forgiveness. My parents' example had a deep influence on me. I came to know reconciliation.

2. *The necessity for forgiveness*

The greatest obstacle on the way to God is the inability to forgive. Each of us knows people who, years ago, were deeply offended, slandered, or unjustly treated, and who were never able to recover from these wounds. They have suffered a great deal from these hurts. They recount the events over and over again with fear, pain, and despair—with reproaches, hatred, or self-pity. Often they become either bitter and hostile or depressive and lethargic. If their wounds appear, for a time, to be healing over, it isn't really so. Underneath the scab, the wound continues to fester. These chronic wounds cannot heal because they have not been suffered through with acceptance and love. Not that everything which has been suffered through has been redeemed: Only that which has been suffered through with love and forgiveness can be healed.

How many people harbor unhealed injuries in their souls! If we're not ready to forgive, at least intentionally, we can go to church as often as we like, recite prayers, read pious books, give generous alms, go on retreats or days of recollection—all for nothing. The whole of life comes to a standstill, like water trapped behind a dam. Yes, a spirit opposed to reconciliation is like a dam which rises up against the natural flow of love with a million tons of reinforced concrete!

That is why we have to learn to forgive. It's impossible to go through life without being hurt or suffering injustice. But we have to learn to live with these realities without damming up the flow of love.

3. The teaching of Jesus Christ

Anyone who doesn't forgive a neighbor nurtures resentment towards God, who created the neighbors and placed them close to himself. We can't separate our relationship with people from that with God. We can *say* it with the Our Father: Forgive us our trespasses *as we forgive those who trespass against us.* Jesus illustrated this petition of the Our Father with a long and dramatic parable (Mt 18:21-35), which I'll try to adapt for you here:

A king wanted to collect outstanding debts from his debtors. One of them owed him 10,000 talents. He must have been the Minister of Finance because this was an unimaginably big sum of money. (Herod's annual income was around 900 talents, so this Minister owed the king more than eleven years' worth of Herod's income!) Since the man was unable to pay, the king wanted to have him sent to prison. The Minister of Finance threw himself at his feet and pleaded, "Have patience with me, I'll pay back everything." This was quite ridiculous because he would never be able to pay it all back. The king realized that the man was shattered and felt sorry for him. He refrained from sending him to prison, let him go free, and in his goodness canceled the entire debt.

The Minister of Finance gratefully took his leave. But he'd hardly walked down the stairs of the palace when he met an official who owed him 100 denarii, a petty debt compared to his own. (It's about as much as an unskilled laborer would have received for a hundred days' work.) But the Minister of Finance turned on him, demanding the payment of his debt. The previous scene repeated itself, this time with roles reversed. The official fell at the feet of the pardoned Minister of Finance and begged him, "Have patience with me; I'll pay back everything." But the Minister refused and had him arrested. The courtiers who were standing around, or who had just come with the Minister from his audience with the king, witnessed his hard-heartedness in great consternation. They went to the king and told him what had happened. The king was furious. He sent for the Minister of Finance and thundered at him, "You scum! I canceled that whole debt of yours because you begged me. Shouldn't you have had pity on this poor fellow, just as I had pity on you?" He called for his Secret Police, who wouldn't stop at torture, and had him taken away.

Jesus concluded the parable with the clear message that his father will deal likewise with all those who don't forgive their sisters and brothers from the heart.

There is an enormous contradiction in the fact that we constantly ask God to forgive us our sins but are not prepared to forgive our fellow humans. How can we hope to receive forgiveness if we ourselves don't forgive our neighbor?

4. From the heart

Jesus asks expressly that we forgive from our heart. That isn't easy. If, for example, someone has deprived me of a large portion of my inheritance, I certainly feel angry with him. I can tell myself a hundred times that I forgive him. My resentment, however, will continue, especially if my inheritance remains in his hands. Forgiveness from the heart has taken place only when resentment, hatred, and pain have been transformed into reconciled love for the

defrauder. That doesn't happen by itself. We have to learn, therefore, how to forgive from the heart.

The first step is to forgive intentionally—to say, "I forgive this
person." The intention to forgive isn't to be undervalued. For many
people it is impossible to utter this little sentence. They can't bring
themselves to forgive. The intention to forgive lies within our freedom, no matter whether resentment remains or not.

As a second step we admit our resentment and face it, "I have forgiven, but there is still resentment in me. I continue to feel it. It's
there, but I can let it be."

We should never try to change our feelings. Every direct influence
on our feelings suppresses them. But we can, without harming our
psyche, change our actions. For example, when I notice that in my
rage and anger I fantasize about killing the person who has hurt
me, I can tell myself that I'm not going to kill that person. I may
well admit to myself that I would like to kill that person. The feelings that arise in me are allowed to do so and just to be. On the
other hand, I'm free to choose my actions. So, I don't have to kill
the other. It's the same with forgiveness. I can genuinely have the
intention to forgive and yet calmly face the fact that my resentment
towards the guilty person is still there.

Then comes the decisive step. We know it already from our efforts
so far. If I can look at my unreconciled feeling and let it be, I can
turn unhesitatingly to the present. The feeling can remain, but I'm
no longer preoccupied with it. I turn my attention to the healing
power. Resentment, anger, bitterness, self-pity, and resignation are
not healed by permanent preoccupation with these feelings. I must
get in contact with my center, God. Reconciliation comes from
there.

Depending on the extent of the hurt received, the resentment needs
to be cleared away bit by bit, layer by layer. The remainder will
burden us less and less, will become hardly noticeable and finally
completely disappear. Then we have in truth forgiven from the
heart.

5. Hurts from our parents

Our deepest hurts originate from our childhood and are connected
with our parents. A lack of love in earliest childhood; authority

conflicts; parental absence through work, divorce, or death—these leave deep wounds which we can't easily process, work through, or even forgive. However, reconciliation is possible and is vitally important.

Reconciliation with our parents depends on us. Our hurts don't lie in them but in us. It may sound harsh, but it isn't our parents who should change in the first place. The problem lies in us, in our hearts.

The greatest pain isn't the hurt which is engraved in us. The most bitter pain is that we can't love the one who has hurt us. This is a deep spiritual torment.

One often hears youth or young adults declare, out of resentment toward their parents, that they have learned their lessons from their childhood and won't make the same mistakes with their own children. It's a common experience that these very people do repeat the mistakes of their parents. As long as one has not forgiven one's parents, the same patterns of action will recur, whether one wants it or not.

We project the problems encountered with our parents on all other people. Only when we have cleared up our conflicts with our parents will we be free human agents with regard to others. Anyone who's been allowed to look deeply into God's loving providence knows that everyone of us has received from God the parents we need in order to advance on the way to God.

I'm convinced that we should not solve our problems in meditation, but look on God. From him come strength and grace. In addition, the stillness brings up everything that has not yet been reconciled, suffered through, and redeemed. However, I believe that there is an exception with regard to our parents. Even people who are otherwise well able to solve their problems in life find, when it comes to their relationship with their parents, that large unresolved chunks of resentment get stuck in them. Such people usually cover up these deep-seated hurts by a certain indifference, inexplicable callousness, lack of memories from early childhood, or by a mysterious resistance in dealings with parents or others. These conflicts that have not been cleared up block our way to God. Stillness could make them surface. If, however, these feelings are covered by a massive concrete slab of suppression, one can fool oneself and not let them reach one's consciousness. That's why I sometimes ask retreatants to allow their parents to come close to them. I recommend, for example, that they imagine father or mother meditating next to them, or allow memories from early childhood to surface, so that the suppressed feelings toward their parents can manifest themselves.

The way to deal with these deeper problems is the same as before: renew the willingness to suffer, allow the feelings to surface without being preoccupied with them, and return to the present. It is important not to escape to the mental level and begin to brood, but—while being in contact with the present—to suffer and to redeem the feelings that arise. I have personal experience of how much healing has taken place in this way. I recommend this exercise only to retreatants who have been meditating on a daily basis for some two or more years. It isn't easy to remain in the present when faced with these seething feelings. I also recommend putting a photo of one's parents on the bedside table every now and then, as a sign that they are always welcome there. It isn't for nothing that we're told in the Ten Commandments to honor our parents.

With deeply religious people, we find painful hurts caused by the Church. Many serious, engaged Christians have been deeply wounded by representatives of the Church. The abuse of ecclesial authority creates many wounds, and that is regrettable. In such a case, too, forgiveness has to be learned. It's also essential to forgiveness that we forgive ourselves. To forgive others, God, and oneself are parallel paths. Every act of forgiving, therefore, is also an act of forgiving oneself.

Everything that happens—and also the way it happens—takes place in order that we may be led to the Father on the straightest road possible.

6. Another memory

In Part V of this book I recounted my abduction in Argentina in 1976. I would like to add a further experience. During the months of my abduction, I underwent a profound purification of which I only became aware after almost two years. I also experienced a sequel which has to do with forgiveness.

Although denounced as terrorists at that time, my fellow Jesuit and I have been shown to be completely innocent of those charges. We

knew that a certain person had spread the rumor about us and, because of his authority, had made the accusation credible in wide
circles. According to later testimony by witnesses, this person had
denounced us—in front of the officers who kidnapped us—as
having been active in terrorism. Only shortly before the abduction,
I had said to this man that he was playing with our lives. He must
have been aware that his denunciation would mean our certain
death. I don't need to say more; I often thought that our story was
so incredible that I would not have believed it myself if somebody
had told it to me.

My feelings of helplessness, rage, and resentment towards this person and his clique during our captivity might easily be imagined.
But I prayed the whole time for him and his accomplices. Many
things cleared up during those months, but the rage itself only partially dissolved. Day after day I prayed for these men and asked
God that my way of the cross might be for their good. I did this
resolutely and with the intention to forgive them, even though my
feelings were completely opposite.

After my release, I went to North America. For two years I tried to
make the facts public in order to be rehabilitated, for our cause and
reputations to be restored. I had more than thirty documents in my
possession which proved in black and white the human rights of-
fences that had been committed against us.

Nothing doing. All doors remained closed.

After one and a half years, I abandoned my intention to return to
Argentina and went to Germany. From that moment on, I asked all
who were working on this matter not to continue to engage themselves in clearing up of the injustices. I no longer needed it. Rage
and helplessness had lessened and only returned sporadically. My
dealing with these feelings remained the same. I faced them again
and again and prayed to God for the guilty persons. Distance—and
the fact that I no longer needed rehabilitation in the public
eye—also helped. It was nonetheless very painful that in spite of
distance, lies, calumnies, and unjust actions against me did not
cease.

Four years after my abduction, my Order asked me to lead the
so-called Tertianship for a group of young Jesuits. Tertianship is
the last phase of the young priests' spiritual formation. By way of
preparation, I made a thirty-day retreat. On the last day, during a

walk in the forest, I asked myself what corrections or changes I was due to make in my life. I was suddenly struck by the realization that I had forgiven my persecutors, yet I was still carefully guarding the evidence against them in a closet. Apparently, the thought of being able to use these documents against them one day was still in the back of my mind. I went home and burned them. This was an important step.

During those times I often thought of St. John of the Cross, whom I generally held in high esteem. He had been kept imprisoned for months by his brothers. I also knew that Jesus Christ had never been rehabilitated in his day. His apostles and the faithful recognized the truth, but for the general public, he remained a criminal executed for his misdeeds. Eight years after my abduction I had to go to Rome to take part in a three-day conference of directors of our Tertianship courses for Europe. During a break, the Superior General of our Jesuit Order asked me if everything was now in order. Asked in this way, I took it that he was personally interested in me. I told him everything—or nearly everything—and stressed my desire that he should not do anything more to repair injustice. I had my work, was contented, and free of the need for any clarification of those former events.

During this conversation, a very deep pain, probably worse than I had ever experienced before, rose up in me for the last time. It was no longer anger, but pain. I could not hold back my tears in front of my Superior General. From then on, I feel truly free and can say that I have "forgiven from my heart." Since then, I no longer feel resentment, anger, or pain regarding those events. On the contrary, I feel only gratitude for this experience that is part of my life. That process of purification lasted fully eight years. At the end, even the last remnants of resentment were taken away. Perhaps this can serve as encouragement for those who have been through similar experiences and who find it hard to forgive.

II. INSTRUCTIONS FOR MEDITATION

We have only three more days. This is the moment when retreatants direct their eyes toward the future. Return to normal life approaches, and the cares and interests of the coming weeks make themselves felt. Unnoticed, the impression creeps in that the retreat is almost over and that it's appropriate to slacken the usual regimen a little. I'd like to advise you not to fall into this trap. If you have followed the retreat conscientiously, you have been led into greater depths, whether you feel it or not. It would be a pity to leave this depth before the time is over. You would be like a mountaineer who, because he is more or less at the top, turns back a hundred yards below the peak of the mountain.

You may even be feeling an aversion to the retreat. That is a sign that something has begun to move. It would be worthwhile to stay with your purpose.

Apart from this, I hope that you meditate at least six hours a day, keep the silence faithfully, don't read or converse, spend much time with nature, and are enjoying yourselves.

III. DIALOGUES

8.1 EMIL

EMIL. I woke up this morning with a huge lack of enthusiasm. I know this from normal life. Usually I then throw myself into work and no longer feel it. The price I pay, I expect, is my restlessness. I have to remain active and occupied; otherwise this lack of enthusiasm returns. Today, instead of work, I threw myself into meditation. I got going with full energy in order not to feel any lack of enthusiasm or perhaps even my loneliness. I pushed myself into it and concentrated with great effort and total will-power until I was exhausted. Until now I had not been aware of the connection between my lack of enthusiasm and my activism.

RM. Now it's dawned on you.

EMIL. Exactly. I realized that the reason for my powerlessness lies in the will-power with which I try to cover up my listlessness and loneliness. I feel like a youngster who tries to drown his loneliness in loud, throbbing music. I tried that with constant activity and now, in the retreat, with tense and dogged concentration.

RM. You discovered your defense mechanism.

EMIL. At first I got scared. Then I remembered what you said about how to deal with feelings. I could look into myself and say, "Well now, I'm just listless. It's unpleasant, but that's how it is. I feel lonely and that's all right." I could stay in my feeling of listlessness. It was a strange experience. For the first time I felt at a distance from the feeling. It was there and I was there, too. I felt that I was there, but that I wasn't identified with my listlessness. For the first time it was no longer threatening. I could let it stand. It was a liberating experience. Afterwards I could meditate much more freely and in a relaxed manner.

8.2 MATT

MATT. During my meditation I'm always made aware of my relationship with my wife. I try to stay in the present, but my relationship with her constantly comes to my mind and gives me no peace.

RM. The relationship burdens you.

MATT. Yes. I feel it hanging over me like the Sword of Damocles. What depresses me most is that she no longer expects anything from me, as if she had somehow already given up. Her only expectation seems to be that I look after the children at certain times so that she can be with her friends more often. I do that regularly and willingly. Our interactions, however, are totally lifeless. I wanted to take a new job and to make the decision together with her, but it was impossible. She doesn't want to speak about it.

RM. Would this new job have cost you more time?

MATT. Not more time, perhaps, but more energy.

RM. She was afraid that you would have even less time and energy for her and the children.

MATT. Yes, but she didn't want to talk about it.

RM. You had hoped that she would agree to the new job and be ready to accept the consequences together with you. She probably felt threatened and doesn't want to talk about it because she had no hope that you would be aware of how frightened and threatened she feels.

MATT. Possible; yes, we have drifted quite far apart recently. . . . *[A long pause follows.]* Communication between us is more or less non-existent.

RM. You can dare a new beginning.

MATT. How?

RM. Turn your attention to your wife. You can show by little gestures that you are aware of her presence in your life. Just to give an example: does she like it when you bring her flowers?

MATT *[short pause].* Yes, she does.

RM. The flowers themselves are not very important; what is important is that she realizes that you're attentive to her. Make a conscious effort to let her be at the center of your life. For example, never leave the house without being there for her for at least two minutes, giving her attention, and saying a warm goodbye. As you arrive home, devote your attention first of all to her until you sense how she's feeling. Be sensitive as to whether she has something to say to you, whether something is depressing her, or whether she wants to communicate something. At other times, too, give her your time and attention generously. Be with her for awhile, without any other motive.

MATT. She doesn't tell me what's weighing on her.

RM. Couldn't that be your fault?

MATT. Should it be my fault that she doesn't share with me?

RM. We all want to express ourselves. If she gets the feeling that she isn't being listened to or accepted, she'll close up. She may have given up expecting you to pay attention to her and to accept her as she is. She probably thinks that you don't understand her.

MATT. Yes, she says so. *[Pause.]* I talk a lot about my work. I have business problems and talk a lot about them.

RM. You see, that's how she finds no space for herself. Create in you a space for her so that she can express herself. Keep quiet when you're with her so that, slowly, something can come from her. In this quiet, you must turn your attention to her—not to her problems, but to her.

MATT. This last part I don't understand. How shall I place her and not her problems in the center?

RM. Let's imagine she wants to tell you something about the children, her relatives, or her friends. Don't pay attention to the problem, but stay with her. Let her be the center of attention and focus on how she experiences her feelings and problems with the person concerned. Don't get involved in her difficulties, but focus your attention exclusively on her. Accept her. Stay with her. Don't condemn her, don't even judge what she says. Let her be as she is. Try not to convince her of something or to change her. Don't try to help her. The desire to help produces a pressure that would no longer allow you to be free in your interaction with her. Should she criticize you, don't defend or justify yourself. Give her your full attention and love, freely, without any other intention than to be with her.

MATT. That's new to me.

RM. It's the same as with meditation. Let me explain this parallel to you a little more clearly. As in meditation you don't occupy yourself with your problems, but focus your attention on the hands or the presence of God, so you turn your attention to your wife and stay with her. Don't distract yourself with her thoughts and problems, but remain with her as a person. As in your relation to God, you need not change or achieve anything, but can simply be there without any other motive, so it is the same towards your wife. Just let her be there, and you too just be there without any other aim. This will only succeed if you let go of your work problems. Just as in meditation, remain empty so that she can find a way to you and room for herself. Your sensitive attention will give her new life and new joy. Whether in meditation or with her, remain there without any other aim and without having to achieve anything for God or for her.

MATT. Does this analogy mean that I don't make room for God in meditation, that I only want something from him and judge him, but don't look at myself? Am I also so full of myself during my meditation?

RM. Hmm. . . .

MATT. You spoke of faults that are given to us so that we can learn from them. Well, then, I want to learn from my faults.

8.3 DOREEN

DOREEN. During the last two meditations I was constantly preoccupied with something. I have a rash on my forehead and on my nose; I can't take it very well that people notice it and stare at it. They often ask about it because it's really very noticeable. I would like to hide myself. I'm constantly thinking of what others might think about it. Today I looked into the mirror and realized to my horror that the rash had become worse. I do visit the dermatologist regularly, but it's uncertain whether he can help me. This sickness gives me no peace. It is constantly coming up in my meditation.

RM. You are ashamed because of this rash. You fear people will make fun of you.

DOREEN. Yes, laugh at me . . . not in my face, of course, but behind my back. I suspect that they smile and talk about whether this sickness isn't psychological. Because of my job I'm often out in public and experience this rash as a threat.

RM. A constant threat.

DOREEN. I feel inhibited.

RM. Look, Doreen, you have this rash. It's a health problem. It isn't your fault. If, as you suspect, there is a deeper psychological reason for your rash, it doesn't depend on your good will or bad will for it to heal. It has been given you just like your good qualities.

DOREEN. Yes.

RM. Look into yourself. Listen there whether you can stick with your rash and so with yourself.

DOREEN. Yes, now I'm beginning to realize. . . . I myself can't accept the rash. *[After a few minutes in silence, she weeps. After that, again a longer pause.]* . . . Yes, thank you very much. I'm calmer now.

8.4 ROBERT

ROBERT. I try to remain present. At the beginning of the meditation I'm awake all right. Then I fall into a land of vagueness. I feel dazed. That passes over into dozing, and at the end of the meditation I don't know anymore whether I was conscious or not.

RM. You feel you're in a foggy state.

ROBERT. Yes, and it was that way also this morning during my meditation. At the beginning I was fully present. Slowly, that changed. I can't describe it very well. I began to doze off, and then I fell asleep.

RM. Only when you woke up did you notice that you had gone off.

ROBERT. Exactly. Something similar happens to me when I'm studying. I read and read and follow the text, and I understand it. But afterwards it's all gone, and I don't remember what I've read. I think it is a weakness of my memory.

RM. Weakness of memory.

ROBERT. Yes, and I'm afraid that this will make it impossible for me to complete my studies.

RM. Look, Robert. In your case, it isn't weakness of memory, but passivity. If you read only passively, it isn't surprising that you can't retain anything. Real study implies being active. One has to summarize what one has read, repeat it, speak about it with others, and, if possible, present the material to someone else. Then you actively take in what you read, and won't have any problem with concentration. The same applies to meditation. If you're only passively awake, you become dull, befuddled, and dreamy. That isn't contemplation. Contemplation is active looking and listening. The contemplative attitude is an alert attentiveness with a lively interest, "What do I discover here? What is happening? What comes through to me from reality?" It isn't wanting to reach something, but active eagerness. It isn't wanting to know something, but a lively interest in what is true, in what is essential—in reality. When you talk to your girlfriend you don't fall asleep, do you?

8.5 FELIX

FELIX. I meditate a lot and do so consistently, but I get tired very quickly during meditation. I find it strenuous.

RM. It tires you.

FELIX. Yes. After the meditation I'm worn out. I feel oppressed and feel a dreadful weight on my chest. I have to protect myself against it, draw the line.

RM. You have to become defensive.

FELIX. Yes. I feel pressured by the demands.

RM. By the demands.

FELIX. Yes; by these exaggerated demands.

RM. You feel demands.

FELIX. Yes; by your demands to be perfect and totally God-centered; to love my enemies from the heart; to become empty; to allow everything to surface; to remain always in the present, and to suffer everything. For me these are unattainable ideals, excessively high goals which depress me and make me feel small.

RM. You experience what I say as a challenge and a demand. You are threatened because you feel under pressure to live up to it.

FELIX. Yes; it's intimidating and I resent it. You are speaking of unattainable ideals. They stifle me and I have to defend myself against them.

RM. This pressure comes from my demands.

FELIX. From the discrepancy between what I can do and these demands to be perfect.

RM. Hmm.

FELIX. You also say that we don't have to achieve anything, but then comes this "must." You must be God-centered, you must become empty, and so on.

RM. Felix, I don't know whether you have noticed that I never, or almost never, say "must." I've never said that you must be perfect, or demanded of you to be God-centered. We have been created God-centered—that's what I said—and when we come back to this God-centeredness, we'll find happiness. I only show the direction to make us conscious of our state and see where we are and where we ought to be. I also speak of fullness and emptiness. When someone becomes empty, God fills him. That does not mean that you have to empty yourself. You can postpone the self-emptying to a later date. God will then fill you later. I've invited you to let everything be as it is. Renounce these ideals and try to come into the present.

Everything will be given you at the right time. Try to allow yourself to be as you are. Now can you imagine that the pressure you feel comes from yourself?

FELIX. I still find that difficult. What is certain is that I always make high demands on myself.

8.6 LUIS

LUIS. I was awake for some time during my meditation, then my attention flagged. The meditation became monotonous. Heaviness came over me and I began to doze off. I became tired even though there wasn't any reason for it. That does happen to me sometimes.

RM. You don't know how to deal with your tendency to doze off.

LUIS. No, I'm helpless when it comes to my drowsiness.

RM. You begin to doze off because your attention becomes passive. Our attention is active, for example, when we play table tennis because we have to react promptly to our opponent's movements. In times of danger, too, our attention is active. We experience this active attention whenever something absorbs us. However, when we watch TV in the evening, our attention becomes passive if the program isn't exciting enough. Our attention is passive during a conversation that doesn't interest us, in which the other person speaks in a boring voice or carries on and on. Our attention is passive when we're under the pressure of "must" or "ought to," but have no personal interest in the matter. There's great danger in passive attention while driving a car; the driver could slowly fall asleep on a long monotonous stretch of road.

Meditation depends on active interest. If you're fully with it, your meditation becomes exciting and absorbing, even when nothing is happening. *Being* and *being there* are in themselves attractive and exciting.

The hands are a superb help toward this active interest. When we feel the flow in the center of the palms, attention becomes more and more intense. But under the pressure of "must" and "ought to," our attention weakens and sooner or later leads to our dozing off.

8.7 AMY

AMY. On the whole I'm doing fine, but today I was at my wits' end and didn't know what to do. I was lost and unconscious during my meditation. Nothing worked. I couldn't feel my hands anymore either. When I don't know at once how to react I feel terribly insecure.

RM. Insecure.

AMY. I don't know how to continue my meditation. I wanted to ask somebody, but that wasn't possible at that moment. So I felt lost.

RM. At such moments, come back to the awareness of your body. That will bring you back to reality. Then you are there. You can also pay attention to your being there. With that you are in the present.

AMY. After a while I began to make friends with my condition. I told myself, "Nothing is working, but that's not bad." At that moment I became aware of my hands again.

RM. That's right. "Nothing is happening, but I'm there." When you look at the present—at yourself—at such moments, then you are back with yourself, with your reality. We find security in the awareness of "I am" or "I am here." Then one no longer feels lost. One is *here*. The awareness of being brings us a sense of security and belonging.

We look for external securities, which provide only momentary relief. When they cease, our insecurities return. True certainty lies in being. It can't be taken away. From it we can act with a sense of security. We can always remain in contact with our being, or return to it. As it becomes gradually more conscious, so it changes into being in the presence of God, where external threats touch us less and less.

AMY. Whenever I'm unable to get to the awareness of my being I'll begin by becoming aware of my body.

RM. That is the way.

8.8 CHARLES

CHARLES. At the beginning of the retreat I did very well. I was nearly always intensely there. In a short time I came to inner stillness, to being almost without thoughts. Often my breathing was so quiet, it was almost as if I weren't breathing at all. Time went by in a flash and I could have sat there forever. It was easy and refreshing, and a quiet joy flowed through me. But then, on the fourth day, everything changed. I didn't know what was happening. Everything came to a standstill. I could no longer recollect myself. I didn't feel restless, only desolate and powerless. I lost the ground from under my feet. It was different from the way I've experienced my psychological crises. I had therapy at one time, which wasn't easy but which came to a good conclusion. I feel love for my parents now and wouldn't want to have missed anything that happened during my childhood, not even the conflicts which I experienced.

Although things didn't go well for me from the fourth day on, the state of my soul was quite different from the time when I went through a psychological crisis. I wasn't tempted to run away either. I returned steadfastly to the name, but the name was empty and desolate. I couldn't do or know anything. I also experienced a colorless boredom. Suddenly, however, I could tell myself, "Well, so I can't do anything. I don't know anything, but I also don't have to do or know anything. I am as I am." That relieved me. In spite of this the heaviness and desolation are still there.

RM. You are on the right way. Carry on courageously.

8.9 HELEN

HELEN. I experienced something interesting. I was wide awake and attentive in my hands and with the name. After a while I experienced pain in my knees. My recollection deepened and the pain got stronger. During the moments when my recollection slackened, the pain became more endurable. The deeper I got into my hands, the greater the pain was. Can that be so?

RM. Yes, that can be. Something wants to be redeemed. The process takes place more easily the more fully you're in the present. It's important not to pay attention to the pain, but to remain wide awake in the present. You don't have to make yourself suffer intentionally. Sit in a way that your knees don't hurt. When you see clearly that your pain does not come from bad posture, but from some inner process, then the most sensible thing to do is to endure the pain. It could also happen that you enter even more deeply into recollection and that then the pain will suddenly cease. The pain is nothing but the physical reality of inner darkness.

8.10. SUSAN

SUSAN. During the last meditation I experienced a lot of inner movement. It all started with a feeling of deep sadness. I compared myself to others and felt inferior and envious—feelings I've known for a long time. When I was in therapy some time ago, I worked through a lot of this. Sometimes I also felt contempt. Several of these emotional states have already come up. I was afraid that I would suppress them, and therefore I faced them and stayed with each feeling for a little while. Some of them soon dissolved, others stayed longer.

RM. Something got moving in you.

SUSAN. I'm glad, as it were, that that's true. I think that in my meditation there is often more intense movement than there was in my therapy. Or aren't I doing things right?

RM. It's right that you don't want to suppress anything. But you want to work actively through your feelings and so you're glad when they come up. Therefore, you unconsciously lure them, you conjure them up and remain with them for too long, because your interest is focused on them. Focus your interest on God, on the awareness of the present. Focus on the essential, on your deepest center, there where God is your foundation. It isn't your feelings that are important, but God.

To be consistent, I should say that we don't have to be interested in our feelings. Since we all like to suppress our shadow, I suggest that we look at our feelings for a short moment, only long enough to acknowledge them and to befriend them. That usually takes only a few seconds. Then we should return to the present, to our hands, and to the name without any further delay. When we're with the name we stop being self-centered.

8.11 LORRAINE

LORRAINE. I notice two different ways in which I'm distracted during my meditation. There are times when I begin to think. Then I follow my thoughts or worries until I catch myself and return. In such a situation I remember my thoughts and they're related to each other. They develop by association. I'd call them active thoughts.

Then there are other thoughts which I'd call passive thoughts. They happen much more independently. They show themselves like a film or like daydreaming. When I become conscious of them, I can't remember any more what I've been thinking, or the images and dreams I've had. Afterwards, I'm often very alert and without thoughts. I experience an awake state of being and my spine feels supported by a power from below.

RM. Your cares or desires are hiding behind what you call active thoughts. Your passive thoughts in reality indicate lack of attention and alertness.

8.12 EMMA

EMMA. I found it hard to come to you for the interview today. During my meditation yesterday I was suddenly seized by intense sexual cravings. They frightened me. I actually wanted to give the time to God. Then these sexual desires came up in me. I was thinking of a young man to whom I'm very attracted, not because of love but because of lust. I was obsessed by some pretty obscene images. I wanted to return to awareness, but every attempt was unsuccessful. I tried umpteen times and did my best—all to no avail. I started panicking because I was being drawn into something against my will. I was powerless against these images and feelings and felt humiliated because my intention to focus on God proved much weaker than this fantasy.

RM. You rejected your fantasy.

EMMA. Yes, after all, it came up during my meditation.

RM. Isn't that normal?

EMMA. I don't understand. How can you say that that's normal?

RM. The sexual drive is something natural and healthy. You ought to thank God that you are healthy. If you have a natural sexual side it's natural to become aware of it from time to time.

EMMA. But I don't want it.

RM. That's your problem. If you reject your sexuality, you reject something that comes from God and was given to you for your well-being. Not only is sexuality in itself a gift, it is also right that it should show itself repeatedly in desires, images, and emotions. What you make of these desires is quite a different thing.

EMMA. Exactly. I want to get rid of them.

RM. Yes, but you wanted to push them out of the way entirely. You can thank God that you have a healthy sex drive and that it makes itself felt. All these things have a right to be there. And everything that comes is allowed to come.

EMMA. Then I should open myself to all these temptations?

RM. No, what you do with them is another matter. Look, a married woman can fall in love with another man. That in itself isn't morally wrong. If she accepts this, she only accepts her healthy sexuality and emotional life. The question is what she does with it. If she says to herself, "Yes, this is a natural consequence of my nature, but I'm married and I want to love my husband and want to remain faithful to him," she may find it very hard to let go of the feeling of being in love, but if she does so in all honesty, her love for her husband will deepen. She has suppressed nothing, but has channeled it in the right direction. When someone has consecrated himself or herself in celibacy to God, it doesn't mean that that person will no longer experience sexual desires. Rather, when one becomes aware of one's sexuality, one acknowledges it and directs it with renewed dedication and love toward God and toward the service of people.

EMMA. That is what I really wanted to do, but I don't succeed.

RM. I have the impression that you not only rejected dwelling on your sexual desires, but also your sexuality as such. It's enough if you try to return consistently and with all your senses to the present. Then faithfulness to your intention is already there. Eventually you'll be given that these fantasies will fade away in the face of your efforts to return to the present.

EMMA. I didn't realize that, with my behavior, I was rejecting my sexuality as a whole.

[The following day.] Our conversation yesterday was a relief and has given me inner peace and clarity. During one of the meditations that followed, a scene from my past suddenly presented itself. I remembered how I was molested by a man for whom I had high regard. I was so shocked that I was paralyzed in this situation and couldn't give a sign of my displeasure. But I felt such disgust for him that I became nauseated. If I 'd only resisted! *[Pause.]* I've never been able to speak about it. *[Pause.]* It wasn't a rape as such, since it didn't go beyond his advances.

RM. But you felt raped.

EMMA. I felt really terrible. . . . *[She cries; after a while she calms down, but remains silent for a long time.]* . . . Thank you, I'm so relieved now. I'm glad that I could express it.

[After several days she speaks about her meditation. At the end of that dialogue:]

RM. Emma, may I come back to our conversation of a few days ago?

EMMA. Yes, gladly.

RM. Can you forgive the man who molested you?

EMMA. Yes, . . . *[hesitating]* forgive . . . *[pause]* . . . Not completely, I think.

RM. You feel resentment and rejection.

EMMA. He really hurt me badly.

RM. Allow this hurt to be. Don't suppress it. Try, though, to get in touch with yourself and to see whether you can forgive him by intention, at least—later perhaps from the heart.

EMMA. I could try.

RM. You can become reconciled with him in your heart without speaking to him personally. You can forgive him without his having to know about it. This forgiveness is important for your relationship with God. God, too, forgives you everything.

EMMA. I sense that I'm due to forgive.

8.13 ROSA

ROSA. Recently I've been well in touch with my hands and have clearly felt the center of my palms. To begin with I always feel warmth and can sense my skin. Slowly there was a flowing. I felt in passing as if my hands were fused together, or like a ball. Sometimes they were bigger, at other times further away. A few times they were quite near. During the last few days I've felt a connection between my hands and my abdomen and then my heart. I experienced them as quite alive and always in connection with the center of my palms. This continued for awhile. Now I can feel this flow throughout my whole body. Everything has become one. With my attention I'm in my hands, but they form a unity with my whole body. My whole body feels the streaming intensely. Shall I continue to pay attention to my hands?

RM. Yes, continue to pay attention to the hands. This union with the streaming through your body is a good experience. The attention can spread to the whole body. Awareness of your body is in any case one with that of your hands. But don't let your attention slip from your palms; always begin with your hands. It is from there that this integral experience of the streaming is established.

When you've experienced this unity, the time has come to pay more and more attention to the name and to the present itself. This experience of the body forms an integral part of the consciousness and is like a solid foundation, but only the foundation. The way continues. Focus your attention more and more on the awareness of the spiritual reality—that is, on the present and on Jesus Christ himself.

8.14 RUTH

RUTH. I don't know what's happening to me. I often find myself not breathing, just sitting without inhaling at all. That frightens me because it's dangerous, or rather impossible, not to breathe.

RM. In this case it isn't dangerous. When we run or perform heavy work our body needs a lot of oxygen, which it obtains through heavy breathing. When we walk we use less oxygen, and when we sit or are lying down we use even less. When we're engaged in intensive intellectual work, such as solving a mathematical problem, our brain burns up a lot of oxygen. Simple attention, however, uses up very little oxygen. This attention is more a matter of the spirit than of the brain. The spirit needs no oxygen.

When the attention is very intense, breathing stops for a while and one is under the impression that one has forgotten to breathe. We use the expression "breathtaking" when we're fascinated by someone or something. In meditation, not to breathe is a sign of intense attentiveness. We say that we are recollected. Don't pay attention to the rhythm of your breathing, but remain with all your senses in this deep experience of the present. The body brings in the air it needs in due time.

8.15 ALAN

ALAN. My knees and my back are hurting during meditation. Yesterday I was afraid I was getting a cold. I felt feverish. I often question myself whether I meditate correctly or whether I make too much of an effort. Today a fly was circling round me, and I tried unsuccessfully to chase it away. It annoyed me. Then it was too hot and sticky, and I couldn't sit. I also had some thoughts that I wanted to write down. I try to return to the present, but am gone again in no time.

RM. Something always crops up.

ALAN. Yes, that's what I feel, too.

RM. Alan, you are much too preoccupied with yourself. Look at God, focus on the present, on what is there. Listen into your hands, remain with the name, and don't forever circle around yourself

8.16 MARIO

MARIO. I was outside and was jogging. I gradually noticed a lot of things I'd never been aware of before. Simple things, like plants, flowers, sounds, trees, animals, and clouds. I noticed them as never before. Everything was intensely present, or rather, for the first time I was intensely present. Everything I looked at became alive. I could just linger over everything for a long time. Nothing pushed me on. I felt a relationship with everything and couldn't stop being amazed. Then I was no longer surrounded by individual plants and animals, but by nature itself. Perhaps life itself. I felt alive. I experienced reality itself. I became completely speechless and started to cry. I haven't cried like this for years. I wept with wonder. It wasn't sadness or self-pity but immense admiration and joy. I don't know how long I stood there. I walked on, and behind the first hill I discovered a hunter's blind, which I climbed at once. The weather was mild, and deep stillness was spread all around me and over the whole landscape. I experienced an incredible vastness and felt one with nature. I think I've never felt the presence of God as clearly as I did then. I was free, and quiet joy was flooding through me.

RM. It was beautiful.

MARIO. I'm aware that this experience was the result of meditation during the past days. Although the individual hours were tough, I nevertheless gained peace and quiet which, it seems to me, prepared me for this grace. This experience means a lot to me because I've gained a deeper understanding of what is meant by contemplation. The presence of God was given to me wholly and entirely, without any effort on my part. It was simply there. Perhaps this experience will help me to let go of myself more completely whenever I meditate too doggedly or want to achieve something.

RM. You can remember this experience sometimes so that it continues to be a source of orientation and openness. We read in the Old Testament how the Israelites were reminded of their fundamental experiences: the liberation from Egypt, the encounter with Yahweh on Mount Sinai, Jacob's Well. We all have our own history and can get in touch with our moments of grace. They are given us so that in desert times we can remember the spring of water. But don't try to force anything. Don't expect, either, that this grace will be given again in the same way.

8.17 INEZ

INEZ. I feel oppressed in meditation, as if my chest has been fitted into the bodice of a dress that's too tight. I don't know what it is. I'm sure there are some feelings behind it, but I can't gain access to them. I presume that it's disappointment, but all I feel is this tightness. It's a permanent feature of my meditation. I try to look at it and let it go. Nothing, however, changes. Whether I look at it calmly or with agitation, it is all the same. The tightness is always there.

RM. You would like to know where it comes from.

INEZ. That's it.

RM. Do you connect it with your mother?

INEZ. With my mother! . . . *[lengthy pause]*. . . No, she was good . . . She was a good mother . . . Let's say, outwardly the relationship was good . . . inwardly it wasn't so good. She was very fond of me. She always wanted to be near me, and I had the impression that she was infatuated with me. She always wanted to have me around her. She looked after me, but expected my love in return. When she had done something for me, she always asked in an indirect way what she would receive from me in return. I felt used, even abused, and wanted to keep my distance. Her closeness oppressed me and gave me no room to breathe. I was angry with her and still am angry with her again and again.

RM. She restricted you like that too-small dress.

INEZ. Exactly. . . . It dawns on me that what I feel during my meditation is the same tightness that I used to feel in her presence.

RM. You can see it that way.

INEZ. Yes, it's clear to me now. The oppression is still fully there, . . . *[pause]* . . . and yet I feel a bit relieved. Something has dropped off me . . .

RM. It is no longer an unpredictable threat.

INEZ. No, it is my burden I have to carry *[five minutes' silence]* . . . I feel this burden and I'm willing to carry it . . . *[again a longer silence]* . . . This tightness is still there and I'm asking myself what I'm doing with it . . . *[again a pause]* . . . Yes, what am I doing with it?

RM. Have you forgiven your mother?

INEZ. That wouldn't change anything.

RM. That doesn't matter. Forgive her first. Think that she, too, had her limitations; that she wanted to love, but that she herself had not reached the point where she could love you selflessly. And try to forgive her. That won't change your feelings, but it's the first step toward enabling you to forgive from your heart. Then we'll talk again.

INEZ *[the following day].* After our conversation yesterday, I went out and cried bitterly. Then I vacillated between the feeling of rage at having to forgive her and the feeling of compassion for her. I was fighting with my mother in my mind, and I was reproaching her. Then I wept for a long time. This morning I was able to forgive her. I wept again, but felt relieved already. Now I feel sore and exhausted. At the moment I don't feel that restricting tightness.

RM. Take your time. When you go to your meditation again, allow your mother near you. Let her be close to you. Imagine, for example, that she is sitting beside you, meditating. Listen into your hands. She is allowed to remain there with you. You may feel the tightness, but don't be preoccupied with it. On the one hand, allow the oppression to be there without wanting to reject it, or wishing it away, or thinking it through. On the other hand, be completely focused on your hands, on the present. Everything that comes from her to you may come, may disturb you, may hurt you. Don't worry about it; allow it to come. Center with all your senses on your hands and so on the present. Look at what is coming from the present to you. No oppression will come from there. It will be something quite different. Look at what comes from there.

INEZ. I'll try.

8.18 FREDDY

FREDDY. In my meditation I'm very occupied with my work and my future. I return at once, but shortly afterwards I'm again thinking of my activities.

RM. You're very attached to your work.

FREDDY. It's very important to me how my work will proceed.

RM. More important than God.

FREDDY. I don't see it like that. God is more important to me. For his sake, I came to make the retreat.

RM. Yes, in your intention he takes first place, but you have not yet let go of your work and you are clinging to it inside.

FREDDY *[thoughtfully]*. Perhaps . . .

RM. You are like so many husbands with their families. They love their families and sacrifice themselves for them. They work day and night so that the family can be provided with everything. In the meantime, their wives and children would be happy with less, if only the husband and father would have more time for them. For the husband, the family takes first place, but because of all his caring for them, he doesn't have time to be with his wife and his children.

Isn't the same happening to you with regard to God? You work and labor for God, but in meditation your thoughts are on your work—which, ultimately, you do for God. But God doesn't want your thoughts. He simply longs to be with you. He wants you to give him your attention. Your work and your future are in his hands. Try to put God first in this way, too.

IV. REVIEW & TRANSITION TO THE NINTH DAY

Look back over the Eighth Day. I'm not going to give you any instructions for your review. By now you will have a sense of how it went.

In the Introductory Talk of the Ninth Day, I'd like to entrust to you once more the name of Jesus Christ. I confess that it's a personal request. Ignatius gave us Jesuits the name of Jesus. It was very important to him. During our first centuries, the Jesuits celebrated the Feast of the Order on the Feast of the Holy Name of Jesus. They marked all their houses and all their writings with the word *Jesus*. Later, devotion to the Heart of Jesus became central for us Jesuits. This is really no different. The name of Jesus Christ has been given to us Christians "from above." The angel entrusted it to Mary at the Annunciation. I would like to place the Name on your heart so that you may learn to love it for the whole of your life.

I wish you a wonderful Ninth Day.

NINTH DAY

I. INTRODUCTORY TALK:
THE NAME OF JESUS CHRIST

1. Two decisions

During my youth I made two important decisions. I was fifteen years old and received a strict military training in a Hungarian officers' academy at Marosvásárhely in eastern Hungary. Besides the normal secondary schooling, we were given theoretical and practical military training. It was a hard life, ruled by discipline. We slept in large dormitories, and were awakened early in the morning with a trumpet call. We had to jump out of bed immediately and stand motionless until the end of the call and the National Anthem that followed it. The winter was icy cold, and we stood freezing in front of our beds. During these minutes, questions of the meaning of it all overwhelmed me. "Why do I have to stand here so uselessly? What sense does it make?" The questions didn't give me peace, and I began to look for reasons. "It's important for you to get through the academy with good marks," was my first answer. It didn't take long before the question of meaning bothered me again. "Is it so important to get through the academy with good marks?" After I'd endured the National Anthem a few times more, a second answer suggested itself. "I want to go through the school because my parents expect it, and I don't want to disappoint them. I love them, and so I do it for them."

When a few more days of morning cold, trumpet call, and National Anthem had passed, I realized that the motivation for enduring the whole thing out of love for my parents was insufficient. My parents will not live for ever, I thought. What meaning remains if they're dead? I have no idea why my existential life problems arose exactly during these minutes in the freezing cold. But I still see myself standing motionless in front of my bed wrestling for the meaning of my life, and see the non-commissioned officers going around looking for someone to shout at. My next attempt at explanation produced the motivation that I wanted to live, grow up, and start a family.

Hearing the National Anthem in the cold dormitory yet again, I had the feeling that this also could not be the ultimate meaning of my life. A few more days passed, and I reached the conviction that God must be the ultimate foundation and reason for my life. With this answer the questions ceased. It had not become easier to get up, but I was more motivated. This decision, or rather insight, became my guidepost for the years of my youth.

The second decision was a continuation of the first. It was a few weeks before the bombardment of Nürnberg of which I spoke in the introduction to the Fourth Day in this book. We were about fifty officer cadets in Hungarian uniform, together with some of our own officers. Only the trainers were German. According to Hungarian custom, all soldiers were marched to church in formation every Sunday, separated according to confession. In the Third Reich, of course, this was not the custom. But we were led to church by our officers as at home. I still see vividly our marching every Sunday into the Sacred Heart Church of Erlangen. Before this I had been accustomed for years to go to Communion on Sundays. I would have liked to do the same in Sacred Heart Church. But I met with a serious difficulty. Most often I sat between my comrades in the middle of the pew. The seating order was not supposed to be changed. In order to go to Communion—and Confession beforehand, as was then customary—I would have been obliged to make five of my comrades get up four times to let me out and in. I was very conscious that the execution of this "ceremony" could bring much scorn and derision on my head. Derision regarding religious convictions would have fit perfectly into the demoralized atmosphere of these last months of the war. Added to this was the fact that I was the only one from our group who wanted to go to Communion.

In this situation, questions of meaning again besieged me. For three weeks I fought for an answer. Was going to Communion only a routine rite for me? Was everything only the child's faith I had inherited which, without the support of the family, had no more power? I stood alone. The war had scattered our family in all directions. I didn't even know whether my parents were alive or dead. I was seventeen and had to decide for my own life.

My discovery that the answer depends on the person of Jesus Christ was a decisive step toward a solution. Who is he? Is he really God as I had heard and learned? Where do I get an answer? I was no theologian and had no one who could have advised me. I asked myself, "How shall I know that all I heard about Jesus Christ is true?" With hindsight I can see that it was good to be thrown back on myself. But at the time it was difficult. I remembered the sermons I heard in my homeland and my religious classes at school. I reflected on the events of the life of Jesus. My existential question became, "But how do I know that it is all true? How can I be certain that the story of Jesus is so true that for his sake I can endure the scorn of my colleagues?" What if the story of Jesus of Nazareth isn't true? There were moments of doubt and of weighing all the pros and cons. After three weeks of inner search, I reached the conviction that the life of Jesus as it has been written and passed down, is important for me. The living faith (of my parents and other important people) carried weight with me. Their witness could not give me absolute certainty in this question, but it was sufficient for me in order to make a conscious decision for Jesus Christ. I reflected for a while and decided to believe in him.

From then on Communion was no longer a problem for me. I was able to let my comrades get up for me as often as necessary without feeling awkward. Their scorn wouldn't have prevented me, for I knew my way and stood by it. But, contrary to what I had feared, I never heard the least disparaging remark from my comrades. That was worthy of respect in the chaos at the end of the war.

The decision for Christ became the foundation of my life. Later I passed through many crises, and there were many more situations in which the grace of God strengthened me. The relationship with

Jesus Christ developed in several phases and became simplified. I found the way to the name of Jesus through long and intensive contact with Scripture. It contains the whole Christian mystery. When at the end of this book I testify that it is this name that has been given to us, I would like to recommend it to retreatants as constant companion not for a few days only, or for a time, but for the whole of life. It is an inexhaustible treasure. This is my way, and it is my privilege to pass it on.

2. From Jesus of Nazareth to the risen Christ

The relationship of the apostles to Jesus Christ had to go through a painful but important transformation from a relationship with Jesus of Nazareth to one with the risen Christ. Their example is important for us, for we are led on a similar journey.

Jesus Christ had touched the apostles profoundly at the beginning of their vocation. Their immediate following of his call is the proof. During the years of his public ministry, they grew closer to him. His person in its humble and accessible humanity was an incredible light for them. Through words and miracles, through his vitalizing radiation and his unfathomable love, he became the center and meaning of their life. Then, like lightning out of a serene sky, there suddenly came for them the arrest, his unexpected condemnation, his cruel way of the cross, and the finality of his death. They must have been depressed beyond imagination. The foundation of their lives was taken from under their feet. To understand their dejection, one needs to keep sight of Jesus' days in the tomb, while they knew nothing of the resurrection. Then the sudden joy: He is there! He meets them, eats and drinks with them, but he is different from what he was before. He disappears and comes again. With the Ascension and Pentecost the apostles have to take leave of the human form of Jesus for the last time. The risen Lord remains present all the same. They experience him always and everywhere. He is present in their daily life in an inexplicable way. He is there more intensely than before. The Spirit of Christ lives in them. The risen Lord is Jesus of Nazareth, but no longer in his palpable, comprehensible human form.

The Christian is led to a similar transformation of the image of Christ. We get to know Jesus Christ of necessity through the pictures, parables, and stories of the Gospel. We come to faith through the witness and example of our fellow human beings, through parish communities, eucharistic celebrations, days of retreat and similar meetings, events, or books. These are comprehensible and concrete. But all this points beyond itself to the ever-present Christ who is living and at work, always and everywhere. Slowly we discover the kingdom of God within us. Jesus Christ doesn't merely remain an external partner. He becomes more and more the incomprehensible but also ever-present one, who lives within us and is nearer to us than we are to ourselves. As time goes on, this immediacy, which no longer knows a form or figure, grows.

Gradually we're led to the awareness of the presence of Christ in our consciousness. We learn to look at our present, and in it, at the formless presence of Christ. We learn to look at our own reality, and in it, at reality itself, the all-embracing, formless reality of him in whom everything was created.

We can't bring about this transformation ourselves. It is a gift. But we can remain attentive. It is given by Jesus Christ who has come to lead us to the Father, not only through exterior signs and witnesses, but by showing himself to our inner selves. He "enlightens the eyes of our heart" (Eph 1:18) so that we recognize him. The inner access to this communion is opened up to us in the name of Jesus Christ. In his name everything is given. It bears the power of his person. In his name he and his redeeming power are present. Turning to him is the way. From initial forms and figures we are carried to interior awareness, even to union with him. In Christ we become one with the Father. But the transformation of our relationship with him is painful. We are invited to let go more and more of concrete forms of experiencing him within ourselves, that we might discover his universal presence in ourselves and in all things.

John and Paul, the two great theologians of the New Testament, see the center and summary of their proclamation in this truth. Both show us that the way of the Gospel leads to mystic union with Jesus Christ.

3. "Becoming one" in the Gospel of St. John

Becoming one with the Father in Jesus Christ is the central message of the Gospel of John. It is the aim and summation of his Gospel. John describes the life of Jesus in twelve chapters. He then devotes five chapters (13-17) to one single evening's conversation in order to summarize the message of Jesus once again. In Chapter 17, he again summarizes Jesus' goal and will in the form of a prayer to the Father. He first expounds his relationship with the Father and speaks to the Father about his relationship to the disciples (Jn 17:1-8, 9-19). Finally, he affirms that the goal of his mission embraces all mankind (Jn 17:20-26). The chapter presents the mystic union—becoming one with him and the Father—as the ultimate goal. After this, Jesus stops teaching. He has said everything. He is silent and wants to confirm what he has said with the testimony of his death and resurrection (Chapters 18-21).

The last passage of John 17 summarizes the message of Jesus Christ and the experience of John. The last part of this prayer is clear and simple: all must be one as the Father is one in Christ and Christ is one in the Father. All shall reach this oneness. That's the whole message. Everything comes together here. The duality of the material world, of discursive thinking, of images and representations, is overcome. Human understanding can't comprehend this:

> I pray not only for them, but also for those who will believe in me through their word, so that they may all be one, as you, Father, are in me and I in you, that they also may be in us, that the world may believe that you sent me. And I have given them the glory you gave me, so that they may be one, as we are one, I in them and you in me, that they may be brought to perfection as one, that the world may know that you sent me, and that you loved them even as you loved me. Father, they are your gift to me. I wish that where I am they also may be with me, that they may see my glory that you gave me, because you loved me before the foundation of the world. Righteous Father, the world also does not know you, but I know you, and they know that you sent me. I made known to them your name and I will make it known, that the love with which you loved me may be in them and I in them. (Jn 17:20-26)

The statement is so clear, that I don't need to add any further commentary. Only one remark: Jesus identifies the Father with his name. To make the Father known and to make his name known is one and the same. We may conclude from this that—for us also—becoming one with Jesus Christ is closely linked to becoming one with his name.

4. The "mystery" in the Pauline Letters

The central theme in the Letters to the Romans and Galatians is grace or justification. In the Letters from prison Paul formulates this theme using the word *mystery*. The mystery is the plan of the Father who created all things in Jesus Christ and has taken us into the mystery. He writes in this sense, "The mystery" is "Christ in you" (Col 1:26-27). We in Christ and he in us. We are members of Christ (1 Cor 12:12). We live "in Christ." Christ lives through faith "in our hearts" (Eph 3:17). Paul himself became wholly Christ. No longer is it Paul who lives, but Christ lives in him (Gal 2:20).

5. The name of Jesus Christ

The name of Jesus Christ stands for his person. Through it we unite ourselves to Christ himself. Whoever repeats his name with reverence is being filled with him. The name is like Peter's eye contact when he walked toward Jesus on the water. Because of this, I recommend repeating the name of Jesus Christ until it sinks into our hearts and is uninterruptedly present there. The name leads us to Jesus Christ. There are times when he gives us consolation and encouragement on the way. With consistent repetition of the name, there will also be times when we experience neither sublime feelings nor sensible strength through the name. These are "desert times," by which term I don't mean to describe routine or mechanical repetition of the name, but rather a state that in a particular way aims at deepening the relationship with Jesus Christ. During this stage of purification we are in awareness, but the repetition of the name is desolate and sterile. We're being led into greater depth, our feelings grow more independent, and dark zones are traversed. If we repeat the name steadfastly during these times—while listening and surrendering—Jesus Christ takes possession of us and penetrates our whole life. While we are becoming instruments in his hands, he transforms us more and more into himself. We become Christ on earth. In Latin we speak of *alter Christus,* "an *other* Christ," "*completely* Christ."

Many pray the Jesus Prayer, like the Russian pilgrim, as a petition for mercy. I describe repeating the name "Jesus" when exhaling and "Christ" while inhaling. It isn't a petition; it is simple "eye contact" when we address him by his name. The Russian pilgrim wandered through the landscape. We're sitting in stillness, in the quiet present. While saying the name and directing our awareness to the center of the palms, we come to more alert attentiveness. As I have already said, these three elements become wholly one and strengthen the awareness of the present. The present, thus perceived, is the first sign of the presence of Christ in whom everything has been created. If we continue walking this way, we are led to union with Christ. That's why I recommend repeating the name of Jesus Christ for more than just a transition period. The name of Jesus Christ isn't a means to an end. If we try to reach quiet recollection through this name, we are degrading his person, making him only an instrument. The repetition of his name turns us to his person, and that is already the goal. We encounter Jesus Christ *in his name* and not *through his name.*

I end with a legend. Legends generally complement historical truth through a story told in order to illuminate the meaning of an event. They express the inexpressible in symbols. Ignatius, Bishop of Antioch in the Second Century, was condemned to be thrown as food to the wild beasts in Rome. In a letter (still extant today) he begged the Christians in Rome not to do anything to save him from this cruel death. He wanted to be ground by the teeth of the wild beasts. So it happened. He died torn to pieces by the animals. That is the historical kernel. The legend that grew out of it tells us that the Roman soldier who led him to execution and saw with what courage he died, opened the body after death to find out his secret. He found written on his heart in gold the three letters I H S. These were the letters of the name of Jesus: *Iesus Hominum Salvator—* Jesus, Savior of Humankind. The truth of this legend is great: whoever bears Jesus in his heart lives by the strength that animated Ignatius of Antioch.

II. INSTRUCTIONS FOR MEDITATION

Dear Retreatant! I'd like to encourage you to go on spending this time in complete silence. Continue as you have done until now. Don't yet think about the end of the retreat. It could be that individual meditations will get more difficult again. Don't come away earlier from your meditations, and don't be content with fewer half-hours than before. You'll see that the practice brings its reward. Don't slacken the silence. This is an important time.

III. DIALOGUES

9.1 MARK

MARK. This morning I was really able to be present. I felt great harmony between the sensation of my hands and that of my breathing. Later I was more distracted. But I never know whether I am properly directed or circling around myself. When I feel into my hands, I am with myself. Isn't that being self-centered?

RM. There's a great difference between circling around oneself and being with oneself. We circle around ourselves when we have thoughts like, "Am I good enough?" "Have I done some thing wrong?" "How am I progressing?" "Shouldn't I be much further along?" "Can I succeed in this or that?" "Have I done something to make me guilty?" To enter into these questions means circling around oneself: They make us self-centered.

To come to oneself is always linked to awareness. When in awareness, you are necessarily conscious of yourself. The path takes us there. The Gospel says that the kingdom of God is within us. When we look at our self and are wholly present, everything that is *related to* the self disappears at once. What remains is awareness of the self. If we then continue to listen into this consciousness, we are no longer aware of the *self,* we're aware of *being.* But that is a long way. Only in these depths of the soul do we become aware that we are in God and God in us. That is a very great grace which we ourselves can't achieve. I say this only that you understand where the way leads, and that to come to oneself isn't something of secondary importance. Anyone who comes to awareness and is conscious of the *I Am* is directed to God, for he alone is the deepest center and the ultimate foundation of the self.

9.2 LILIAN

LILIAN. I was wholly there in meditation, very awake, and fully turned inward. I was totally with myself, and found in myself—I don't know how—a gentle and quiet point. It drew me further into stillness. I had to be very quiet myself in order to remain with it. I felt neither wishes nor thoughts. I was only interested in remaining there. It was a very sober and simple state. It lasted for hours during recent days. I often forgot time completely.

RM. You have found a great treasure.

LILIAN. Yes, it is a gift. I'm only unsure of it because of something I've noticed always more clearly during these last months.

RM. . . . during recent months.

LILIAN. Yes, I've lost access to Scripture meditation. It hurts my conscience, and I fear having gone astray, that I'm moving away from Jesus Christ.

RM. It upsets you.

LILIAN. Yes, it upsets me, because Bible meditation used to lead me to Christ and always brought me back to him. Now there's an obstacle, some preventing factor which I don't recognize. I can no longer pray with Scripture. I keep trying, but it's impossible. I feel inwardly drawn to Jesus Christ and find constant "eye contact" with him. It's too much for me now to read the Gospel; it seems to demand a lot of activity, and I only want to be present. On the other hand, I feel guilty because I've lost the connection to Scripture. I can't meditate the way I used to.

RM. What you are experiencing now is a much deeper contact with Jesus Christ than what you have experienced through the events, images, and reflections of Bible meditation. Until now you endeavored to come to him, and now you are simply with him. That is greater. The time for Bible meditation is over for you and won't return.

The Church teaches us that the life of prayer develops. After vocal prayers come meditations which lead to a conversation with God. This colloquy develops into an immediate looking at God-Present. It's called "prayer of simplicity" or active contemplation. This is what you're experiencing now. You need only look at him, and Jesus Christ himself guides everything else.

LILIAN. And Sacred Scripture?

RM. Sacred Scripture, God's message, is already in you. He himself lives and acts in you. You need only keep this vital contact, and everything will flow from you without your working at it. The power of Jesus Christ holds you. Trust it, surrender to him. It isn't Sacred Scripture that is over for you, but the discursive approach to it. Jesus Christ, the living Word of God, is in you. You can read and study Scripture (it's not that which will be impossible for you). But in prayer you no longer need to work actively and discursively with a text as you used to do in reflective meditation. That is finally over for you. Your contact with Jesus Christ has become more immediate.

LILIAN. Shall I then give up trying?

RM. Don't on any account try to return to reflective meditation. You can try to come to your quiet point or to this inner attentiveness to the presence of God and remain with it. Later you will be drawn still further into it. When your attention is held effortless by grace, you don't need to make any other effort.

9.3 JIMMY

JIMMY. I was very recollected in meditation. Then I suddenly heard the person next to me getting restless. He moved and breathed more heavily. I felt restlessness radiating from him. I was disturbed, and when it didn't stop, I was annoyed. First I felt it was something positive to have discovered that my neighbor's unrest led to my annoyance. In this sense, he was only the occasion for my annoyance, for which I really had no reason. I asked myself then whether I should beg his pardon.

RM. You wanted to prove to yourself that you had no reason to be annoyed.

JIMMY. Yes, I looked for arguments to discern why my feelings were unreasonable.

RM. Yes, but in this way your reasoning comes between you and your feelings, and you're cut off from them. You won't feel them anymore, not even when they are still there unconsciously. You want to keep your feelings at bay with your reasoning. You feel anger and want to rationalize it away.

JIMMY. Yes, there's a parallel to my daily life. I often control my feelings with arguments.

RM. That must be very strenuous.

JIMMY. Yes, but what else should I do?

RM. First you noticed your neighbor's restlessness. Shortly afterwards, you became aware of your anger. Until then it was excellent. Then came the wish to get rid of your anger. Instead of displacing the anger with reasoning, you can say to yourself, "The anger is there, and whatever is there is all right to be there." Look with kindness on your anger. "How do I feel this anger?" That's unpleasant, but with it you're already in awareness. And being in awareness, you'll soon have quiet. Looking at feelings shouldn't take so long that you become occupied with them; otherwise your reason will at once intervene. As soon as you can look at your anger, return to meditation: to the hands, to the name, to the awareness of the present. Enter into it with all your senses. When you succeed, take care that you stay in awareness without looking right or left.

JIMMY. Will this free me from my constant rationalizing?

RM. Yes, in this way you learn to stay with yourself without being cut off from your feelings. Your anger can remain, but you don't occupy yourself with it. It will slowly dissolve.

9.4 HARRY

HARRY. Meditation is going well.

RM. You are satisfied.

HARRY. Oh well, I'm not wholly satisfied. I often have the feeling of missing out on something. I wish it went better. I'd like to be able to sit there—doing nothing and being there without obstruction. Yesterday many images and pictures came. They were like daydreams. They were pleasant representations. I was okay with all of them. And I often miss just this in meditation. I'd like to exist in well-being and don't want to be disturbed. I remember having often been happy in meditation. That happens very rarely now, or even never of late. I feel a sense of losing my time, of disappointment and dissatisfaction.

RM. You'd like to be quiet and undisturbed.

HARRY. Yes, and I miss it in meditation.

RM. This puts you in a bad mood.

HARRY. Yes.

RM. This dissatisfaction is there underneath during ordinary time also.

HARRY. I would need to feel into that . . . perhaps I am more disappointed than dissatisfied . . . *[short pause]*. Yes, but also dissatisfied.

RM. The question is whether you seek God or your feeling of happiness.

HARRY. Hmm . . . *[pause]* . . . I have to say it with inner pain and resistance . . . *[pause]* . . . I realize now that I didn't seek God at all, but my well-being . . . *[pause]*. . . . That's terrible.

RM *[keeps silent]*.

HARRY. I believe there's also a connection with my fear of pain. . . . I have often noticed that I dread pain. I defend myself against it. But I didn't know that it's part of my striving for enjoyment and well-being.

RM. Surrender to God. Try to serve God, praise him. That brings true happiness. Enter deeply into awareness of what exists, so that you forget yourself. Remain fully in awareness. Consistent attentiveness to the light of the present will lead you out of this state.

9.5 ROSALIND

ROSALIND. For days I was very quiet, awake, and nearly without thoughts in meditation. Suddenly a lot of fear rose up in me. My pulse raced, I sweated, and panicky terrors overwhelmed me.

RM. Fear.

ROSALIND. Yes, I thought of my mother. The thought suddenly came, what would it be like if she were to die. This hit me deeply, and I was stunned. I didn't really find much reason for this fear, because she's much healthier and full of life now than two years ago. I wanted to return to awareness, but it didn't go well. The image kept returning that my mother could die.

RM. And the fear also.

ROSALIND. Yes, it was there most of the time. The thought of her death was hanging threateningly over me, and I didn't know whether I could admit it. Another thought came like a flash: what would happen to my son Andy if I were to die? He's my only child and is now twelve. My terror increased. I felt sorry for him.

RM. Is it a question only of him?

ROSALIND . . . *[long pause].* . . . I can't admit the thought that I will die myself.

RM. It's taboo for you.

ROSALIND. Yes, that's why I keep getting into a panic.

RM. Hm. . . . Let's leave this alone for now.

ROSALIND *[next day].* I've continued with meditation. I'm calmer, but I can't look at death.

RM. Not yet. The fear is still too great.

ROSALIND *[on the third day].* I'm blocked somehow. The thought of death isn't prominent now, but hangs like the Sword of Damocles over me. I'm more clearly aware that the thought of my mother's death and the fate of my son are only ways in which I'm being led to my own problem. I'm ready to work on it, but I don't have any idea how to go about it.

RM. You can try to allow the thought of your own death to come closer to you, if you are resolved to come back with all your senses to the present and to being. That's important, because these will give you strength to admit this threat and endure it.

ROSALIND. Agreed. I've felt countless times that contact with my center gives me the security with which to face anything.

RM. I suggest that you help yourself with role-playing.

ROSALIND. Role-playing?

RM. Well, it's now the middle of August. Imagine Christ saying to you, "Look, Rosalind, for next year, I need you elsewhere. That's why I'd like to call you away from this earth. You could still live longer, but I need you now. If you agree, I'll allow you to get cancer in September. At the end of September it will be proved to be malignant. In October you'll undergo an operation which won't bring much improvement. At the end of December you'll die."

Ask yourself whether you can say yes to this. Picture to yourself how you will fare during this process in September, October, and into December, and see what feelings arise in you. You can also imagine how your mother, your husband, and your son take part in the funeral.

Do you want to try that?

ROSALIND. Well, I can try.

RM. Remember that it's important not to fall into thinking or brooding, but to let your feelings come and learn to endure them. Don't do this during meditation, but in between.

ROSALIND *[on the fourth day]*. No feelings have come. It's astonishing, but I feel nothing.

RM. Keep at it.

ROSALIND *[after ten days]*. I've come to dialogue every day now for ten days. On the fifth or sixth day my feeling of fear began to erupt. It's still seething in me, but I'm glad that I dared the role-playing about my death. I still can't properly deal with the thought of my death. But I have a hunch that there's a way out of this panic.

I suspect that something of importance has also happened in my relationship with God. I have an inkling what it can mean to make the world relative and to place my foundation and security in God and not in this world. I experienced for a moment that God is the First, that God is Reality, that we don't have any abiding home here. . . . It's still so new and more like a premonition than a security. . . . I can hardly dare to say it, but I could imagine that I'll have still more zest in living now. I feel freer with my environment, and just because of that I can love and act with more engagement. I don't have to expect everything from the situation, don't have to attain something through all my actions. Before this, I didn't know about this freedom and independence from the world. But I have a suspicion that it could become like that.

9.6 BERNARD

BERNARD. You asked somebody to imagine her mother sitting beside her, so that her feelings toward her mother could come up. I asked myself whether I, too, live in a relationship I can't face directly. Strangely enough, I thought of myself. So I looked at myself—discontented Bernard. Funnily enough, I was able to look at him after just a short while. I saw how this Bernard is discontented. I could let him stand, or better, sit there. For the first time in my life, I could distance myself from the feeling of discontent. My discontent was less absolute than before.

RM. You have felt that you aren't this feeling.

BERNARD. Exactly. Until now I was so engulfed in my discontent, so identified with it, so possessed by this feeling, that I had no distance from it. I didn't look at my discontent, only at the surroundings I thought caused it. Now I experienced distance. I sensed that I have this feeling of moodiness, but it isn't me. "I'm myself," I felt. The discontent disturbs me, but that isn't me.

RM. You know, Bernard, I have a good friend who runs a small business. Once he was in arrears for a prolonged period of time. He had no money to pay the workmen and to buy raw material. The banks besieged him about his debts. His clients couldn't pay. He was under severe pressure. He couldn't even distance himself from it at home. The children lost their contact with him, and his wife looked on anxiously. He was occupied with his problems day and night and immersed in the panic of his life. At last his wife persuaded him to take a weekend off. He told me later that he drove out into nature and lay down under a tree. He saw there how, above the crown of the tree, beautiful white clouds were moving along. He looked on for awhile.

Then, watching the continuous flow of the clouds, he thought that the clouds had flown by in the same way a hundred years ago, and would do the same a hundred years from now. He had the insight that these clouds knew nothing of his monetary problems. They knew nothing about his business—neither those that passed by a hundred years ago, nor those which would pass by a hundred years from now. In this way he was able to look at his hopeless state in a relative framework. The objective problems remained, but he no longer identified with his worries. He was he, and the problems were problems. He could switch off, and could tackle his problems with serenity.

BERNARD. Yes, exactly the same happened to me. My discontent is still there. It's all right for it to be there. But I am me. I'm at a distance from it.

RM. Dwelling in the center of our being frees us still more from unnecessary identification with the world. It enables us to be what we are, and feel free and be responsible toward the world.

9.7 CARRIE

CARRIE. When I come into deeper recollection, fear rises in me. I become frightened at what else might still come. I don't know what I might meet in this new land. I could find myself at the edge of an abyss with no way to go forward.

RM. You feel threatened by the unknown.

CARRIE. Exactly, because I have no idea what's lurking in me. It could be that something will come up that I can't cope with, or can't come back from. I am afraid and fasten the bolt shut.

RM. You are also shut in then.

CARRIE. Yes, that's my problem.

RM. What abyss could open before you?

CARRIE. I don't know, and that makes me insecure.

RM. Carrie, if I didn't know you, I'd have to say that this fear is a signal that you really shouldn't go any further. You would have to stop the meditation and approach this abyss at most with the help of talk-therapy. But since I do know you, I can assure you that the gulf isn't so dangerous.

CARRIE. Isn't dangerous?

RM. Your psychological stability guarantees it. Otherwise we would never have begun this retreat. You also have last year's experience. Since your last retreat you haven't had any more doubts that your place is in your Order. You've cleared up that relationship that was still an acute problem for you last year. You lead a balanced life and are content on the whole. Isn't that true?

CARRIE. Yes.

RM. That's a guarantee that the abyss is only a kind of gray zone where a few isolated feelings and shadows are still lying. You may have a few difficulties, but you can traverse this dark zone.

CARRIE. Sure?

RM. Sure. You may continue to feel afraid, but that shouldn't keep you from going on. Underneath this gray zone, from which the fear comes, lies the presence of God. There you find the indwelling of the Blessed Trinity. You have the feeling that it will get worse the deeper you go, but that isn't the case. It's merely a feeling of fear. In the center, in the ground of your soul, God is dwelling and waiting for you.

And you're also going into this depth with the name of Jesus. Nothing can happen to you. Salvation and security are in the name of Jesus Christ. He protects you. Remain faithfully with his name, and he leads you across the abyss. If you still fear, express the awareness, "I am now afraid again." Look at this fear until you can say, "Well, the fear is there. But I'm also there. I am not the fear, it is just there along with me. That's all right." In this way you can relativize it. Then return to the present and the name. Entrust yourself to the name of Jesus. If the fear is too great, you can also stop for a moment until it has decreased. But then return courageously with the name into silence. Meet your fear with calm. Nothing can happen to you. You are on the right way.

9.8 EDWARD

[Edward is a highly regarded priest who radiates a great deal of love and kindness and is spiritually very serene.]

EDWARD. I am getting on fine and I'm content. But it's a tough time for me. I feel nothing in meditation. That's all right. I know I must not force myself to feel anything. A general meaninglessness lies over me like a thick blanket of cloud. Nothing interests me. I sit and sit and don't want to go away either. It's something very heavy and desolate. I have no doubt that God is present. But I don't experience him. Deep within me there's a kind of calmness or composure, but I feel lost all the same and desperate. I don't know how I should meditate, I just sit there and try to come into the present. I'm awake, but couldn't say what's happening in meditation. I have the impression that it's all the same whether I meditate or not—it doesn't depend on me.

RM. You are passing through a dark tunnel, you know that light exists, but you can't see it.

EDWARD. One could describe it that way.

RM. Well, Edward, you have to pass through it. You are held fast by grace.

9.9 KATIE

KATIE *[begins to weep]*.

RM *[Is alert and present, but says nothing. The weeping lasts five minutes]*.

KATIE. I don't want to go on meditating . . . *[weeps]*.

RM *[continues to listen]*.

KATIE. I shall never again meditate.

RM. Never again.

KATIE *[no longer weeps, but speaks only after a long pause]*. From childhood I have felt a love for God . . . *[speaks slowly]* also for Jesus Christ and the Mother of God . . . my parents brought me up that way, and I have never rebelled against God. . . . I had no reason to do so. I had a happy childhood. I always loved to go to church and prayed because I wanted to. . . . When I entered the Order, I knew it was right. I felt from within that God was calling me. I have been in the Order for thirty years and never regretted it. I like my work and I lead people to God with conviction . . . *[pause]*. But what happened now is terrible.

RM. You have experienced something terrible.

KATIE. It was cruel. I shall never be able to say it.

RM. You can't let it pass your lips.

KATIE. No . . . Never!

RM. Hmm . . . *[pause]*.

KATIE. I shall never again meditate *[pause]*.

RM. You got into a panic.

KATIE. I tried to say the name of Jesus, and a voice sounded in me as if I were saying something different, but I certainly did not want it.

RM. It was against your will.

KATIE. Yes, it was dreadful. I don't think I ever used this word against anyone.

RM. It was swearwords.

KATIE *[weeps]*.

RM. It seemed to you like blasphemy.

KATIE. Yes, it was that, but I didn't want it. Somehow it came from deep within me.

RM. You did not want it, but it was simply there.

KATIE. Yes, I believe I must never meditate again. I don't want it to happen a second time.

RM. Look here, Katie, it is no sin. You haven't done anything evil. This blasphemy was deep within you and wanted to be redeemed. You had no suspicion that there is still hidden in you something against Jesus Christ. During meditation you were able to look more deeply into yourself, and so it could come to the surface. It was there before. Now you can be freed from it.

KATIE. Yes? And how am I going to be freed from it?

RM. Precisely by going back and continuing to meditate. Most likely it will come up a few times more, but you remain with all your attention with the name, and gradually everything is redeemed and you are free from it.

KATIE. But I can't let a blasphemy come.

RM. It's the intention that makes a blasphemy, not the mere words. If you renew your intention of praising God, even a swearword becomes praise of God. All your life this blasphemy has had, consciously or unconsciously, a disturbing effect on you and your prayer life . Now you can be freed from it. Only let it come out. So go and continue meditating. You can tell Jesus Christ that the swearword is still in you and that you have to let it out, but that you have no intention to blaspheme against him.

KATIE. If that's the only way. . . .

RM. Yes, it is the only way.

9.10 LARRY

LARRY. I have the impression that I remain at the surface. A lot of distractions from daily life come up. At one time it's a quarrel that took place two weeks ago; then I remember unfinished work. Suddenly an image from my work stands before my eyes; then a scene of a traffic jam or a plan I could never carry out, then the face of a friend whom I'd like to see, or of a neighbor who gets on my nerves.

RM. You feel set upon by worries about ordinary life.

LARRY. That's right. Not great worries. But they're persistent. I wouldn't really call them worries, but rather the normal routine thoughts that buzz around in my head.

RM. If your thoughts tend there, it means that your interest has remained clinging to your normal life.

LARRY. I don't quite understand.

RM. Look, Larry, contemplative prayer demands full commitment and intense surrender. It doesn't only demand that you turn your immediate attention to your hands, but that you direct your whole interest from without to within. "The kingdom of God is within you," says the Gospel. It's necessary to let go of ordinary life, its cares, and the world itself, in order to be able to turn our interest wholly within.

For the duration of the meditation you have to renounce the world completely and turn inside with your whole heart, your whole interest, and all your intention. Where your heart is, there your attention will be. If you don't make this turnabout, you'll notice that your attention runs away. You can bring it back a thousand times. As long as you haven't renounced the world, with your heart still clinging to something else, you won't succeed in remaining in meditation.

We have to let go of everything for the kingdom of God, even if only for half an hour. A radical turning to God is necessary. Then you'll be able to remain in the present.

9.11 GABY

GABY. I'm sad in meditation. When I begin to meditate, I feel sick after a while, and I burst into tears. I ask God to help me but have the feeling he doesn't do so. I pray in vain. He doesn't hear it. It doesn't seem to be important to him how I feel. Then, when I go to my room, I cry for whole nights. *[She begins to weep.]*

RM. You're in a bad way.

GABY. No one cares about me.

RM. You weep a lot.

GABY. Yes, when I think how much I have to suffer, sadness and pain rise up in me.

RM. You're sad about your state.

GABY. Yes, it makes me suffer.

RM. You find suffering hard.

GABY. Yes.

RM. I think that could be your problem.

GABY. That I have a lot to suffer?

RM. Not that you have a lot to suffer, but that you feel sorry for yourself. You surrender to your hurts and wallow in your wounds. You bore yourself into your unhappiness.

There are people who can't admit their pain. They think they need to control it. They suppress their hurts and become hard. They find it difficult to cry. The pain remains unresolved and depresses them constantly. Weeping is healing for them, because they can let go and give expression to their feelings. In this way the pain is worked through. The wound becomes a scar. That is in order.

Your problem is different. You suppress your pain not with harshness, but with self-pity, and keep circling around yourself. You moan inside yourself and don't get away from yourself. The pain and self-pity grow, and you feel worse and worse. You lose all reverence and respect for yourself. This self-pity is a sign that you don't stand by yourself and your life. You suppress your pain with complaining.

GABY. And what should I do against it?

RM. Accept first of all where you stand. Don't give any more importance to your tears, and don't nurse your wounds. Turn wholly to God. Be interested in him. Remain with determination in the awareness of your hands and with his name, whatever your own state. The more you pay attention to him, the less your wounds and tears will interest you. Then you'll be free and be able to meet God, people—and yourself also—with joy.

Stop being occupied with your weeping. It doesn't help. Stand by your destiny and make yourself ready to suffer whatever falls to you to suffer.

GABY. That is new to me. I always thought that weeping helps me. I have to let this work in me.

9.12 HELEN

HELEN. I can't say much. I've already said at various times that I am doing well. Nothing much happens with me. I am with my hands, my breath, and the name. Since I've been meditating for a long time already, and have also passed through more difficult times, I'm glad to be allowed to experience a quiet and peaceful stretch of the way. The name gives itself to me with reverence and love. I don't have any feelings, but it's often serene and clear in me. If it weren't the case, I am also ready for that. It's good as it is. My meditation has become very simple in recent years.

I just remembered one thing . These last few days I've become aware of a vital place or point above my heart on the right. It's like a current.

RM. On the right side.

HELEN. Yes, on the right.

RM. Where the wound of Jesus is?

HELEN. Yes, I now realize that the wound of Jesus was on the right side of his heart. Shouldn't I pay attention to it?

RM. Oh yes, you can stay with it.

HELEN. Shall I always stay with it?

RM. Whenever you feel this place, stay with it. When you don't feel it, return first to your hands, and when you feel it again, direct your attention to this heart-stream.

HELEN. Then I shouldn't pay attention to my hands any more?

RM. When you feel this place, you don't need to pay attention expressly to your hands. They're already included. But don't do this with other places in your body, only with the heart-stream.

9.13 TOBIAS

TOBIAS. When I sit there in the group and meditate, I often compare myself with the others. One is already more advanced than I, another has made fewer efforts, I seem to be ahead of a third, and so on. I'm conscious that I often compare myself with others. My impression that others have gone further makes me moody, envious, and jealous, because with me it's tough going. I'm conscious that I am still at the beginning. If I sense myself ahead of others, then competition, criticism, or contempt rises up in me.

RM. You always experience yourself in relation to others.

TOBIAS. Yes, and I can't put that aside. I'm trying to cure myself of it, but I don't succeed. This behavior pattern is deeply ensconced in me and I'm helpless when it comes down to it. I live constantly in comparisons. During meditation, I think it's ridiculous if it seems to me that I meditate better than others. I feel guilty that I'm glad when others don't get on well. Or vice versa, I envy someone who's getting on better. And I really don't know at all how the other is progressing.

RM. You want to be freed from these comparisons.

TOBIAS. Yes, they disturb me. But I'm powerless against them.

RM. It's an important step that you are conscious of your urge to compare yourself. As far as meditation is concerned, turn to yourself. Look within. When you feel, "I am here," you have found a foundation that doesn't depend on others. When you look at the presence of God in the depth of your soul, you find something that rests in itself and isn't related to others. This quiet point doesn't have to be confirmed or supported from outside. It stands by itself. Then all comparisons fall away. They're no longer necessary, no longer interesting. You can let the others be as they are. You don't need to judge them, put them into categories, or change them. By looking at the presence of God in yourself and experiencing yourself grounded in this presence, you become free from comparisons.

9.14 ALBERT

ALBERT. I made a surprising discovery in meditation. I was with the heart-stream and spoke or heard with every breath the name of Jesus Christ. I did get along well for months, and I was intensely present. A few days ago, when I was with the name, I became aware that I say the name of Jesus Christ, but I still see him outside myself. Yes, I discovered that my orientation to him is related to an imagined representation of Christ. I can't explain it very well. I felt I had reached a turning point, and that I was invited to drop my image. Jesus Christ is here. He is in me, I told myself. Somehow I succeeded in looking within myself as if trying to pay attention to how he is in me. I was looking then at him and myself at the same time. I could pay attention to the "if" and "how" of his presence in me.

RM. Looking at him and looking at yourself have become one.

ALBERT. Yes, in between I prayed to him, "You can show me how you are in me." There were no more words, only this looking at my present with the interest of feeling his presence in my own.

9.15 AMBROSE

AMBROSE. I'm appalled at my pride. I realized like a flash that I always find myself better than others. I mean, I understand everything better and meditate better and am further along than others. I remain in my self-complacency. I'm conscious that I'm convinced inside that the others ought to admire me, and even that God should approve of me.

RM. Hm.

AMBROSE. I've known for some time that I'm proud, and I tried hard to change. I had the feeling I was making progress, but now I notice that my pride has taken on more subtle tricks which I can't see through. I find myself looking for recognition unconsciously, as if through a back door. How can I expose these tricks and overcome them?

RM. You don't need to examine these mechanisms. Turn to God and tell him that you are proud and can do nothing about it, that he alone can heal your pride. Tell him, "Lord, I'm wholly at the mercy of my pride. I'm powerless, but I am your child, and you care for me. You free me from my hidden vices, which constantly set traps for me. My only desire is to remain with you and leave all my cares to you."

AMBROSE. To trust in him.

RM. Pride and arrogance are the most "pleasant" vices. One doesn't need to overcome them.

AMBROSE. How is that?

RM. Because they can't be overcome.

AMBROSE. Why?

RM. Should anyone overcome them, he could say with full pride, "I have gained the victory."

AMBROSE. That would be the height of arrogance.

RM. Pride and arrogance can only be dissolved by pure grace.

AMBROSE. Yes, I understand—we can keep our eyes on him, until he himself dissolves our pride.

9.16 BEATRICE

BEATRICE. Since yesterday, nothing is going right with my meditation. I can't sit down, and when I do, I can't recollect myself. I'm very restless.

RM. You can't put up with yourself.

BEATRICE. Yes, and I know why. . . . I know my period's due. It sets my nerves on edge.

RM. You reject it.

BEATRICE. Yes, I don't want it because it makes me sick. I have to lie down; I'm sick and I detest it . . . *[pause]*. . . . Yes, I don't want it.

RM. With this you reject your womanhood.

BEATRICE. That's true, I suppose, but that's how it is.

RM. Look, Beatrice, your period is coming now. Accept it and allow it to come. Tell yourself that it's welcome and even something good. Stand by your womanhood and your body. Be prepared to accept that it's a bit unpleasant, but that it belongs to you as a woman. Accept it with love. Permit your body to be weaker, permit the period to make you sick and set your nerves on edge. Allow everything that comes, to come as it may. Accept that you have to shorten your meditation.

BEATRICE *[next day]*. Here I am again. I did prepare myself for my period. It did, in fact, come. I find it a wonderful experience that half the tensions are gone. I no longer feel that dreadful inclination against my period, against my body, my womanhood. I would never have believed that only a fraction of my sufferings comes from the period itself. It came from my resistance to it. I've been able to look at it, and I told myself it was going to be painful, and that's all right because I'm a woman. I could stand by it. I went to meditation, couldn't meditate, and told myself it's natural that you can't meditate now. I went into the kitchen to do some work. Later I lay down on my bed. It wasn't much better, but that was all right. I saw how I don't accept the limitations of my body and ignore them. I take painkillers because I can't accept the restrictions my period imposes on me. I believe this experience will be a compass for me in other situations as well.

I also realized concretely through this experience what it means to live in the present. I really was in the present even though I couldn't meditate.

9.17 CLEMENS

CLEMENS. I don't dislike going into the chapel, but I meditate better in nature. I'm more relaxed, more present, and feel better. Nature uplifts me, and I come more easily into the presence of God. Is it right if I meditate outdoors?

RM. Nature is indeed an excellent place to encounter God. Farmers who still work quietly in nature, without much machinery and overhead, become contemplatives. The desert fathers retired completely into nature and into the desert. They became contemplatives. We, however, live under stress, but nature provides a balance. We relax there, and get rid of all demands made on us. That's why I recommend during the first days of retreat to go out of doors often.

Meditation is recreation, and recreation meditation. One who meditates properly, rests, and one who really rests is led to contemplation. Meditation and rest converge on each other until they become one. But nature also offers distractions. It liberates us from our cares but can also distract us from our center. To go into complete solitude is more recollecting. The motionless calm and resolute repetition of the name lead us more into the depth than would a relaxed walk in nature.

IV. REVIEW & TRANSITION TO THE TENTH DAY

Dear Retreatant, take a look back at the Ninth Day just completed. You are now quite practiced in doing this.

The Tenth Day, or rather the last day, shall serve us as preparation for the time after retreat. Now, after a long silence, you are internally more calm and serene than you would be if you had been occupied the whole time with your problems. In the last Introductory Talk, I'd like to prepare you briefly for the way back to normal life.

TENTH DAY

I. INTRODUCTORY TALK:
RETURN TO DAILY LIFE

1. Alternating between resting and activity

We have been walking together for nine days, and we're now coming to the end of the road. The question arises, how to continue after the retreat.

We lived in the desert, far away from daily worries and activities. The desert is a place of encounter with God. With the marketplace of the world at a distance, what's really essential comes to the fore. This journey into the desert is both tough and attractive. It captivates all those who sense that it may open the road to the presence of God. However, time doesn't stand still, and we have to return now to our daily routine. If this desert has been a true experience, we will not be able to forget it again. Like a mysterious piece of music that won't fade away, but continues to lure us, the experience creates a sound tension between desert and day-to-day life, between the retreat and our busy preoccupations. This is healthy. This way two important poles of our life are kept united. Indeed they belong together, just as inhaling and exhaling do. A healthy life consists in this: Moving out from and returning to yourself. A balanced person can get up in the morning and find his joy in going out to be creative and, together with others, to make and shape his world. Returning home at night, he also comes home to himself. He looks for security and intimacy in his family. A person who doesn't enjoy going out in the morning is closed up and self-centered. He is truly sick in soul. And a person who doesn't look forward at night to returning home in order to relax, to relish the company of dear ones or just be by himself, is a busybody. He is running away from himself. A healthy human being feels the need, in rhythmic alternation, to move out and to return to himself again.

Only at the depth you have reached in yourself will you encounter another person. A restless activist who continuously runs away from herself, unable to stay at home, is incapable of encountering other people in a true sense. By necessity, her relationships will remain superficial. Her restlessness doesn't admit encounters on a deeper level. Only the words of a person who is in touch with her center and who cultivates this contact steadily—only such a person will be able to touch the soul of her neighbor.

We also experience this kind of alternation in the retreat. Once you have spent some time in the desert, then the inner call to creativity, activity, and responsibility for the common good returns. If you make a retreat in this sense, you will look forward to quiet at the beginning and, at the end, to a return to your daily life.

2. Contemplative prayer after the retreat

Just as I asked retreatants at the beginning of the retreat whether they're ready to be guided, so I tell you now, at the end of our days together, that guidance is coming to an end. The time has now come for personal assessment, independent from the retreat master. Anyone who has found his or her way in contemplative prayer, and is prepared to continue in it, should now meditate out of his or her own conviction.

Before I give concrete suggestions as to how to carry on with the practice of contemplation, let me answer a question that is frequently asked, "Should I meditate exclusively in this way or should I also practice other forms of prayer?" There are many ways, of course: Vocal prayer with the help of prayer books, Bible meditation or reflection on a particular topic. Some pray the rosary or the Hours of the Office. Still others engage in quiet, spontaneous conversation with Jesus Christ. "Shall I give up all that and only meditate?"

According to the teaching of the Church, our prayer life develops just as does human life itself. The child will first use formulated prayers: the Our Father, the Hail Mary, and others—we call this *vocal prayer.* A youth will ask questions about life and look for answers. *Mental prayer* will correspond to this state—Bible meditation, reflection, examination of conscience, or "revision of life." If religious growth goes hand in hand with the rest of human growth, then slowly *affective prayer* will develop—a person will speak freely to God in prayer about his problems and share with him his deeper feelings. Dissatisfaction and rebelliousness against God fit in here, as well as gratitude and love. The heights and depths of the inner life find their expression in prayer. If this exchange is unfolding further, a state will be reached where the various feelings more and more blend into one single and enduring attitude. Some call it surrender, others love or loving trust. The name is secondary; different authors call it *simple prayer* or *active contemplation,* and define it as "loving attention to God" (Tanquery). It is a looking without words, thoughts, or a multitude of feelings. It has been my endeavor in this book to introduce the reader and retreatant to this form of prayer. After it comes contemplation itself. That is pure grace.

With the description just given, we're now able to answer the question about the form of prayer: Every person, according to the level he or she has reached, will sense how to pray. In the course of time, prayer will slowly develop from vocal, to mental, then to affective, and finally to simple prayer. In case you have been led too quickly to a level of prayer not yet corresponding to your state of development (as can happen with contemplation), it's up to you to correct this by returning to earlier forms. If you are ready to go to the next level, it will come to you—as an inner necessity—to move on spontaneously to the form of prayer you desire.

Whoever feels the need to continue contemplative prayer in daily life may find the following suggestions helpful.

1. Above all it will be useful to keep certain priorities in mind:

   - The first priority is sleep. We must give the body the hours of sleep it needs. If you've decided to get up half an hour earlier in order to meditate, you also have to go to bed half an hour earlier. Otherwise you'll fall asleep during meditation. Your sleep is better in bed. You can't be fully awake in meditation when you are sleepy.

- The second priority, in my opinion, is to give your body the exercise it needs—sports, walking, running, doing yoga, gymnastics, or whatever it may be. This especially applies to students and others who spend their working hours at a desk. Exercise is important for life and is listed here before prayer. Without it, you're in danger of ruining your body.

- The third priority is prayer. We will come back to this later.

- The fourth priority is giving time to the people with whom we live, either in the family, religious community, or the group with which you share a home. This isn't necessarily a matter of a lot of time, but of giving it freely and generously. Otherwise, you cannot live together as human beings.

- The fifth priority is work, which in any case takes enough of our time. But it should be listed at the end: Other priorities shouldn't be neglected because of work.

2. If you wish to continue with meditation I suggest that you create somewhere in your house a "meditation corner," a place you enter only for meditation and prayer. There might be a candle, a cross, an icon or other pictures, or flowers. In the course of time you will love to go there. This corner will somehow acquire the atmosphere of recollection and surrender, and in times of meditation, it will deepen your recollection and surrender.

3. When should you meditate? It's highly recommended to find periods of time that are regular and protected. Early morning offers us favorable hours before the phone rings or visitors come—something the rest of the day won't give you. We are preoccupied with daily worries, and we tend to postpone the beginning of meditation under small pretexts. Still, there are people who meditate in the evening. In parishes, the early afternoon is often the most favorable time.

4. How much time should one give to daily meditation? For the kind of contemplative prayer taught in this book, at least half-an-hour is recommended. Otherwise you won't reach the kind

of calm which will permeate the whole day or could guarantee ongoing growth towards contemplation. Experience shows that in the long run, people don't persevere if they settle for periods of prayer that are too short. An hour's meditation daily, however, provides a solid foundation for a growing access to the presence of God.

5. It's an effective help to meditate in a group. Meeting once a week, or every two weeks, for an hour's meditation with others provides remarkable support for daily contemplative prayer.

6. Skipping regular meditation for a while often can't be avoided, for instance, during vacations, while attending conferences, paying visits to friends, etc. That is all right. When, after such a break, you start meditating again, you may not find it easy to get back to your accustomed rhythm of meditation. My suggestion on such occasions is that you take a full afternoon off—or at least half of one—in order to meditate two, three, or four times. This will help start your daily meditation flowing again in its accustomed rhythms.

7. Once in a while, you may find yourself in an extremely hectic situation. If you try to sit immediately then and meditate, you'll get even more nerve-wracked. Rather than using meditation time for other purposes, you should engage in preparatory exercises, like going for a walk or slowing down, till you get back fully into awareness and recollection. Another suggestion might be to do some relaxation exercises or to move through your respiratory channels (as described in the Second Day at the beginning of this book). As soon as you are able to sit down quietly again, contemplative prayer proper can begin.

3. Contemplation outside of prayer

Contemplation is not only a form of prayer, but also a state of life. Once you are led into contemplation, you are contemplative—in prayer as much as in your other occupations. The quiet times of prayer are necessary in order to get into contemplation. Without such periods of prayer, you won't be led into contemplation unless a special grace is given. Once contemplation has begun, however, it will gradually spread, permeating and transforming all of your life. It's just like becoming an adult: once you are adult you are so, whether you're working or resting.

That's why we can say that we have been striving to learn not only contemplative prayer, but contemplation itself. And so we may continue our endeavors after the retreat and even outside our periods of prayer. I want to demonstrate this now by recalling what we have learned and how it is not just tied to times of prayer.

We have learned to *live in the present*. To live in the present means, always, to be completely there where you are. Many people live with only a fraction of their attention given to their momentary activities, because they keep chasing down lots of tangential thoughts. They linger in their past, unable to leave it behind, or—looking ahead—live always in a future which has not yet come. They think of whom they have to phone, of what they have forgotten, and in the process get distracted from the present moment by needless worries. They are unable to switch off. We ourselves have experienced how many distractions assailed us during meditation. To live in the present means to be 100% present where you are. This you can continue to practice outside your times of prayer.

We have learned to *suffer what life has placed on our shoulders*. During the retreat, suffering came almost exclusively from our unconscious, since contact with the outside world was cut down to a minimum. Now, after the retreat, the outside world is there again. The way of dealing with suffering, however, remains the same. We can continue to learn how to welcome everything life imposes on us. This, too, is an attitude that concerns all of life and not only the hours of prayer.

We have learned *acceptance*. We have learned to let things be, to just look at and tolerate what's not pleasing or even disturbing. We have learned to look at ourselves and accept ourselves just as we are. We have even learned to let God be God. To accept doesn't mean to say, merely, that I accept something: That's only an intention to accept something. True acceptance means to look at something and to be able to leave it as it is—that is certainly a task for our daily life! If you allow your fellow human beings to be as they are, you have discovered the art of living. Not to become passive, but first of all to accept the facts, so that you may act, not with intolerance, but with love.

During this retreat we have become more aware of how many thoughts we harbor in our heads, and we have learned a little how to *handle our thoughts*, with all their superfluous baggage. That, too, we can continue in daily life, which brings no fewer unnecessary thoughts than do our hours of prayer! But in our hours of stillness, we've sharpened our awareness of the multitude of thoughts swarming in our heads. Meditation proceeds like our daily life, but in slow motion. Nothing different from our daily life is happening, but we can more easily recognize what actually is going on.

We have learned *to handle our feelings.* That is no different outside or inside prayer.

One fundamental task in the retreat was to renew constantly our attitude of surrender, divine service, and adoration. These three basic attitudes find their parallels in our interpersonal relations. Now, in daily life, we have good opportunities to practice them toward others. One by one, let's take a closer look at these three attitudes.

- *Surrender* in interpersonal relations means that we give ourselves completely, one hundred percent, in even the short times we want to spend with our neighbors. Let's say someone asks you for directions on the road: Give him that little time completely. You should be with him totally, accept him totally, and give him total attention.

- *Divine Service* in interpersonal relations means our readiness to serve others. Readiness to serve is the opposite of tyranny, of greed for power and domination. Instead of forcing your own will on someone, ask the other what he or she desires you to do: That person will make a request, and you are prepared to carry it out. That's exactly what we have tried to do in prayer before God. In daily life we can try to do it with other people.

- Neither is it different with *Divine Praise,* except that we encounter human beings with an attitude of reverence, not with adoration. This perhaps is the most important element in our dealings with others—not to treat them as objects, not to overestimate ourselves, but to acknowledge their dignity as human persons and meet them from a stance of humility. Here also, what we have learned in prayer before God, we can now carry on in daily life as we continue our learning process.

We have learned *to become independent of results.* In daily life, too, this remains an important challenge. Independence from results does not apply to everything. In the outside world we often have to pay attention to results. Still, in interpersonal relations we can find similarities to our attitude in contemplative prayer. We don't love people with the expectation of receiving love or reassurance in return. To love others means to love them unconditionally. It is as with the rays of the sun. The sun simply radiates on its own, whether or not you reflect the rays. The sun simply shines, because this is its nature. To love people means that we love them because love is our nature, and not in order to receive something from them in return. This is a splendid task for our daily life.

And finally, thanks to our constant return to awareness, we have been trained in *relating to reality*. We have learned not to proceed from our ideas and imagination, but constantly to "listen" into reality and allow ourselves to be affected by what exists independent of us. With time, this lesson will help us grow our roots more deeply in reality. In our day-to-day activities, we can at all times continue to practice attentive listening to everything that comes from the world around us.

II. INSTRUCTIONS FOR MEDITATION

This time I don't have to say much about meditation. Stick to your hours of stillness. Slowly come to the end of your retreat. You may direct your attention to the time just ahead of you after the retreat, but do this not as part of the meditation, but outside of it. For the conclusion of the retreat it is a good idea to spend a longer period of time in adoration.

III. FAREWELL DIALOGUES

10.1 DOMINIC

DOMINIC. During the past six months I have had a great time. At home, with my family, everything is fine, and we like each other. It's a source of joy for me. You know, it was not always like this. There is vitality in my work, and much of what flows into the ordinary day is fully alive.

RM. You have a wonderful time.

DOMINIC. Yes, I'm surprised myself, because for years I have been struggling with frustrations. I used to get irritated and often felt depressed. I couldn't find my place, continuously compared myself to others, and suffered from inferiority feelings. All these problems are "gone with the wind."

RM. A lot has changed.

DOMINIC. I meditated only off and on, but it went well that way.

RM. Only off and on.

DOMINIC. Yes, I had such a fine time that I used to tell myself: Everything is really there, thanks to my creative inspiration and the love for my family.

RM. . . .so that the hours of stillness were no longer necessary.

DOMINIC. Isn't it that way?

RM. If you feel that way. . . .

DOMINIC. Yes, really, I do feel that way and that is why I have consciously dropped meditation.

RM. It's not clear to me why you meditated earlier. As long as you were in bad shape you took time for God regularly, for years. Meditation was really important for you. And now, while you have a grand time, it's not important anymore. I ask myself whether you meditated just for your well-being. This wouldn't have been, in the first place, a true search for God, as you've often professed, but a search for your own satisfaction. You've achieved your well-being, and then you discontinue the hours of stillness. You aren't interested in finding God, but in your own comfort and a pleasant feeling about self.

DOMINIC. Yes, but my life is now one big river of joy and strength. I consider my life itself to be my prayer. That's why I don't need to take extra time for it.

RM. That's exactly the problem: Your strength and your joy are coming from God. They are gifts of God, not God himself. You're no longer interested in God himself. You don't have any more time to spare for him.

DOMINIC. You want to say that I'm looking for the gifts of God and not for God himself.

RM. Yes—you see, if you really seek God and not just your own well-being, you won't stop taking time for hours of stillness, in order to be there completely and alone for God. If you really have been led closer to God, you'll feel yourself being pulled toward silence where you can devote yourself to God alone. If you don't feel that, you are still looking only for yourself.

DOMINIC. I'll try to let what you've said speak to me.

10.2 ERWIN

ERWIN. I'm afraid I am selfish in my meditation. I do renew my intention to be present for God. That doesn't seem to be solid enough. It's not fully genuine. If I look honestly into myself, I have to admit that I want to be happy, and that's why I meditate.

RM. You feel that you are selfish.

ERWIN. Yes, I make constant efforts to meditate well. However, the truth is that I don't meditate for God but for myself.

RM. Your inner reality is not congruent with your intention.

ERWIN. Yes, this is my experience.

RM. You feel you should drop your desire for happiness.

ERWIN. At least give it second place.

RM. It's enough if you renew your intention to be present for God and try to stay with him. Your desire for happiness doesn't have to vanish. It will become one with your longing for God.

ERWIN. It will become one with the love for God?

RM. Certainly! In eternal life we will live totally in and for God, and this will be heavenly bliss at the same time.

ERWIN. My desire for happiness isn't selfish then?

RM. The desire isn't yet purified of selfishness. Your awareness that you are still centered on yourself, your desire to give yourself to God, and the insight that you don't yet fully succeed in your surrender to God—these are indications that you are on the right path. It is, however, enough to renew your intention, again and again, to give yourself to God. Jesus Christ himself is concerned about the purification of your intentions. He himself cares for your eternal happiness.

ERWIN. You mean, my desire for happiness and my intention to serve God don't exclude each other?

RM. No, both will become one.

10.3 EUGENE

EUGENE. For a long time I was struggling with sleepiness during meditation and with a feeling of weakness. I wanted to be "with it," but succeeded only for seconds in being present. The distractions, on the other hand, went on endlessly. I always believed I had difficulties in concentration and suffered from inner powerlessness. When I came to you before, hardly anything changed, except that I felt resistance to listening into my hands. I was annoyed because of this supreme importance given to the hands and felt confused with the multiplicity of directions: the hands, the breathing, the name.

Now in this retreat I've experienced a big turnaround. The sensation at the center of my palms grew very strong. At first I sensed a tingling in my hands. After some days that grew into a current which spread to my whole body. And this grew still much stronger with pronunciation of the name. At the very beginning of the meditation, I felt great power, which brought about remarkable alertness. I hardly have to make an effort at it

This strength keeps me fresh and attentive. I'm able to pay attention to the presence of Christ. Before, this used to be possible only if I imagined the person of Jesus. But as long as the current is alive in me I'm able to be attentive to the person of Christ himself. It's as if my consciousness was suffused in light. The interplay of attention to the hands, breathing, and name has opened a new perspective. I would never want to miss it again. During meditation I experience ever more clearly a current, a strength, . . . and a light. For years I tortured myself with supposed weakness of concentration, and had no idea that it was possible to be freely given such a power.

RM. You are satisfied.

EUGENE. I'm very happy and feel the courage to stick to it. I'm aware that this is only a beginning. I have found a way.

10.4 CARMEN

CARMEN. I've come to the end of the ten days. It cost me a lot of effort—I had to suffer many pains and to struggle with feelings of frustration, since I hardly sensed a thing during the exercises. Nevertheless, I engaged myself fully in the exercises because I wanted to give this way a serious try. And I'm glad that I persevered.

RM. Pulling all the strings, you managed to struggle through.

CARMEN. You're right, pulling all the strings. I really don't feel at home in this kind of prayer and think that it's not my way. After the retreat I'll return to the kind of prayer I was used to: I feel more at home with the Psalms (which I can repeat for days on end), with the Gospels, and with reading books that give me new ideas.

RM. They suit you and will lead you to God.

CARMEN. Yes, I really need it, to converse with Jesus Christ. I tell him how I feel, how I'm longing for him and wish to surrender to him. I need a partner to whom I may turn confidently. I feel more at home with all of that.

RM. You're familiar with the kind of prayer that has served you and you want to continue in it.

CARMEN. Yes, this contemplative meditation remained something foreign to me. I felt unable to warm to it. I believe the ten days have given me the clarity to see that it isn't my way.

RM. I find it perfectly all right that you return to the prayer which touches you inside yourself.

10.5 ERIC

ERIC. My meditation has somehow improved recently. I'm more recollected, attentive, and quiet, and I feel much freer. This has a beneficial effect on my day-to-day life. I'm more calm and find myself to be more tolerant. A few days ago something happened to me that previously would have upset me for days. Against all expectations, I remained unruffled.

RM. You're glad that you are making progress.

ERIC. Yes, indeed, I am glad.

RM. So am I . . . and what about God or Jesus Christ?

ERIC. About God or Jesus Christ? ... The question surprises me. ... I believe everything's fine. The question really surprises me ....

RM. I wouldn't have asked everyone this question, but I see that you're going deeper.

ERIC. I've always tried to put God first in my life, and believe that he is.

RM. But *where* does God come first for you? We Christians always place God in the first place. That's the Christian ideal, the Christian vision—that God comes first. Everyone agrees with that.

ERIC. The insight that God should be first not only in my convictions and world-view, but also in the scale of values in my daily life—this was an important discovery for me a few years ago. I realized at the time that God must hold the decisive place in my decisions and actions. He is first for me only when he takes first place in my concrete motivations. That's valid for everything I do. So I try to live according to the criteria and statements of the Gospel, so that my decisions are determined by him. Is that the answer to your question?

RM. That's very praiseworthy. But you could now take the next step and give God the first place even more definitively.

ERIC. I don't understand. How can I make God's place more central other than by living according to Christian values?

RM. One thing is missing.

ERIC. What is it?

RM. Try to make him the center of your attention. There's a huge difference between placing God at the top of your hierarchy of values and keeping him always at the center of your attention. Contemplation tends to lead one wholly to this constant attention. One tries to place God more and more at the actual center of one's attentiveness. The desire to be always with him is the only care one experiences. One no longer knows any other care than to be wholly directed to God. Everything else flows naturally from it.

ERIC. Don't I do that?

RM. No, Eric, that's not what you do. If I understand you rightly, your attention is still indirectly turned to God. You spoke of your own progress. You are more recollected, freer, and more calm. You have found a balance. All that is good—even very good—but it is still about yourself. That's why I dare to point out a further step to you, the passionate longing, always and everywhere, to pay attention only to God, to listen always to his presence, to place him always at the center of your attention and keep him there, whether in meditation or in daily life.

10.6 DEBRA

DEBRA. I feel good and am aware that I've refueled during these days. The retreat gave me new strength, and I'm very grateful that I can return so often. I'm always waiting for this time long before the dates are booked. After the retreat I can work better for months. But I find that, with time, the strength peters out, and that's a pity.

RM. You fall back into the old routine.

DEBRA. Yes, and then I wait for the next retreat.

RM. You want to refuel.

DEBRA. Yes, I'd like to stay in retreat for ever.

RM. The retreat isn't given to us for protection, like the shade of a tree. It helps to put us on our own feet and learn to live for God and others. We should preserve as a gift the grace received. Being conscious of this and trying to keep returning to this strength, increases it. But many retreatants hang on to the retreat courses like a saving anchor and always want to be refueled. They quickly use up the new strength in daily life, and then they're worse off than before, because they've accustomed themselves to live *off something* and *not for something*. Every help is help toward self-help. If we have been helped, we must learn to make the effort ourselves. That's why I ask everyone who comes for a yearly retreat to continue meditating daily. If we still don't meditate daily, after several retreat courses, then the way isn't important to us.

DEBRA. How does one preserve the strength?

RM. By not using it up for ourselves, but giving it back to God. In simple language, by being alone with God for a period of time every day, devoting ourselves exclusively to him. This is the way to learn to live for God, instead of living on God's strength like a parasite.

DEBRA. I find it difficult to find time every day for meditation . . . *[pause]*.

RM. You're very busy.

DEBRA. Yes, I have a thousand occupations, and they keep multiplying.

RM. You can't set boundaries for yourself.

DEBRA. No, a lot is demanded of me; I help a great many people.

RM. Could it be that besides your willingness to serve, there's also a bit of flight from yourself, or that you are looking for recognition and love?

DEBRA. Yes, the thought had already crossed my mind. . . . I can't easily say No.

RM. To devote an hour every day to quiet meditation is not unattainable and leaves you the remaining twenty-three hours. An hour a day is enough to remain on the path.

10.7 JERRY

Jerry *[hesitating]*. Yes . . . today is our last conversation. I'd like to confess to you that I was never quite happy with your guidance, and have always felt free to go other ways. I didn't always follow your instructions.

RM. You've felt resistance towards me.

JERRY. Yes—resistance . . . *[short pause]* . . . resistance. But I'm also convinced that everyone has to go his own way. I don't believe in having a guru whom one has to follow blindly.

RM. You distrust instructions that don't come from yourself.

JERRY. It could be expressed that way. Besides, for a long time I was dependent on the opinion of my parents and had to learn with great effort to stand on my own two feet.

RM. And now you're able to assert yourself.

JERRY. That's why I often didn't follow your instructions.

RM. Isn't that a kind of negative dependence? To have to react against every kind of authority is also dependence, as much as to feel inferior in face of authority. It's really the same, only the other way around.

JERRY. We should follow God's inspirations and not human directions.

RM. How does one recognize inspirations?

JERRY. One listens to one's inner voice.

RM. God's inspirations appear in our consciousness as thoughts, in the same way as the inspirations of our egotistical self-will. In other words, we never know whether ideas and thoughts that suddenly come to us are coming from our self-will or from God.

JERRY. And how does one discern between one's own thick head and the thoughts that come from God?

RM. Directly one cannot, only indirectly.

JERRY. And how?

RM. Our relationship with God runs parallel to our relationships with human beings. If we can be open to others, we are also open to God. And vice versa. If we don't have much of an ability to be open to others, we can be sure that we are rarely open to God. We have the freedom to choose which persons we want to be open to, and which not. In our case that means that each person can choose a retreat master. When we have made our choice freely and then can't open ourselves to our chosen guide, that's a sign that we don't necessarily follow the inspirations of God either.

JERRY. You want to say that I didn't lay myself open to God.

RM. No, I wouldn't go that far. But I'd say that you can measure your habitual openness to God by your readiness to open yourself to the guidance of the last few days.

JERRY. Then the picture doesn't look good in my case.

10.8 SOPHIE

SOPHIE. I made the retreat last year. Since then I meditate almost regularly three-quarters of an hour a day. It's become a necessity. I miss the quiet time if for some reason I have to omit it. Now, a year later, I'd like to make the retreat according to this book. When I spoke about it to my friends, some of them wanted to join me. A priest also joined us. We five are firmly resolved to retire for the retreat. We have eight free days and a house in a quiet environment at our disposal. How should we best proceed?

RM. You've got courage.

SOPHIE. Yes, we are resolved, and we'd like to have some orientation.

RM. Do all of you meditate regularly?

SOPHIE. Yes.

RM. Do all meditate with attention to the hands, the name, and the breathing?

SOPHIE. Not all, only three of us.

RM. Is someone present who counsels the others?

SOPHIE. I spoke with everyone, also the priest. They're looking to me for orientation. We're all familiar with each other. We can listen attentively to one another. If the need arose, we would be able to help each other.

RM. To start with, it would be helpful for everyone to spend half a day in nature. Anyone arriving exhausted or over stimulated should invest a whole day in this.

Anyone new to this way of meditation should complete the first two days and then remain with the Third or Fourth Day for two or three days. They shouldn't go further until they have reached what the Review of the Fourth Day sets out as necessary for transition to the Fifth Day. I'd give the same recommendation to any who have made this retreat, but don't meditate regularly during the year. This seems necessary to me.

For the others who do meditate regularly in this way, I recommend spending the meditations of one day solely feeling into their hands, even though the name comes up naturally at the same time. After that they should pass on to the name and remain with it as in daily life. They should meditate exactly the same way as they do during the year. In between, for short times, the group or all the individuals by themselves can read part of the Introductory Talk or a few Dialogues.

If you come together once a day, be sure you avoid any discussion. Each one can report how he or she is doing. The others may listen until a report is finished. It would be best not to comment, but if necessary, summarize the report briefly and clearly.

10.9 IRENE

IRENE. Now, at the end of the retreat, I still have a question. I've found my way here and want to continue. I'd like to know what is the most important thing on this way.

RM *[smiling]*. God himself . . . *[pause]*.

IRENE. Yes, I somehow realize that. . . . But I have to ask, all the same, how I am to understand the answer.

RM. We all know that God is first and most important. That's stated in the Gospel, in every catechism, and at the beginning and end of St. Ignatius' book of Spiritual Exercises. This is the foundation and the fulfillment of the retreat, and is expressed at the outset of every single meditation. We are firmly convinced that God is most important.

Then we return to everyday life and direct our attention again to our small world. God moves into second place. He appears only indirectly. To give a few examples: We want to change in order to please God. We plan so that God's plans may be realized. We work through our past, so that obstacles be removed from our way to God. We pursue long processes of discernment in order to discover God's will for us. We work to change the world in order to promote the Kingdom of God. We study theology in order to know more about God. We read spiritual books to obtain the right attitudes. We make retreats in order to calm down and work for God. We seek religious feelings in meditation to become motivated to walk the way to God. In short, our attention is directed to ourselves and our world, so that something may change in our direction to God. But God very rarely takes the first place in our life.

IRENE. That was my great discovery during these days.

RM. The way you discovered, which we walked together, consists in directing our attention to God himself or the risen Christ. Instead of directing our attention to changing the world, we turn it directly to God with the trust that he will give us everything, and that all things will work together for good this way. We let go of the cares of the world and look only at God.

IRENE. I can confirm that. What you talk about was the central theme of my retreat. I became aware that God often takes second place not only in my activities but also in my prayers.

I used to pray to God for a particular grace, and my concern for this grace took up all my attention. I contemplated a topic of the Gospel. In the foreground of my attention was a scene from the Gospel, and the desire to understand the life of Christ frequently took second place. Jesus Christ himself finally took the third place. My attention was only indirectly turned to him.

Now I am returning to work and can't think always of God and neglect my duties in the world.

RM. Through contemplation we don't neglect the world and people. We work in this world like other people, but with fewer cares or none at all. If we keep our gaze always on God without any other intention, we become free from cares. We act from the center of our being and need not worry about anything. This freedom from care doesn't come about through preoccupation with this world, but through ever renewed, single-hearted attention to the risen Christ. The way of contemplation consists in the single-hearted gaze at the presence of God, without any other motive. Changing the world isn't then a means to come to him, but a consequence that follows from coming to him. Looking at God, we are being transformed into his Son. The most effective power toward change in the world is direct, single-hearted, care-free and motive-free gazing at the risen Christ. Everything else flows without any difficulty from this source.

10.10 ROLAND

ROLAND. The retreat went very well. I feel great strength. It flows through my whole body. I feel cleansed as though I'd had a spiritual bath. I could tear up trees!

RM. You're looking forward to your work.

ROLAND. Yes, I feel the urge to become active. I've never before felt such a desire to turn to my tasks, and never felt as creative as I do after these days.

RM. I'm glad. Life is alternating between withdrawal from the bustle of life and devoted engagement with the world.

ROLAND. I would never have believed that quiet can produce such courage and strength for action.

RM. It's wonderful to feel the strength. Go and serve your fellow human beings! Take care! This strength is not your own. It has been given you out of stillness. Treat it as a gift, as a treasure entrusted to you. It is God's strength.

We can use it up like a car using gasoline. At the end of the journey the tank is empty, and we stand there powerless, out of gas. If we use God's strength only for working, for getting something for ourselves with it, we consume it and will sooner or later fall back into our old state. The strength dies down and we lose our breath.

But we can also bring this strength back to its source, and without greedily wanting to hold on to it, we can give it to God day by day. Then God's strength grows in us, and we shall experience it more and more as something enduring, something that remains. Instead of consuming God's strength, we can remain with him, stand in his strength, and act for him from this strength.

ROLAND. Should I work less?

RM. No, I didn't want to say that. I don't mean that you shouldn't go among people with this strength and engage yourself fully for them. I only want to stress that you should not lose touch with the source in your day-to-day life. "Remain in me and I remain in you," Jesus says. This "remaining" isn't just declaration of intent, but staying with one's attention directed to him. This strength is like a flame. It's nourished by attentiveness to God. It has to be taken care of, so that it won't die down and go out. We can't rekindle it by our own strength. We protect and nourish it with daily meditation and the return to stillness. If we make time every day for new contact with the source, we can work much better. We are in the current of this strength, but we don't use it up like a parasite. On the contrary, this strength carries and leads us and allows us to act in a care-free manner. We don't exploit the divine strength, but become Servants of the Most High.

10.11 FABIAN

FABIAN. My experience with the retreat is mixed. The exercises cost me a lot of effort. During the first days I was at the point of leaving several times. Nature did me good, but meditation was foreign and unsatisfactory. The long silence made me calm inside, but I don't really know whether it was nature or meditation that led me to calmness.

RM. You don't see clearly yet.

FABIAN. No, I have mixed feelings. Something about this contemplative prayer attracts me, but so far it hasn't become clear to me whether this is my way. . . . This afternoon I went out of doors to reflect on these days. At the end of my walk, I seemed to find more clarity.

RM. More clarity.

FABIAN. At home I won't be meditating . . . *[pause; then thoughtfully]* . . . I have an inkling that later contemplative prayer could become a way for me. Certainly not now. I don't exclude making a contemplative retreat again in a few years. Yes, I have a hunch that this could be a way. I can't say more right now. The experience of this retreat has to settle first. After a few months, I hope to see more clearly what happened here.

RM. Go back to your familiar form of prayer and try to forget meditation. Whatever is genuine doesn't get lost. It will come back and won't let you forget: If you can forget contemplative prayer, it isn't your way.

10.12 MIGUEL

MIGUEL. I have a leaden feeling inside this morning. I was like somebody under a great burden. It's difficult to get into meditation. I was angry, desperate, and sad. I can't describe it exactly. In spite of this I went forward and resolved to meditate. It took a long time to get into it. Perhaps there's still something of these depressive feelings weighing on me. If I hadn't been in retreat, I would have taken up a book and read, or sat in front of the TV, visited a friend, or stuffed myself with sweets—something like that.

RM. But you didn't do it.

MIGUEL. No, I hope I've learned a bit better to face up to these moods and not run away.

RM. In meditation and retreat we learn fundamental attitudes that are also valid in daily life. There are many simple people who have never heard of a retreat or contemplation and yet instinctively endure their darkness. They also come to contemplation without meditation. Redemption takes place for them in their ordinary life, because they don't suppress their darkness but accept their feelings and the states of their soul.

We're aware of only a fraction of our shadows. If we willingly suffer everything that comes to us, we are purified and redeemed. Then the process of purification goes on not only in retreat. If we allow our original sin to be redeemed only during the ten days of retreat each year, we'll need decades to traverse the way of purgation. Others who constantly undergo purification reach redemption in a year. Meditation is meaningful only when this fundamental attitude informs the whole of life. To live in reality and not run away from oneself—this leads to contemplation.

10.13 SEBASTIAN

SEBASTIAN. I meditate every morning for an hour. The hour is very important to me. I hardly ever omit it, and it sets the tone for the day. Yes, it determines what I do. I seek the will of God. I ask myself every day what God's will is, so that I may do it or know it.

RM. You seek God's will for the day.

SEBASTIAN. Yes, exactly. I want to live my day according to God's will, and I want to come closer to it in meditation. Isn't that right?

RM. Yes, it is right, and yet not quite right.

SEBASTIAN. What's not right about it?

RM. That you are not wholly directed to God.

SEBASTIAN. I really don't understand. I seek the will of God and therefore I'm not wholly directed to God?

RM. *[Is silent.]*

SEBASTIAN. To what am I directed if not to God?

RM. In the last resort, to your own actions. God is to show what's lacking, so that what you do is according to his will.

SEBASTIAN. I still don't understand.

RM. You are still expecting something for your knowledge and your actions. You are not directed to God, but to your life, so that it can be led according to God's will.

Why don't you turn your attention to God himself, without seeking and wishing for other things? Leave it to him to plan your life. Look at God for his own sake, without expecting a gift, a present—or any knowledge, except himself. Give yourself freely, without any other intention, in surrender, service, or adoration, without wanting to bring about any change in this world.

Go a step further. Don't stay on the level of acting and doing. Be there for God. He does everything else.

SEBASTIAN. That is not a spirituality of the active life. That is for contemplative monks. My life is hard and demanding. I must look to achieve something and to make right decisions.

RM. The difference doesn't lie in the choice of a lot or a little activity, but in living with a contemplative attitude or not.

SEBASTIAN. Again, that's incomprehensible to me.

RM. Look, Sebastian, it's good to seek the will of God. It's better to seek God himself. When we are introduced to contemplation we've already gone a long way. Many people live in a kind of rivalry with God. They believe that if they act according to God's will, they will lose out on themselves. So they bargain with God about how far they want to do his will and what God is allowed to demand of them.

Later they discover that God is the real meaning of their life and that he knows what they need. They then realize that he wants only what's best for us. Then comes the desire to do God's will exclusively. They resolve to seek the will of God and fulfil it. The eye is no longer turned to themselves, but to bringing their lives into harmony with the will of God. That's a very high spirituality, but it still has that faint scent of a desire to achieve something in this world.

There's another step: turning one's gaze not on the will of God in our life, but on God himself. This step consists in being there for God, independent of what our life has been or will be. This present and disinterested view amounts to much more than seeking God's will. It is contemplation itself.

SEBASTIAN. Yes, but I have a difficult and active life. I want to direct my activities according to him; that's where my love of God exists.

RM. Jesus says in the Sermon on the Mount, "Seek first the kingdom of God, . . . and all these things will be given you beside" (Mt 6:33). Seeking God first, without any other intention, contains the absolute trust that you will be given everything in your tasks and activities. Unite yourself single-heartedly to the vine, then the power of the vine will flow through you, and you will do God's will in the full meaning of the word. He himself will do it through you, and you won't need to worry about God's will anymore.

SEBASTIAN. I am not yet at the point where I can let go of my worries. I have to seek the will of God with great effort.

RM. That's right. But I show you a perspective so that you can see how the way continues. I show you the next step, how to approach this horizon.

SEBASTIAN. And what is that?

RM. Continue on the way you have begun. But reserve meditation exclusively to being without any other intention. Go to meditation to give this time really to God for his own sake, not linking it with your tasks and actions. Try, also, not to connect any other purpose with your time of meditation—even indirectly. It must belong wholly to God. It must have nothing to do with changing the world. It must be sufficient to itself. God alone suffices.

As long as you haven't discovered this purpose-free, loving existence before God and for God, you haven't yet entered through the door of contemplation. Contemplation is a grace. No one can reach it by his or her own efforts. The longing to be with God in this purpose-free way is the sign that God has begun to give you the grace of contemplation.

10.14 BENEDICT

BENEDICT. Something has dawned on me. I was meditating as usual, and suddenly I felt the present and that I exist—I felt it in a very intense way, unlike any other time. I can't describe it. I noticed that I am wholly present. I experienced the "now," this single moment in which I exist. I can't explain it. I have become more conscious of what "reality" is. I was held in this state for a long time. Yes, I say I was held in it, because I really didn't bring it about or continue in it myself. Frequently before, it's happened that I wanted to prolong an intense state, and at that moment it disappeared. This time it didn't even occur to me to prolong it. I was lost in wonder. I was simply there, present.

I experienced in a new way that I don't have to bring anything about. Everything was given. I felt a calm and tender love. I don't know how it came, it was simply there. Everything was simple and clear, unproblematic, and so real. It was good to be there.

RM. To be there.

BENEDICT. Yes, simply to be there. The surprising thing is that I found in this state for the first time that I don't have to bring anything about. I've told myself that time and time again; it was clear to me in principle. But during this meditation I actually experienced it. Experience is really something quite different from knowing. I was gripped by this experience. I sensed that the whole of life is gift, and that God gives everything, even our endeavor, also recollection. Everything.

RM. It was a wonderful experience.

BENEDICT. Yes, it was. But afterwards something else happened that's important.

RM. What's that?

BENEDICT. Yes, after meditation I went out of doors, still under the influence of this experience. You know I'm a Jesuit and know the Ignatian Exercises, have undertaken them for decades, direct others in them often and with satisfaction. One of my favorite prayers of offering is the one given in the last contemplation (Spiritual Exercises, No. 235):

> Take, O Lord, and receive all my freedom,
> my memory, understanding, and all my will,
> whatever I have and possess.
> You have given them to me;
> I give them back to you.
> Everything is yours;

dispose of it according to your will.
Give me only your love and your grace;
they are sufficient for me.

So then, being out in nature and feeling again this simple existence, and not having to do anything, I said this prayer spontaneously. Suddenly its meaning dawned on me. More than a devout prayer of self-offering, it's the foundation of contemplation. After saying this prayer, one can't meditate in the same way as before. It really depends on surrendering one's understanding to God and remaining in loving wonder. It's really important to surrender the memory and stop being occupied with one's past. He takes all that on himself.

To be occupied with the past would mean that his love is not sufficient for us. To surrender our will means, henceforth, no longer to want anything for him, but to enter more and more into *not wanting* and *letting God act*. According to the mentality of this prayer, even our prayers of petition lose much of their meaning, for his grace and love *suffice*. He takes care of everything. We can surrender to him forever our cares for others. We don't need to implore him for individual matters. All prayers of petition are already contained in our existence for him. Any other kind of petition no longer fits into this prayer. He knows everything and does everything.

RM. You mean, we no longer need to plan or work.

BENEDICT. No, I don't mean that. I only mean that we surrender our worries to him. Yes, our dealings with him change. I can't imagine that we still *work at prayer*—reflect on texts, analyze ourselves, or plan the future. In our relationship with him only the wonder of existence remains. In our work everything comes about without our worrying about it.

RM. You mean one should give up reflecting on texts.

BENEDICT. Yes, that's what I mean. But not for everyone. Meditation on Scripture is indispensable before contemplation. In the contemplative state it's also possible to take a text again and again. It dawned on me that the prayer "Take, O Lord" introduces us into a form of prayer where everything that is thought—memory, will, planning, striving for perfection—has to cease completely. All that is replaced by loving and being. I have rediscovered the meaning of this prayer anew. It is for me the Ignatian foundation of life according to the Exercises, of contemplative life in the life of action.

RM. I can only agree.

10.15 LINA

[She did not take part in the retreat, but has come for a preparatory talk for her next retreat.]

LINA. Since my previous retreat last summer I've been meditating regularly. I have kept on with this form of prayer and say the name of Jesus in connection with my hands. I'd like to repeat this kind of retreat, but don't know whether the contemplative retreat is the right thing for me at present, for I have to make an important decision. *[She speaks for a long time about this decision.]*

RM. Is the decision urgent or not?

LINA. Why is that important?

RM. There are three ways of making an important decision.

We can go the path of reasoning: we write down all the reasons that speak for and against. We weigh them up and decide. This way would have to be complemented with a second one, because it takes no account of our feelings.

The second way leads through the feelings of consolation and desolation. On this path we have to understand that, though thoughts can change quickly, feelings don't. People making a decision whether to get married, or to enter religious life or the priesthood, have various feelings that move them to and fro. The feelings that move us constructively to one side or the other are naturally conscious to us. But the feelings that hold us back, fill us with fear, come only hesitatingly to our consciousness. As soon as they show themselves, our thoughts move to the other choice. For example, if one wants to enter an Order, the thought of renouncing marriage remains in the unconscious. As soon as it shows itself in a sadness or sense of loss, we jump to the other side and think we should marry after all. In this way we now suppress the feelings that drew us to religious life. Every choice means a loss which first has to be mourned. That's why a choice is made by looking first at one possibility until all the feelings of fear, sadness, loneliness, and uncertainty come to our consciousness. Then we change to the other possibility and let all the reactionary feelings of this choice come up. Once the feelings have been accepted and suffered through, we can choose freely. The process is extensive; sometimes we go through it in a retreat, sometimes outside.

Both paths are pre-contemplative ways of decision-making. They have the advantage that they can be used during a definite period of time. If there is a limit to the time, you have to proceed this way. If, however, there is no limit to the time, we can take the contemplative path. It consists in leaving aside any preoccupation with the possibilities of a particular choice, and going into the depth of the soul through contemplation. From there, suddenly, a decisive clarity arises. It's often an immediate conviction. It comes from the center of the soul, from the divine spark in us. This conviction is unshakable. But we can't determine when it will come. It's frequently given during a contemplative retreat. But if not, at least the basic clarity of the soul will increase.

So I say it's worthwhile to use the contemplative decision process. God gives much clarity in stillness. The necessary work of mourning also takes place in a much simpler and more thoroughgoing way than in the pre-contemplative decision process. But the requirement is that you turn off, and consistently abstain from, preoccupation with the process of making a choice.

LINA. I'd like to make my decision in the contemplative manner.

RM. Let someone accompany you, a contemplative.

LINA. Thank you.

10.16 YVONNE

YVONNE. What I want to tell you has no immediate bearing on meditation, though afterwards it had an important impact on mine. During a group dialogue I saw someone listen completely to another person. I can hardly describe it. He was totally wrapped up in the other. It was strange. He didn't seem to hear the other's words, but put himself in the other's shoes. The atmosphere of the group became intense. I suddenly realized that I had never myself listened like that. I always listen critically to the words of others and distance myself, so that I can "judge" their statements objectively.

RM. You've discovered what it means to listen to the person and not to the statement.

YVONNE. Yes, that's right. I then discovered the parallel to meditation. I've never listened to God like that. I have analyzed texts to find out what they wanted to say. I was very quiet, but more to follow my own mind's interest. To listen to God in the way I experienced it here in the group dialogue, is new to me. I discovered for the first time what listening means. It doesn't mean to ask after something in a detached way but to reach out to the hidden reality with tender and attentive love. To be all ears, to be wholly present. Listening not only with the mind, but with the whole body and the whole soul. Listening means to enter with great reverence into the uniqueness of the other, until I feel one with him or her.

RM. Yes, that's it. Only love can listen. Only when we direct our attention beyond the words to the person can we welcome the other as he is. It is only when touched by the other's being that we can listen to him. We are good listeners only when, after listening, we become conscious that we had forgotten ourselves totally. What you say of listening to others is also true of listening to God. Contemplative prayer is listening in this sense. This listening has a strong healing power. It awakens in the other clarity and self-recognition. He feels understood and accepted. This gives him new self-respect and vitality.

In meditation, this healing power of listening comes back to us. We ourselves are being healed from within.

10.17 BRIAN

BRIAN. These ten days have done me good. When I arrived, I was dried up and exhausted within myself. I found quiet here and came to peace. I had been looking for this way for a long time. At last I have discovered it, and I want to follow it. I'm a youth chaplain in an urban center, belong to a religious Order, and am sure of having been called to it. But now, four years after my ordination, I was burned out and empty inside. I had somehow lost contact with myself. My faith, too, had become very weak and seemed almost lost. I suffered great pain every time I found that I couldn't stand behind my words. I did talk a lot formerly, but my words weren't sincere. I was very overworked. I worked and organized for roughly seventy or eighty hours a week and always felt that I should do more.

Since I was caught up in this bustle of activity, I no longer prayed, for all intents and purposes. I didn't have time. The weaker my faith grew, the less I could bring myself to pray. I saw that this couldn't continue, but I couldn't find a way out. I couldn't pray. The inner calm was lacking, so I didn't find the necessary time.

RM. You were in a blind alley.

BRIAN. Yes, and I felt that a change had to come. I found a way that seemed possible in contemplative prayer. Now I'm asking myself how I can continue on this way.

RM. I'm glad that you've found your way. The "shepherd of souls" who wants to help others in the faith must be firm in faith himself. You experienced the diminishing of your faith; it was almost lost. It's understandable that you gave up prayer. I'm convinced that—besides the Eucharist—an hour of prayer is necessary for someone in ministry. Otherwise pastoral ministry becomes superficial, unconvincing, and changes into amateurish activism. An hour of prayer belongs in the life of a pastor.

BRIAN. I had often made resolutions to pray regularly, but couldn't carry them through.

RM. When you have the kind of work that's very demanding, you can't keep up with every form of prayer.

BRIAN. What can one keep up with?

RM. Prayer must lead to quiet. In a restless world, we quickly become restless ourselves. So the form of prayer must have an extraordinary strength to lead us directly and quickly into a great calm. "Come to me," says Jesus, "all you who labor and are burdened, and I will give you rest" (Mt 11:28). If prayer doesn't lead us soon into deep quiet, we can't persevere in it in daily life.

To be able to stick with prayer in our hectic world, we need a form of prayer that relaxes us. If it tires us, we won't be able to keep to the schedule of prayer we decided on. The urge to achieve—and the expectations and demands of our restless world—weary us and dry us up, as you say. Mental activity in prayer tires us. The pastor's prayer must therefore lead him back to his own sources where he can recuperate completely.

And a third point—it's necessary in the pastor's life that God works more and more in him, that he becomes an instrument in God's hands. This happens only through self-emptying. We have to become quite empty in the presence of God. Prayer in the active ministry must be kept free from occupation with problems. These possibilities are offered most fully in contemplative prayer.

BRIAN. Yes, I can see that. I'm convinced of it. My problem is, however, that I really don't have the time.

RM. May I show you how to make time for it?

BRIAN. That would be interesting!

RM. We find ourselves in a dilemma: either you find times for prayer that leads you to quiet, or you must feel dried out, superficial, and unauthentic. If you continue to live in your hectic overworked way, your co-workers will have to suffer severely from your restlessness, and—with time—from your neurosis.

When you say you have no time, I think of all the priests who had the same problem and suffered heart failure at age forty or forty-five. Because they wanted to achieve so much, they worked thirty years less than others. Is that sensible? Does more work get done in this way?

Let me tell you an anecdote. It was 1961, after John F. Kennedy had just taken over the presidency of the United States. He was the first Catholic President of the USA, and had awakened many hopes in Latin America, where I was a young priest, that he would solve the North-South problem. The papers wrote a lot about him, and I read a description of his schedule in the daily paper. Every Sunday he went to Mass at 8 a.m. The day I read that, an ordinary workman said to me that he couldn't go to Mass on Sundays because he had no time. I said I understood, because he probably had more important work to do than President Kennedy, who took time off for Sunday Mass.

"To have time" is relative. Everyone has twenty-four hours in the day. It all depends on what is more important to us. We use our hours accordingly. I once heard a wise saying: "When God created time, he created enough of it."

BRIAN. Do you consider twenty minutes sufficient?

RM. Yes, Brian, twenty minutes can be sufficient for a Christian who is not actively caring for souls and doesn't have an intense longing for God. But if we want to confirm others in the faith, we must invest more. To have no time for God is a sign that God's attraction for us is still so weak that we can hardly be called messengers of God. We shall proclaim ourselves, but not God. We shall strive for our own honor, power, and success.

There's something else. You need an hour of meditation not only because you are a pastor of souls. You need it also because you have promised yourself to God in celibacy. You have renounced a spouse and family in order to have time and attention to give to God and to people. My experience of thirty years in ministry to priests tells me that without the daily hour of prayer apart from Mass, one is hardly capable of living consecrated celibacy. That is not possible even with extraordinary graces.

BRIAN. You have very little confidence in the grace of God.

RM. On the contrary, very great confidence.

BRIAN. In what way?

RM. Grace leads into stillness. The vocation to celibacy consists of a very intense desire to seek God alone. This grace draws so much into stillness, that it's easy to set aside an hour a day for prayer. The great contemplatives have always found time for stillness, and most of them were active.

BRIAN. I must let this affect me.

10.18 NELLIE

NELLIE. We've come to the end of the retreat. A new world has opened to me. Until now I looked for orientation, and now I've found it. I am very content because I've found my way; but I still feel very much a beginner. This lessens my contentment and I feel a certain amount of discouragement. A long pathway lies ahead of me, stretching endlessly in the distance. That depresses me. When shall I arrive at the goal?

RM. You would like to be at the end of the journey.

NELLIE. I feel totally at the beginning. I am still nowhere.

RM. This fills you with fear.

NELLIE. Yes, it makes me afraid that I won't be able to keep up.

RM. Or maybe gives you inferiority feelings?

NELLIE. Perhaps.

RM. Or do you want to say that you need help?

NELLIE. Yes, absolutely.

RM. Help is always there. Trust in God's guidance. He has been at your side until now and has guided your whole life with love. Why don't you trust him to continue caring for you?

NELLIE. Yes, I must learn to trust in God. At times I succeed. But in spite of everything I have the feeling that I am right at the beginning.

RM. That can be a very good feeling.

NELLIE. How can that be?

RM. Look, Nellie, this retreat has shown you a way for your life, as you say. This means you'll be on this path as long as life lasts. We can't grow into the love of God in ten days. It isn't a task to be completed and then left behind. The more we advance on the way, the more we feel at the beginning. We know this from the saints. The nearer they were led to God, the poorer and more helpless they saw themselves—always at the starting point.

NELLIE. And where does this need for help come from?

RM. To need help is in the order of things. It's even healthy. The mistake is that you expect it from outside. You compare yourself with others who, you believe, have gone further than you. Instead, expect help from within, from the Spirit of Jesus Christ who is waiting for you in the depth of your soul. It's sufficient to be on the way. It is quite unimportant whether we are at the beginning or the end of the path. Anyone who has been led to the right path, and walks it, will be led further. Only trust is required, and placing the reins of our life in the hands of God.

NELLIE. I have the feeling I'm not making any progress.

RM. When we place our hand on the head of a child, we can't feel the child growing. But it grows all the same.

NELLIE. Thank you. May I say goodbye with an ancient Christian greeting?

RM. Of course.

NELLIE. Praised be Jesus Christ.
RM. For ever and ever. Amen.

BIOGRAPHY OF THE AUTHOR

Franz Jalics was born in 1927 in Budapest, Hungary, and grew up on his father's estate, setting out to become a professional soldier as his father wished. But at the end of World War II, he spent time in Germany as a refugee and returned to Hungary in 1946, where he completed high school and entered the Jesuit Order. In the early 1950s, he began studies in literature and languages in Pullach, near Munich, Germany, and in 1954 earned his degree in philosophy at Leuven-Eegenhoven, Belgium, after which he spent two years in southern Belgium, teaching in a Jesuit high school at Mons. In 1956, the Order sent him to Chile, and a year later to Argentina, where he remained for the next twenty years. He studied theology and was ordained a priest in 1959.

Fr. Jalics then spent a year in Córdoba, teaching Dogmatics and Fundamental Theology at the Jesuit San Miguel University. In 1963, he became the students' Spiritual Director and began to give retreats. He earned his Ph.D. in theology in 1966, and then became a professor at San Salvador University in Buenos Aires.

At the beginning of the 1970s, Fr. Jalics and two fellow Jesuits went to live in the slums to share their life with the poor. In 1976, an ultra-conservative group kidnapped him and imprisoned him in an undisclosed location. For five months he was their captive, blindfolded and tied hand and foot. He was released without explanation, surreptitiously. He left Argentina late in 1977 and spent a year in the United States and Canada.

His early books include: *El encuentro con Dios* (1970), *Cambios en la fe* (1972), *Aprendiendo a orar* (1973), and *Aprendiendo a compartir la fe* (1978).

Since 1978, he has been living in Germany, devoting himself to leading retreats, and, since 1984, has had his own Retreat House in Gries, Wilhelmsthal, Germany.

In addition to the original German, *Contemplative Retreat* has also been published in

Hungarian	*Szemlélödö lelkigyakorlat* (Manréza Korda, 1994)
Spanish (Argentina)	*Ejercicios de Contemplación* (San Pablo, 1998)
(Spain)	*Ejercicios de Contemplación* (ediciones sigueme, 1998)
Dutch	*Contemplative oefeningen* (Carmelitana, 1999)
English (India)	*Called to Share in His Life* (St. Pauls, 1999)
Italian	*Desiderio di Dio* (Ancora, 2000)
French	*Ouverture à la Contemplation* (Desclée de Brouwer, 2002).